The German and Welsh Origins of the

Charles and Lottie Fetterolf Family

Including Hodge, Reiner, Marsh, Kidson and Skelding

by

Steve E. Troutman & Joan E. Troutman

SUNBURY PRESS

Mechanicsburg, PA USA

Published by Sunbury Press, Inc.
Mechanicsburg, Pennsylvania 17055

SUNBURY
PRESS

www.sunburypress.com

For information about special discounts for bulk purchases, please contact Sunbury
Press Orders Dept. at (855) 338-8359 or orders@sunburypress.com.

To request one of our authors for speaking engagements or book signings, please contact
Sunbury Press Publicity Dept. at publicity@sunburypress.com.

ISBN: 9781-9345-970-8-8 (Trade Paperback)

SECOND SUNBURY PRESS EDITION: December 2016

Product of the United States of America
0 1 1 2 3 5 8 13 21 34 55

Set in Bookman Old Style
Designed by Steve Troutman
Cover by Lawrence Knorr
Edited by Joan Troutman

Continue the Enlightenment!

Cover Photo courtesy of the Troutmans

Table of Contents

Introduction

A Brief History of the Charles and Lottie Fetterolf Family, Including German, Welsh, and English Origins

The Charles and Lottie Fetterolf Family Reunion is held annually on Father's Day. The gathering has traditionally been held at the Klingerstown Fire Company Picnic Grounds. This booklet was compiled in response to interest in family history at this reunion.

The first part describes the Fetterolf connection to Germany, and the migration to Berks, Northumberland, and Schuylkill Counties of Pa. The Fetterolf Family origin is well documented in the book *Rothermel Families in America* , page 119 and 120,by Joseph A. Meiser, 1989. References to the ancestral village home of the Fetterolf's in Wachbach, Germany are also found in the book *Genealogical and Biographical Annals of Northumberland County, Pa.*, page 890 and 924, by Floyd, 1911.

Reiner Family History is also included. The book that provided most of the Reiner history is entitled *Genealogy of the Reiner Family*, Descendants of Charles Reiner and Margaret Mosser, by The Rev. John Lewis Reiner, D.D., May, 1996, published by Docu Data Associates. This book is presently out of print. Interested Reiner family researchers may contact Roger Reiner, at 2274, Route 380, Saltsburg, Pa., 15681 or e-mail: roger.reiner@gmail.com., for more information.

The second part describes the Welsh family origins and the migration from South Wales to Helfenstein, in the Schuylkill County coal regions of Pennsylvania. Family tree roots include the names Marsh, Hodge, Kidson and Skelding. The authors are relying on research as well as oral tradition, passed down by the founding father of this reunion. Charles Fetterolf, himself, spoke of his "grandmother as coming over on a boat, from Wales."

We hope you enjoy reading this book and perhaps it will spark further interest in family history. "To forget ones ancestors is to be a brook without a source, a tree without a root." (Ancient Chinese proverb)

The former Charles and Lottie Fetterolf homestead location in the Mahantongo Valley, photo 2009.

Our Fetterolf Heritage

From Germany to Pennsylvania

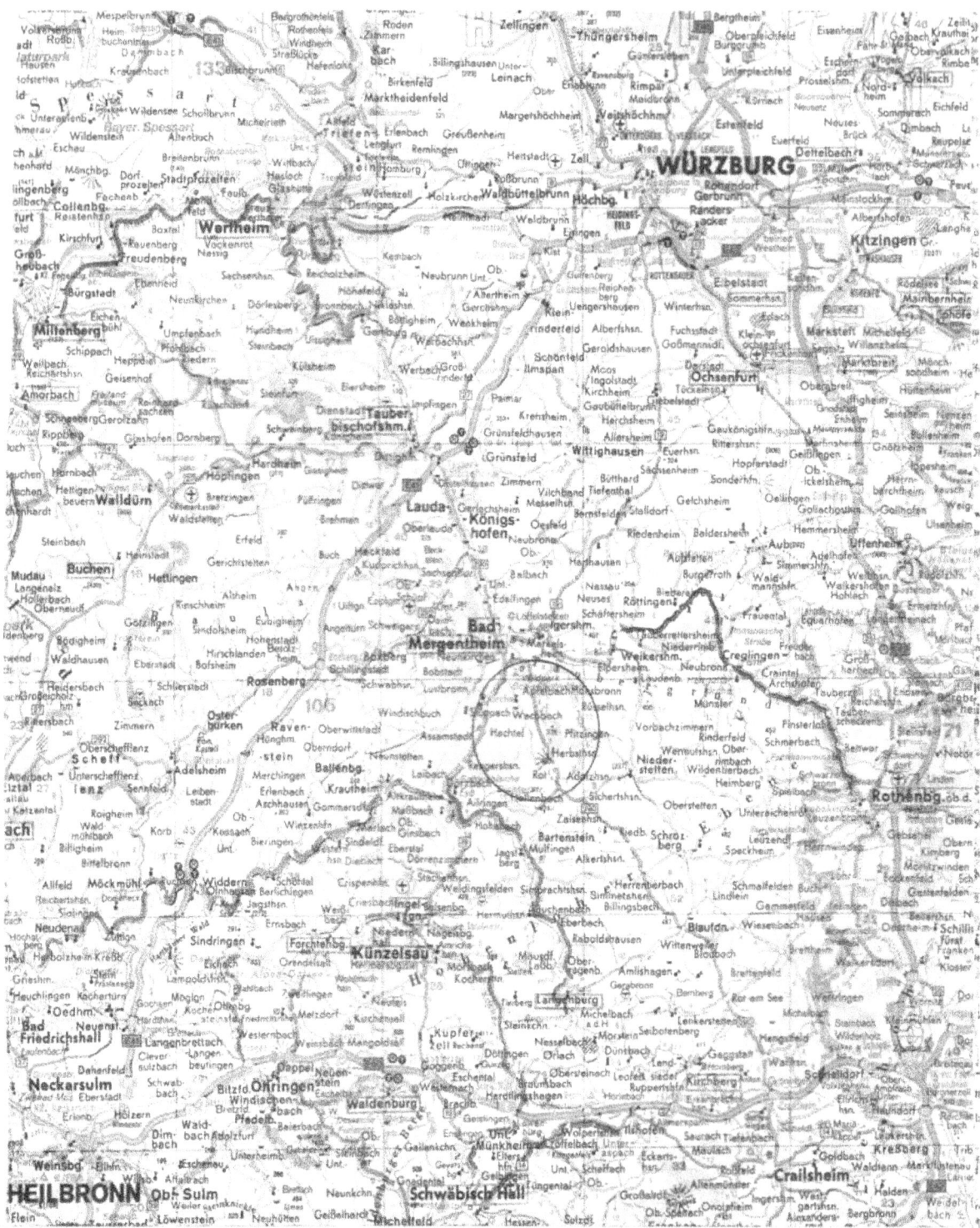

Map of Germany showing location of the villages Wachbach and Hachtal.
The village of Dortel not shown is mid-way between Wachbach and Hachtal.

The Evangelical Church in Wachbach built in 1045. Our ancestor, Peter Fetterolf, the immigrant to Pennsylvania was baptized here.

Die erstmals 1045 urkundlich erwähnte Kirche mit Gadenhaus

EVANGELISCHE KIRCHE WACHBACH

Anita Bengel

Kanzel mit den Bildern von Luther und Melanchthon

A drawing of Wachbach during the Middle Ages. Note the wall around the town with 3 gates. The Adelsheim Castle is centrally located with a water filled moat around it. The Evangelical Church is also nearby.
The armored soldier is depicted on a sign near the church today, as a reminder of the past.

Kleine Skizze aus dem Forstlagerbuch des Deutschordens
(Hauptstaatsarchiv Stuttgart)

The village school, built next to the church and closely associated with the Evangelical Church is seen here connected by a second story walkway. Below may be seen the Rathaus (town hall) and the present day main street.

Das Renaissanceportal des
Schlosses Wachbach

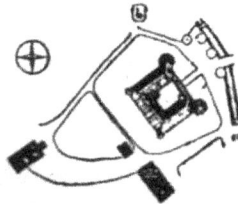

Nordseite des Schlosses mit Zwerchbau

Erdgeschoß des Schlosses Wachbach

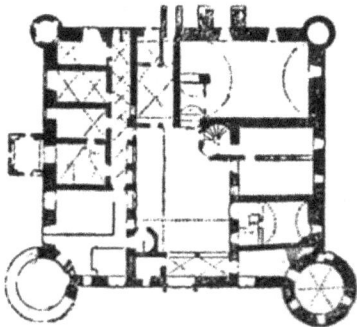

Schnitt durch das Schloß Wachbach
bei Mergentheim

Schloß Wachbach

Adelsheim Castle
with a renaissance style gate,
named after the
Adelsheim Family.

Der linke Eckturm (in der Zeichnung
weiß eingelassen), ist halb abgetra-
gen. Die Gewölbearten (Kreuz- oder
Tonnengewölbe) durch punktierte
Linien angegeben. Die Stützen auf
der Rückseite des Schlosses neueren
Datums.

Skizzen von Architekt Lusin

Leonard Federolf bakery
in Wachbach on Dorf Strasse.

Bäckerei Leonhard Federolf,
heute Freymüller, Dorfstraße,
auch hier ist noch der Brötchen-
oder Brotkasten zu sehen

9

The village of Dortel located mid-way between Wachbach and Hachtel. All these villages are located in a small stream valley separated by only a few kilometers. Below may be seen cherry trees in bloom and a garden with a fence. All these villages are named as being associated with the Fetterolf Family.

Book cover: 700 years of Hachtel History, by Anita Bengel.

GERMAN FEDEROLF ANCESTRY

HERMANN FEDEROLF (born ca 1360 in Hachtel, Germany, 3 miles from Wachbach. In 1404 purchased land in Dortel, 2 miles from Wachbach; price ten Gelders. (Taken From Land Owners Handbook, 1700's).

JEORG (GEORGE) FEDEROLF, born ca 1604 in Dortel, according to Wachbach Church Records. Occupation, shepherd.

DIETRICH FEDEROLF, born ca 1630, son of George, according to Wachbach Church Records. Worked in Adelsheim Castle, Wachbach, as a tax collector. Set rules for Knight's duels. Married twice: first wife Anna; second wife Barbara (married November 19, 1667).

JOHANN JACOB FEDEROLF, born October 15, 1668, son of Dietrich and Barbara, married Agnes Spores.
CHILDREN:
Johann Peter Federolf (3/20/1699-8/15/1784) Anna Maria Rothermel.

GEORGE FEDEROLF JR., supposedly son of Dietrich.

BALSAR FEDEROLF, supposedly son of Dietrich.

Hausnamen

Albrecht, Karl, Balz;
Bätzner, Viktor, Gassenschmied;
Bauer, Johann, Keitel;
Beez, Karlheinz, Kechelfeld;
Benz, Friedrich, Simmeles;
Brand, Hermann, Seitz;
Brand, Berta, Brandwechner (Wagner);
Brunner, Johann, Eugens;
Brunner, Emma, Kirchenbrunner;
Brunner, Josef, Postbrunner;
Brunner, Robert, Brunnenschuster;
Dörr, Josef, Müllerhans (Mühlhans);
Dörr, Johann, Kiefer (Küfer);

Ehrmann, Alfons, Scheierdeckel
Ehrmann, Lydia, Herschlesbaue
Ehrmann, Edwin, Josefsbauer;
Ehrmann, Martin, Burkert;
Federolf, Karl, Hanspeter;
Federolf, Willi, Schlecht;
Federolf, Ursula, Owald (Anwal
Freund, Karl, Schoch;
Gahm, Kurt, Hofbauer;
Herschlein, Erich, Eschenbauer;
Herschlein, Ludwig, Franzenmä
Rupp, Albert, Wimlisbar (Wimli
Rupp, Martin, Gustav;

Bauernhaus Wilhelm Federolf, mit das älteste Haus in Hachtel, aus dem 17. Jahrhundert. Früher und heute.

Farmhouse of Wilhelm Federolf, the oldest house in Hachtel, ca. 1600's, old and new house.

12

FETTEROLF GENEALOGY

JOHANNES LEONARD ROTHERMEL (1/1), son of Johannes Rothermel was born ca. 1690 in Europe. He married Margaretha Zimmerman, who may have been the daughter of General John Zimmerman and Sarah Metzger. They resided in Hassloch, a small village in the German Palatinate. The names of all their known children as well as their birth dates appear in the Lutheran Church records of that village.

It is not know when Johannes Leonard Rothermel and his family migrated to America. He may have died, as some say and was buried at sea on his way to America in 1730, or he may have been the Leonard Röderbill (Rodennill) who arrived at the Port of Philadelphia, October 2, 1727 on the ship "Adventure Galley". Hopefully the recent discovery of Rothermel records in Germany will enable future historians to unravel the mystery surrounding the early Rothermel immigrants.

Nothing is know of Johannes Rothermel's profession or his personal wealth other than the numerous clearances through customs and payment for the family's passage must have required substantial sums of money.

The death dates and place of burial of Johannes Leonard Rothermel and his wife Margaretha Zimmerman are unknown. It is believed that his wife is buried in a family plot on the farm of her son-in-law Peter Federolf. It was the common practice in the 1700's and the early 1800's to bury in private cemeteries on farms owned by the deceased at the time of their death. Unfortunately subsequent owners of the land died not respect these burial plots. Since the plots were not maintained by descendants, the graves became engulfed with briars, weeds, and brush. The new owners removed the tombstones, plowed over the graves and eliminated what to them was an eyesore. It could also be that the tombstones deteriorated with age and were removed because the inscriptions were no longer legible.

CHILDREN:

2/1	Christian Rothermel (1/24/1710 - 1769)	m. Magdalena (Merkle) Hill
* 2/2	Anna Margaretha Rothermel (2/12/1712 - ca 1785)	
		m. Peter Federolf
2/3	Johann Peter Rothermel (2/3/1712 - ca 1785 - twin)	
		m. Sybilla Hoch
2/4	Lawrence Rothermel (2/3/1715 - 1759 - twin)	m. Ursula Kuhns
2/5	Johann Paul Rothermel (12/30/1718 - 1811)	m. 1st Margaretha Maurer
		m. 2nd Sophia Maurer
2/6	Johannes Rothermel (1/21/1722 - 1785)	m. Mary E. Siegfried

Location Map of Fetterolf Ancestral homestead in Siesholtzville, Berks County, Pa.

FETTEROLF GENEALOGY

ANNA MARIA (MARGARETHA) ROTHERMEL 2/2, daughter of Johannes Rothermel (1/1) and Margaretha Zimmerman, was born February 12, 1712, in Hassloch, Germany. Lutheran Church records in the village list her name as Anna Margaretha Rothermel. She married Peter Federolf, born March 20, 1699, in Wachbuch, Germany, and died August 15, 1784. He was the son of Johann Jacob Federolf and Agnes Spores; grandson of Dietrich Federolf; and great grandson of George Federolf.

Since Peter Federolf arrived on "the Thistle of Glasgow" at the Port of Philadelphia, August 29, 1730, early historians stated that Anna married Peter in Germany; furthermore that Johannes Rothermel (1/1), his wife and five sons were aboard the same vessel. Based on the birth year of the oldest child of Anna M. Rothermel (2/2), and Peter Federolf, the authors feel that the couple was married following their emigration to America.

Peter Federolf purchased large tracts of land near Siesholtzville, now Hereford Twp., Berks Co., at the point where the counties of Berks, Lehigh and Bucks meet. In 1759 he was a tax collector for the area in which he resided.

In his will Peter Federolf gave 300 acres of land to his son John and 100 acres to his son-in-law Christopher Bittenbender. Peter and his wife are buried in a family plot on the farm where they resided. The date of Peter's death is given as august 15, 1784. Anna's date of death is unknown.

CHILDREN:

3/1	Catherine R. Federolf (1731 - 7/19/1794)	m. 1st Johannes Siegfried, II
		m. 2nd Abraham Zimmerman
* 3/2	Peter Federolf (1738 - 5/1777)	m. Susanna Seitz
3/3	Jacob Federolf (1746 - 6/1778)	m. 1st Dorothea Brobst
		m. 2nd Catharina Brobst
3/4	Philip Federolf (1746 - 6/1778)	m. Christine Reichert
3/5	Johannes Federolf (ca 1748 - ca 1784)	m. Dorothea Brobst
3/6	Anna B. Federolf (ca 1750 - prior 1784)	m. Philip Hehn
3/7	Maria Magdalena Federolf (3/6/1755 - 8/10/1831)	
		m. Christopher Bittenbender

Rothermel, Federolf, Bittenbender Cemetery
Siesholtzville, Pa.

FETTEROLF GENEALOGY

PETER FEDEROLF 3/2, son of Anna M. Rothermel (2/2), (Johannes Rothermel 1/1) and Peter Federolf, was born ca. 1738, in what is now Berks Co., PA, and died in May 1777, prior to his father's death in 1784. He married Susanna Seitz. They resided in the Seisholtzville area and are believed to be buried in a family cemetery on the farm where they resided. Orphaned at an early age, the children of Peter and Susanna were raised by Peter's parents, Peter Federolf and Anna M. Rothermel. This explains why so many historians omitted one generation when compiling information on the descendants of Peter Federolf and Anna Rothermel.

CHILDREN:

4/1	Philip Fetherolf (ca 1767)		m. Catharine Lesher
4/2	Margaretha Feterolf (4/15/1768 -)		
4/3	I. Adam Feterolf (1/11/1769 - 11/22/1838)		m. Susanna Sheib (Shipe)
4/4	J. Frederick Fetherolf (1/11/1772 - 10/1/1831)		m. Catharine Dreese
* 4/5	J. Peter Fetherolf (6/30/1774 - 11/2/1848)		m. Anna Maria Dunkelberger
4/6	Elizabeth Fetherolf (3/29/1776 - 10/28/1849)		m. Philip Schaeffer

The Douglas Hetrick residence, 2987 Seisholtzville Road, Macungie, PA, 18062. This farm location is approximately one mile south of Seisholtzville. Doug lives adjacent to the Rothermel-Federolf-Bittenbender Cemetery. He described 2 separate prior home locations. The earliest stone pioneer cabin remains as a stone pile ruin. A later stone house with a kitchen fire place and curved stairway is under renovation. The large stone home that he and his family live in is the third house on the farm. See the appendix of this book for a picture of Peter Federolf's log house in Seisholtzville.

This is the pioneer cabin stone ruin.

Small stone 2-story house
With kitchen fireplace,
Open beam ceiling,and
curved stairway.

In later years the small 2-story stone house was used as a grainery before remodeling.

July 4, 1999, Joan Troutman
Visited the Rothermel, Federolf,
Bittenbender Cemetery near
Siesholtzville

In early fall of 2008
Steve and Joan Troutman
and Rev. Mark Rothermel
visited this cemetery location
and found it much more
overgrown. The cemetery
is located on a farm lane
which passes by the earlier
stone pioneer cabin ruin
and the later stone houses.
The cemetery is located
about ½ mile east of the
Douglas Hetrick residence.
It is in a meadow, adjoining
a large farm pond.

Genealogical and Biographical
Annals of Northumberland County,
by Floyd, 1911
Wachbach, Holland as named
below is today Wachbach, Germany

FETTEROLF. The Fetterolf (Federolf, Fetherolf) family, two of whose representatives in Upper Mahanoy township, Northumberland county, are Edward and Daniel Fetterolf, brothers, is of Dutch origin, its founder in this country, Peter Federolf, having been a native of Wachbach, Holland, born in 1699. In 1729 or 1730 he married Anna Maria Rothermel, only daughter and eldest of the six children of Johannes and Sabilla (Zimmerman) Rothermel. In 1730 Peter Federolf and his wife accompanied his father-in-law to America, the voyage being made in the "Thistle," and about 1732 he and his wife and one of her brothers, Leonard and Rothermel, located in Hereford township, Berks Co., Pa., where Peter Federolf acquired a large acreage of what has become valuable farm land, upon which he passed the remainder of his life, dying there. His property was partly in Hereford township and partly in Longswamp township, and he made his home near what is now Seisholtzville, near the line of Lehigh county. Leonard Rothermel located in Perry township, Berks county, before the Revolution, and there died at an advanced age, leaving a large family.

Peter Federolf was a man of more than ordinary importance in his locality, not only because he was a large land owner, but because his successful management of his own affairs showed him entitled to influence and leadership in the conduct of such matters as affected the general welfare. He reared a family of seven children, who became connected by marriage with other substantial old families of the county, and all of whom are mentioned in his last will and testament (on record in the courthouse at Reading, Will Book B), made July 19, 1784, and probated Sept. 16, 1784, showing that he died during the summer of that year. The witnesses to the will were Henry Bortz and Christopher Schultz, the executors Paul Groscup, of Rockland township, who was the testator's true and trusty friend (he was the ancestor of Judge Peter Grosscup, the Federal jurist of Chicago), Jacob Fetherolf, the eldest son, and Christopher Bittenbender, blacksmith, a son-in-law. In later years this Christopher Bittenbender obtained the original Federolf homestead, on which is located the Federolf private burial ground, where the emigrant ancestor, Peter, is buried, as well as Christopher Bittenbender, his wife, and some of their children. The will sets forth that the son Jacob was to have three hundred acres of land;

the son-in-law, Christopher Bittenbender, one hundred acres of land; the six children of the son Peter, who predeceased his father, three hundred pounds of money (divided between them); that the son Philip, deceased, left one daughter; that the daughter Catharine was twice married, first to John Siegfried and after his death to Abraham Zimmerman; that the daughter Barbara married a Hehn (name now spelled Hain); the daughter Magdalena married Christopher Bittenbender, who was a blacksmith and farmer, and who as previously noted eventually acquired the old homestead of Peter Federolf, which remained in the Bittenbender name until 1908. About 1840 a valuable find of iron ore was discovered on this property, and some of the Bittenbenders became wealthy thereby, the ore mines being worked until the early eighties.

Jacob Fetherolf was born Feb. 16, 1762, and died April 6, 1823; he is buried at Wessnersville, Berks Co., Pa. His wife Catharine, born May 12, 1760, died Jan. 10, 1849. (There was a Jacob Fetherolf, son of Peter, who died in Albany township in 1823, and whose will is on record in Will Book 5, page 412. He left sons John and Peter.)

The will of a Peter Fetherolf of Berks county who died in 1840 is also on record (Will Book 8, page 242). He died without sons, and John S. Kistler and William Mosser were the executors.

Johann Peter Fetherolf, ancestor of the Northumberland county branch of the family, was born June 30, 1774, in Hereford township, Berks county, and was one of the six children of Peter Federolf, son of the emigrant Peter Federolf, mentioned in the latter's will. He came to this region before his marriage and here wedded Anna Maria Dunkelberger, who was born Sept. 2, 1772. They lived for some years in Cameron township, where their children were born, later settling on a large farm in Upper Mahantango township, across the line in Schuylkill county, which Mr. Fetherolf purchased from a man named Carl, who got the best of the bargain. He did not tell Fetherolf that there was a mortgage upon the property, which he (Fetherolf) was obliged to pay, so that the transaction proved an expensive one. Nevertheless, he became a most successful man, and by the time of his death had accumulated a large estate. His original tract in Upper Mahantango township is now divided into three farms, the one on which the first set of buildings was erected, and on which Johann Peter Fetherolf, lived, being now the property of William Mattern. When he came to the Mahantango Valley the Mahantango creek was alive with fine fish, and he and his family found them an acceptable addition to the larder in those days when variety in food could not always be obtained even by the well-to-do. Johann Peter Fetherolf died Nov. 2, 1848, his wife on Feb. 7, 1853, and they are buried at the Salem

See addendum p. 21

(Herb) Church, located immediately across the Northumberland county line in Schuylkill county, where some of their children also rest. In religious faith the family were all Lutherans, Johann Peter Fetherolf was a saddler by trade, and he was a short-set man physically. His ten children were: Samuel, Peter, John, Joseph, George, Joseph (2), Daniel, Mrs. Josiah Geist, Mrs. Joseph Dunkelberger and Mrs. John Zimmerman. We give some account of the six sons who reached maturity.

Samuel Fetterolf, son of Johann Peter, was born Oct. 11, 1800, and died March 29, 1880. He was a worker in a fulling or carding mill, where wool was manufactured, the old establishment standing on the Little Mahantango creek. Later he owned and operated a grist and saw mill, and he was a large land owner, having 360 acres of land at County Line, in which region he was a most useful and influential citizen, being a man of extensive business interests. In his grist and saw mill he gave employment to a number of hands, and he built a number of dams or retaining walls, upon which he expended considerable money, and which also afforded work for many men. He also built a large brick house and several barns. His example and encouragement were powerful factors for good in the development and betterment of his section, in more than a material sense. He was a pillar of the church of his choice, he and his wife being active members of the Evangelical Association, and they are buried side by side at the Bingaman meeting-house near County Line, the Lower Mahanoy Church of that denomination. Mrs. Fetterolf, whose maiden name was Rachel Maurer, was born Dec. 15, 1807, daughter of John Maurer, of Lehigh county, Pa., and died Sept. 21, 1889, at the home of her son Daniel. Their ten children were: Elizabeth, Mrs. Peter Kehler; Catharine, Mrs. John C. Renn; Sarah, Mrs. George Kehler; Hannah, Mrs. Isaiah Kiehl; Lydia, Mrs. John D. Deibler; Felix, whose wife Elizabeth died Aug. 30, 1900, aged sixty-four years, six months, ten days; Daniel; Samuel; John, and Elias. Of this family,

Daniel Fetterolf, a farmer of Lower Mahanoy township, Northumberland county, born July 1, 1835, has been an agriculturist all his life. In 1860 he began farming on his own account in Dauphin county, at County Line, being a tenant for ten years. In 1870 he purchased his present farm, a tract of eighty-three acres which was formerly the John Kohl homestead (it was much larger in Mr. Kohl's time). Mr. Fetterolf has since occupied and cultivated this farm, and he has prospered steadily, in 1907 building the attractive frame residence which now adorns the property. In politics he is a Republican, and he has served as election officer and filled the position of supervisor in his township. His wife, Sarah,

was a daughter of Joseph and Mary (Shutt) Spotts and granddaughter of John Spotts. Two children were born to Mr. and Mrs. Daniel Fetterolf: Amelia (deceased) married Jacob H. Schaffer, and their only son, Charles F., is mentioned elsewhere in this work; Alexander was accidentally killed in a runaway, when a young man.

Peter Fetherolf (tombstone inscription Fetterolf), son of Johann Peter, was born Jan. 6, 1806, and died March 16, 1861. He lived in Upper Mahantango township, Schuylkill county, following farming. He married Sarah Reiner, born Feb. 26, 1805, who died Sept. 13, 1887, and they had children: Harris, Peter (who was an undertaker), Elias, Hettie, Katie, Mary (married Nelson Knorr) and Elizabeth (married Isaac Knorr).

John Fetherolf, son of Johann Peter, was a farmer. His first wife, whose maiden name was Maurer, is buried with him at Kimmel's Church. She was the mother of Peter, Daniel and Jesse; and by his second wife, who was a sister of the first, he had one son, Frank Dengler Fetherolf, named after his sponsor, Frank Dengler.

George Fetterolf, son of Johann Peter, was born March 11, 1809, and died Dec. 31, 1888. By trade he was a shoemaker, but farming was his principal occupation. Through his wife he obtained the homestead of his father-in-law, Johann Nicholas Rebuck, which was located in Upper Mahanoy township on the public road between Rough & Ready and Urban, now owned by Edward Fetterolf, grandson of George. His wife, Polly (Rebuck), born March 30, 1810, was a daughter of Johann Nicholas Rebuck (1771-1855) and his wife Magdalena Wolfgang (1777-1859). She died aged eighty-five years, three days. Mr. and Mrs. Fetterolf are buried at the Salem (Herb) Church, which he served in the offices of deacon and elder. They were the parents of ten children: Adam and Emanuel are mentioned later in this article; George is a resident of Illinois; Gabriel lives at Heplers, Schuylkill county; Dinah died unmarried; Amanda married George Wolfgang; four died young, George and three who were older than he.

Joseph Fetherolf, born May 25, 1813, died July 11, 1882. He married Abby Rice, who was born April 12, 1815, and died Dec. 24, 1890, and they were farming people in Upper Mahantango township, living near Heplers post office. Their children were: Joseph, Daniel, Samuel, Alice, Hettie, and Amelia (married James Thomas).

Daniel Fetherolf, son of Johann Peter, married a Miss Miller, and they had one daughter, Katie, who married Henry Herb. Daniel Fetherolf died at a comparatively early age, of smallpox, and he and his wife are buried at Klinger's Church. (There is a Daniel Feterolf buried there, born April 27, 1804, died Aug. 13, 1830.)

Adam Fetterolf, son of George, was born May

27, 1834, in Upper Mahanoy township, of which his brothers and sisters were also natives, and has passed all his life there, being now one of the oldest residents of that section. He received his education in the German subscription schools conducted during his boyhood, and worked for his parents until he reached the age of thirty, soon after the Civil war commencing farming for himself on his father's place, where he continued to live and work for eight years. In 1877 he purchased his present place, to which he removed at that time, and which consists of 105 acres of valuable land. He is a Democrat in political connection and a Lutheran in religion, he and his family belonging to the Lutheran congregation at the Salem (Herb) Church, which he served as elder four years. In 1867 he married Mary Brown, daughter of Michael and Peggy (Erdman) Brown; ten children have been born to this union: Sarah, Lydia, Nathan, Mary, George Henry, David, Harriet, Wilson, Victor, and one that died young.

Emanuel Fetterolf, son of George, farmed his father's homestead, of which he became the owner. It is located on the public road between Leck Kill and Klingerstown, the latter being his post office. He was a useful man in his district, serving as school director, and he was an active member of the Lutheran congregation at the Salem Church, which he served as deacon and elder. He was a Democrat in politics. He died Nov. 26, 1894, aged fifty-seven years, ten months, six days, and is buried at the Salem Church. Mr. Fetterolf married Catharine Knorr, daughter of John and Catharine (Schadle) Knorr, and since his death she has become the wife of Nathan Steely, of Schuylkill county. By her union with Mr. Fetterolf she was the mother of seven children: Catharine married Samuel Ressler and they live in Upper Mahanoy township; Edward is mentioned later; John M. died at the age of twenty-seven years, unmarried; Daniel C. is mentioned later; Emma J. married Samuel Schmeltz and they live in Schuylkill county; two died young.

Edward Fetterolf, a farmer of Upper Mahanoy township, was born there, on his father's homestead, Oct. 2, 1867, and attended the township schools during his boyhood. He was reared to farming, working for his parents until he reached the age of twenty-four, and in the spring of 1891 began cultivating his grandfather's place, where he lived for fifteen years. He then purchased the fine farm he now owns and occupies, which contains fifty-eight acres along the road between Leck Kill and Line Mountain. It was the old John Diehl homestead. Mr. Fetterolf has made a number of improvements on this property during his ownership, and he also owns the homestead of his grandfather, George Fetterolf, now comprising 127 acres. He is a prosperous, enterprising and highly respected citizen of his dis-

trict, where he has been chosen to the office of school director, in which he has been serving for the last five years.

In December, 1894, Mr. Fetterolf married Cevilla Snyder, daughter of Levi Snyder, of Upper Mahanoy township, whose wife was a Diehl. They have no children. Mr. and Mrs. Fetterolf are members of the Salem (Herb) Church, and he has served as deacon.

Daniel C. Fetterolf, now farming his father's old homestead in Upper Mahanoy township, was born there Feb. 7, 1871, and received his education in the local common schools. Farming has been his occupation all his life, and he worked for his parents until he attained his majority. In the spring of 1895 he began working the home place on his own account, purchasing the property from his father's estate. This place was formerly the homestead of Paul Brosius, from whom George Fetterolf purchased it for his son Emanuel, father of the present owner. The house was built many years ago and was remodeled by the late Emanuel Fetterolf. The barn was erected in 1904 by Daniel C. Fetterolf, to replace the one destroyed by fire May 10th of that year. The farm contains 110 acres, which Mr. Fetterolf has under profitable cultivation. He is an industrious and intelligent worker, and has taken his place among the progressive farmers of his district.

On Dec. 26, 1903, Mr. Fetterolf married Lydia Rebuck, daughter of Jonas and Rebecca (Malick) Rebuck, and they have had two children, Minnie G. and Lottie D. Mr. Fetterolf and his family are Lutheran members of the Salem Union Church, located just across the Northumberland line in Schuylkill county. Politically he is a Democrat.

In 1943, Willard and Verna Mattern purchased their farm from William and Verna Mattern. The only thing that changed was the middle initial, according to the new owners. This is probably the farm referred to on p. 19 of this history by Floyd in 1911. Peter and Anna Maria are buried at Salem, near by this farm. S.E.T.

FETTEROLF GENEALOGY

J. PETER FETHEROLF 4/5, son of Peter Federolf (3/2), (Anna M. Rothermel 2/2, Johannes Rothermel 1/1), and Susanna Seitz, was born June 30, 1774, in Hereford Twp., Berks Co., PA, and died November 2, 1848, in the Mahantango Valley of Schuylkill Co., PA. He migrated to Cameron Twp., Northumberland Co., PA., where he married Anna Maria Dunkelberger, born September 2, 1772; died February 7, 1853. She was the daughter of Clement Dunkelberger and Anna M. Gurtner. A saddler by trade, he purchased a large farm in Upper Mahantango Twp., Schuylkill Co., PA. Peter and Anna Maria are buried in the Salem (Herb) Church Cemetery, near Klingerstown, PA.

CHILDREN:

5/1	Joseph Fetterolf (infant)	
5/2	Elizabeth Fetterolf (11/19/1797 - 11/26/1874)	m. Josiah Geist
5/3	Samuel Fetterolf (10/11/1800 - 4/29/1880)	m. Rachel Maurer
5/4	Hannah Fetterolf (3/20/1803 - 9/30/1863)	m. Daniel Zimmerman
5/5	Daniel Fetterolf (4/27/1804 - 8/13/1880)	m. Sarah Miller
5/6	Johannes Fetterolf (9/19/1805 - 12/3/1887)	m. 1st Katie Maurer
		m. 2nd Mary Maurer
* 5/7	Peter Fetterolf (1/6/1806 - 3/16/1861)	m. Sarah Reiner
5/8	George Fetterolf (3/11/1809 - 12/28/1888)	m. Mary P. Rebuck
5/9	Joseph Fetterolf (5/25/1813 - 7/11/1882)	m. Abigail Rice
5/10	Rachel Fetterolf (5/1/1815 - 6/25/1884)	m. Joseph Dunkelberger
5/11	Maria Magdalena Fetterolf (3/8/1818 - 1875)	m. John B. Zimmerman

Photo courtesy of the Hereford Township Heritage Society. This photo is found on page 186 of "Early Times in Hereford Township". The log home of Peter Federolf was located on the southeast corner of Siesholtzville Road and Hunter Forge Road. In the photograph, the log house is identified with an arrow. The chimney can be seen coming out of the center of the roof. The log house originally had a dirt floor. The building has now been removed.

Pictures of Salem Church taken in 1912. The iron fence is plainly visible on the one.

These four Fetterolf stones at the Salem Church in Rough and Ready, Pa., are near the township road fronting the cemetery. The Peter Fetterolf stone carved in 1861 by Rev. Isaac Stiely, is a classic example of Stiely's style of decoration and format.

Hier Ruht
Johann Peter Fetherolf
Geborne 30 June
1774
und Starb 2 Nov.
1848
alt 74 yahr, 4mon.
und 2 tage
Text: ? 6-18

Hier Ruht
Anna Maria
Geb. Dunkelberger
Ehegaden von
Johann Peter
Fetherolf
Geborne Sept. 2
1772
und Starb Feb. 7
1853
Alt 80 yahr
5 monate, 5 tag
Text: Phill.? 1,21

J.Peter Fetterolf, son of Peter Fetterolf and Anna Rothermel, b. June 30, 1774 in Herford
Twp., Berks County, d. November 2, 1848 in Schuylkill Co., bur. Salem Church.
Migrated to Cameron Valley and married Anna Maria Dunkelberger, b. Sept. 2, 1772,
d. Feb. 7, 1853.

Hier Ruht John Peter
Fetterolf
Sohn von Peter and Maria
Fetterolf
Geborne am 6 tn, Janner
1806
Starb am 16 tn, Mar.
1861
Alt 55 Jahr, 2 Monate
(Days unreadable underground)

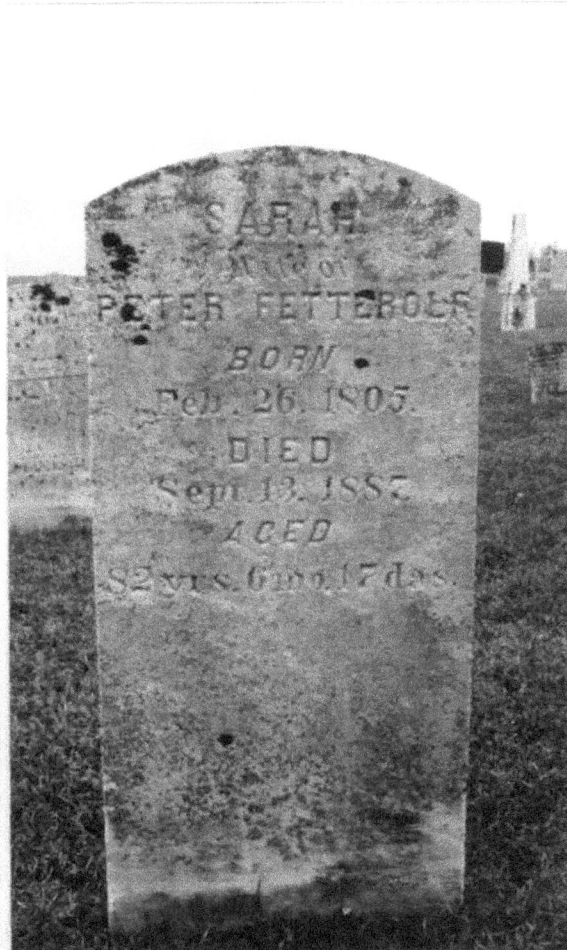

SARAH
Wife of
PETER FETTEROLF
BORN
Feb. 26. 1805.
DIED
Sept. 13.1887.
AGED
82 yrs. 6 mo. 17 das.

Peter Fetterolf, son of Peter and Anna Maria Dunkelberger, b. January 6, 1806, in
Cameron Valley, d. March 16, 1861, in Mahantongo Valley, married Sarah Reiner,
b. Feb. 26, 1805, d. September 13, 1887, bur. Salem Church, Rough and Ready, Pa.

Rev. Isaac Stiely carved Peter Fetterolf's stone, (1806-1861). Rev. Stiely founded the
Salem Church and preached there the rest of his lifetime. He decorated the gravestones
with hearts and flowers motif as found on early birth certificates. The Stiely grist mill he
operated stood along Mahantongo Creek near where Donnie Stiely lives today. Isaac was
familiar with sharpening millstones and he carved many markers for his parishioners.

FETTEROLF GENEALOGY

PETER FETTEROLF 5/7, son of Peter Fetherolf (4/5), (Peter Federolf 3/2, Anna M. Rothermel 2/2, Johannes Rothermel 1/1) and Anna M. Dunkelberger, was born January 6, 1806 in Cameron Twp., Northumberland Co., PA, and died March 16, 1861 in Upper Mahantango Twp., Schuylkill Co., PA. He married Sarah Reiner, born February 26, 1805; died September 13, 1887. They are buried in the Salem (Herb) Cemetery near Klingerstown, PA.

CHILDREN:

*	6/1	Harrison Fetterolf (12/23/1829 - 4/26/1906)	m. Lucinda Brosius (1842 - 5/2/1899)
	6/2	Peter Fetterolf (8/5/1830 - 12/29/1894)	m. Henrietta Hepler (10/15/1835 - 6/16/1912)
	6/3	Louise Fetterolf (11/10/1833 -)	
	6/4	Elizabeth Fetterolf (1/30/1836 - 1913)	m. Isaac Knorr
	6/5	Catharine Fetterolf (9/19/1837 - 12/18/1914)	
	6/6		
	6/7		
	6/8	Mary Fetterolf	m. Nelson Knorr
	6/9	Elias Fetterolf (2/5/1849 - 1/5/1925)	m. Lovina Miller (10/2/1854 - 1/24/1903)

Huntersville Christ Independent Church, established 1805. Church is located on what was once the main road between Mowry and Lavelle, Pa. Several generations of Fetterolfs are buried here.

HARRISON FETTEROLF 6/1, son of Peter Fetterolf 5/7 (Peter Fetherolf 4/5, Peter Federolf 3/2, Anna M. Rothermel 2/2, Johannes Rothermel 1/1) and Sarah Reiner, was born December 25, 1829 in Cameron Twp., Northumberland County, Pa. and died April 26, 1906 in Lavelle, Schuylkill County, Pa. He married Lucinda Brosius, born 1842; died May 2, 1899. They are buried in the Sunnyside Cemetery.
CHILDREN:

7/1 August Fetterolf (1871- (Sunnyside Cem.)   Jemima Hodge (1881- 1916)
   CHILDREN: (Thirteen children; three died as infants)
     8/1 Charles A. Fetterolf (4/20/1897-6/10/1972)   Lottie E. Reiner - Leck Kill (Jacobs Cem.)
     8/2 Martha Fetterolf (1899- 1918)   John H. Hepler
     8/3 Frank E. Fetterolf (7/2/1901-7/ /1954)   Elsie M. Maurer
     8/4 Elnora Fetterolf (10/28/1902-2/14/1980)   Rathmus M. Minnick
     8/5 Althesta Fetterolf (4/24/1906-   William Adams
     8/6 Wesley T. Fetterolf (6/13/1907-3/3/1982)   Irene N. Kehler
     8/7 Clayton H. Fetterolf (10/18/1908-   Beatrice M. Evans
     8/8 Harvey L. Fetterolf (8/24/1911-5/ /1950)   Catherine Reinoehl
     8/9 Clyde W. Fetterolf (6/2/1914-5/27/1985)   Ruth E. Leiser
     8/10 Archie G. Fetterolf (4/6/1916-   Maude Brosius

CHARLES A. FETTEROLF 8/1, son of August Fetterolf 7/1 (Harrison Fetterolf 6/1, Peter Fetterolf 5/7, Peter Fetherolf 4/5, Peter Federolf 3/2, Anna M. Rothermel 2/2, Johannes Rothermel 1/1) and Jemima Hodge, was born April 20, 1897 and died June 10, 1972. He married Lottie E. Reiner, born March 24, 1896; died August 1, 1973.
DESCENDANTS:

9/1 Pauline M. Fetterolf (3/27/1916-3/16/1978)   Clement L. Masser
  10/1 June M. Masser (5/30/1936-   Willard W. Haas
    11/1 Faith L. Haas (1/16/1955-   Darrell G. Klinger
      12/1 Douglas M. Klinger (2/6/1975-
      12/2 Andrew D. Klinger (6/1/1978-
    11/2 Audrey A. Haas (12/15/1955-   Barry L. Bahler
      12/1 Denise M. Bahler (4/19/1983-
      12/2 Will G. Bahler (2/28/1985-
    11/3 Stephen W. Haas (11/12/1957-   Virginia L. Zimmerman
  10/2 Mark C. Masser (10/13/1941-   Arlene M. Willier
    11/1 Lamont M. Masser (6/2/1970-
    11/2 Nolan L. Masser (12/13/1972-
  10/3 Diana G. Masser (3/30/1945-   Byrant R. Klinger
    11/1 Jeffrey B. Klinger (11/5/1967-
    11/2 Wayne G. Klinger (8/13/1971-
    11/3 Ann M. Klinger (10/12/1976-
  10/4 Joan E. Masser   Steve E. Troutman

FETTEROLF GENEALOGY

HARRISON FETTEROLF 6/1, son of Peter Fetterolf (5/7), (Peter Fetherolf 4/5, Peter Federolf 3/2, Anna M. Rothermel 2/2, Johannes Rothermel 1/1), and Sarah Reiner, was born December 15, 1829, In Cameron Twp., Northumberland Co., PA, and died April 26, 1906, in Lavelle, Schuylkill Co., PA. He married Lucinda Brosius, born 1842; died May 2, 1899. They are buried in the Sunnyside Cemetery.

<u>CHILDREN:</u>

* 7/1   August Fetterolf (1871 -)   m. Jemima Hodge (1881 - 1916)

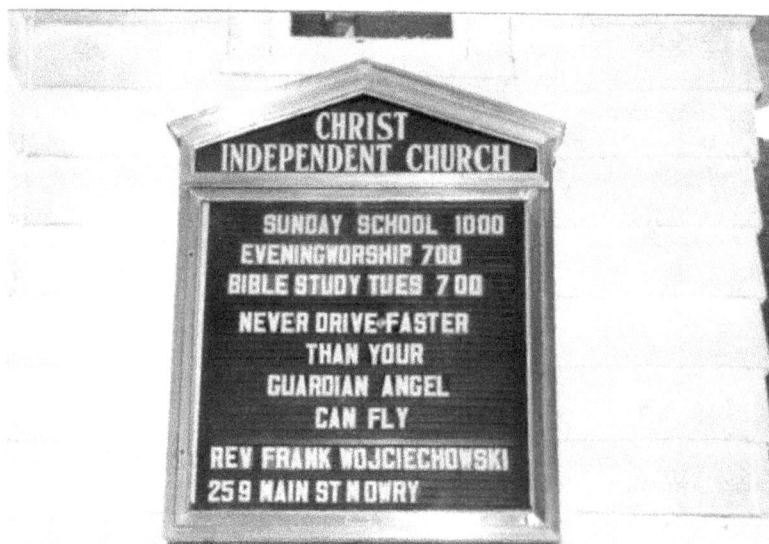

Huntersville one-room school house, west of the church.

FETTEROLF GENEALOGY

AUGUST FETTEROLF 7/1, son of Harrison Fetterolf (6/1), (Peter Fetterolf 5/7, Peter Fetherolf 4/5, Peter Federolf 3/2, Anna M. Rothermel 2/2, Johannes Rothermel 1/1), and Lucinda Brosius, was born 1871; and date of death is unknown. He married Jemima Hodge, who was born 1881; and died in 1916.

CHILDREN:

* 8/1 Charles A. Fetterolf (4/20/1897 - 6/10/1972)   m. Lottie E. Reiner
  8/2 Martha Fetterolf (1899 - 1918)   m. John H. Hepler
  8/3 Frank E. Fetterolf (7/2/1801 - 7/1954)   m. Elsie M. Maurer
  8/4 Einora Fetterolf (10/28/1902 - 2/14/1980)   m. Rathmus M. Minnick
  8/5 Althesta Fetterolf (4/24/1906 - 2/20/1989)   m. William Adams
  8/6 Wesley T. Fetterolf (6/13/1907 - 3/3/1982)   m. Irene N. Kehler
  8/7 Clayton H. Fetterolf (10/18/1908 -)   m. Beatrice M. Evans
  8/8 Harvey L. Fetterolf (8/24/1911 - 5/1950)   m. Catherine Reinoehl
  8/9 Clyde W. Fetterolf (6/2/1914 - 5/27/1985)   m. Ruth E. Leiser
  8/10 Archie G. Fetterolf (4/6/1916 - 6/3/1996)   m. Maude Brosius

Fetterolf Family Genealogy Prepared by the Katie (Fetterolf) Rothermel Family

Charles A. Fetterolf (1897-1972)
Son of August and Jemima Hodge Fetterolf,
Standing on a horse, at the crossroads in Gowen City. Pa.

Photo courtesy of Mr. and Mrs. Kenneth Minnich, 3835 Road Meadow Lane, Hatboro, Pa.

The Charles and Lottie (Reiner) Fetterolf Family

Front Row: Iva (Saltzman), Lottie, Charles, Katie (Rothermel)
Back Row: Mae (Fetterolf), Elda (Kahler), Pauline (Masser), Mark Fetterolf,
Anna (Specht), Ethel (Kimmel)

FETTEROLF GENEALOGY

CHARLES A. FETTEROLF 8/1, son of August Fetterolf (7/1), (Harrison Fetterolf 6/1, Peter Fetterolf 5/7, Peter Fetherolf 4/5, Peter Federolf 3/2, Anna M. Rothermel 2/2, Johannes Rothermel 1/1) and Jemima Hodge, was born April 20, 1897, and died June 10, 1972. He married Lottie E. Reiner, born March 24, 1896; died August 1, 1973.

DESCENDANTS:

9/1 Pauline M. Fetterolf (3/27/1916 - 3/16/1978) m. Clement L. Masser
  10/1 June M. Masser (5/30/1936 - m. Willard W. Haas
    11/1 Faith L. Haas (1/16/1955 - m. Darrell G. Klinger
      12/1 Douglas M. Klinger (2/6/1975-
      12/2 Andrew D. Klinger (6/1/1978 -
    11/2 Audrey A. Haas (12/15/1955 - m. Barry L. Bahler
      12/1 Denise M. Bahler (4/19/1983 -
      12/2 Will G. Bahler (2/28/1985 -
    11/3 Stephen W. Haas (11/12/1957 - m. Virginia L. Zimmerman
  10/2 Mark C. Masser (10/13/1941 - m. Arlene M. Willier
    11/1 Lamont M. Masser (6/2/1970 -
    11/2 Nolan L. Masser (12/13/1972 -
  10/3 Diana G. Masser (3/30/1945 - m. Bryant R. Klinger
    11/1 Jeffrey B. Klinger (11/5/1967 -
    11/2 Wayne G. Klinger (8/13/1971 -
    11/3 Ann M. Klinger (10/12/1976 -
  10/4 Joan E. Masser (5/20/1952 - m. Steve E. Troutman
    11/1 Michael S. Troutman (1/12/1978 -
    11/2 Valarie E. Troutman (9/23/1980 -

9/2 Mae I. Fetterolf (1/14/1918 - 11/11/1987) m. Ralph L. Fetterolf
  10/1 Eleanore K. Fetterolf (12/8/1940 - m. Ray A. Williard
    11/1 Kent R. Williard (4/21/1961 - m. Lori Leffler
      12/1 Ryan K. Williard (1/4/1984 -
    11/2 Kelly M. Willard (4/27/1967 -
  10/2 Mary J. Fetterolf (4/2/1949 - m. Glenn L. Schreffler
    11/1 Eric G. Schreffler (12/18/1970 -
    11/2 Scott R. Schreffler (1971 -
    11/3 Kristy A. Schreffler (6/9/1976 -

9/3 Elda E. Fetterolf (8/9/1919 - m. Dwight A. Kehler
  10/1 Joyce E. Kehler (11/21/1942 - m. Larry J. Gooding
    11/1 Steven J. Gooding (2/10/1967 - m.
      12/1 Grant Gooding
    11/2 Lara J. Gooding (9/5/1970 -

Elda Edna Fetterolf Kehler born Aug 9 /1919 , Klingerstown , pa ----- died Aug 24 / 2009
Married---- Dwight Albert Kehler born Feb 25 / 1921 pitman , pa ----- died April 21 / 1982
Joyce Elaine Kehler Gooding born Nov 21 / 1942 Pitman , Pa -----------xxxxxxx
Married -- Larry James Gooding born --- Flint , MI March 5 1943 -----------xxxxxxx
Steven James Gooding , born Holy Redeemer Hosp in Huntington Valley pa ---- 2 / 10 / 67
Lara Joy Gooding " " "" """"""""""""""""""""""""""""" 9 / 5 / 70
Steve married Leslie Gaskill on 12 / 30 1995
Grant James Gooding born in Bryn Maur hosp 1 / 16 / 98
Sarah Joy Gooding born "" "" "" """""""" 10 / 27 / 2000

FETTEROLF GENEALOGY

9/4 Mark D. Fetterolf (10/22/1921 - 2/20/1985)   m. Lorraine C. Reinoehl
    10/1 Carol E. Fetterolf (3/2/1944 -   m. Roger L. Hess
        11/1 Matthew Hess (8/11/1970 -
    10/2 Peggy G. Fetterolf (4/17/1946 -   m. Herbert J.F. Borchet
        11/1 Beth A. Borchert (12/24/1969 -
        11/2 Heidi J. Borchert (6/30/1973 -
        11/3 Carolyn A. Borchert (9/24/1979 -
    10/3 Dennis M. Fetterolf (8/3/1948 -   m. Brenda Frounfelter
        11/1 Michael D. Fetterolf (12/23/1968 -
        11/2 Samantha J. fetterolf (11/22/1972 -
    10/4 Charles J. Fetterolf (4/12/1951 -   m. Linda S. Haas
        11/1 Brian C. Fetterolf (4/17/1977 -
    10/5 David M. Fetterolf (3/24/1956 -

9/5 Anna M. Fetterolf (8/9/1923 -   m. Leon Specht
    10/1 Franklin L. Specht (10/19/1942 -   m. Sandra L. Lesher
        11/1 Wendy A. Specht (10/19/1964 -   m.
            12/1
        11/2 Eric F. Specht (6/1/1969 -   m. Tammy
            12/1 Jordan Specht
            12/2 Jared Specht
    10/2 Jack L. Specht (5/19/1944 -   m. Yvonne D. Klouser
        11/1 Shannon L. Specht (10/3/1968 -
        11/2 Shane L. Specht (8/12/1971 -
        11/3 Somer A. Specht (2/10/1975 -

9/6 Katie A. Fetterolf (3/26/1925 -   m. Stanley J. Rothermel
    10/1 Randall C. Rothermel (4/20/1949 - 4/23/1949)
    10/2 Rhonda R. Rothermel (11/27/1950 -   m. 1st Donald F. Rhoades, Jr.
                                        (m. 4/25/1970) (D)
                                m. 2nd Bill Stout (m. 5/10/1991)
        11/1 Todd A. Rothermel (2/17/1969 -
        11/2 Daniel C. Rhoades (5/12/1971 -   m. Gina (m. 12/23/1997)
            12/1 Celena L. Rhoades (4/23/1997 -
        11/3 Travis J. Rhoades (10/31/1976 -
    10/3 Susan J. Rothermel (12/3/1953 -   m. 1st Barry Jandla (m. 6/7/1975)
                                          (D)
                                m. 2nd Douglas MacWade
                                      (m. 3/17/1984) (D)
        11/1 Allison N. MacWade (11/16/1985 -
        11/2 Kyle D. MacWade (1/11/1987 -
    10/4 Kristine A. Rothermel (4/12/1961 -   m. Robert W. Perry, Jr.
                                      (m. 9/27/1985)
        11/1 Jonathan C. Perry (8/25/1986 -
        11/2 Shawn P. Perry (11/3/1990 -

Fetterolf Family Genealogy Prepared by the Katie (Fetterolf) Rothermel Family

33

9/6   Katie A. Fetterolf (3/26/1925 -   m. Stanley J. Rothermel
                                                                    (m. 9/28/1946) (b. 11/27/1925)

10/1   Randall C. Rothermel (4/20/1949 – 4/23/1949) (d)

10/2
       Rhonda R. Rothermel (11/27/1950 -   m. 1st Donald F. Rhoades, Jr.
                                                                    (m. 4/25/1970) (D)
                                                                    m. 2nd Bill Stout (m. 5/10/1991) (D)

              Todd A. Rothermel (2/17/1969 -   m. Kristine Ann Muzslay
       11/1   (m. 9-23-2006)
                                                                    (b. 7-29-????)
       11/2
              Daniel C. Rhoades (5/12/1971 -   m. Gina Kane
                                                                    (m. 12/23/1997) (D)

                     Celena L. Rhoades (4/23/1997 –

                     Daniel Rhoades (5-31-2000 -

                     Logan Rhoades (9-12-2003 -

       11/3   Travis J. Rhoades (10/31/1976 -

10/3   Susan J. Rothermel (12/3/1953 -   m. 1st Barry Jandla (m. 6/7/1975) (D)
                                                                    m. 2nd Douglas MacWade
                                                                    (m. 3/17/1984) (D)
                                                                    m. 3rd Merrit Baker
                                                                    (m. 10-17-2004)
                                                                    (b. 4-5-????)

              Allison N. MacWade (11/16/1985 –

              Kyle D. MacWade (1/11/1987 –

10/4   Kristine A. Rothermel (4/12/1961 -   m. Robert W. Perry, Jr.
                                                                    (m. 9/27/1985)
                                                                    (b. 11/17/1960)

       11/1   Jonathan C. Perry (8/25/1986 –

       11/2   Shawn P. Perry (11/3/1990 –

m = married   b = birthday   d = died   D = divorced

FETTEROLF GENEALOGY

9/7 Iva F. Fetterolf (7/21/1927 - 9/15/1982)   m. George H. Saltzman, Sr.
    10/1 George H. Saltzman (8/25/1954 -   m. Kathi Morgan
        11/1 Dennis G. Saltzman (7/29/1982 -
        11/2 James A. Saltzman (12/21/1984 -
        11/3 Randy Saltzman (8/18/1987 -

9/8 Ethel H. Fetterolf (3/4/1931 -   m. Charles J. Kimmel
    10/1 Ronald G. Kimmel (8/17/1948 -   m. Brenda J. Leitzel
        11/1 Erin N. Kimmel (7/16/1983 -
    10/2 Linda S. Kimmel (10/31/1951 -   m. James V. Smith
        11/1 Brandon J. Smith (8/1/1974 -
        11/2 Eric J. Smith (5/16/1979 -
    10/3 Rickey C. Kimmel (7/8/1955 -
    10/4 Karen L. Kimmel (5/21/1957 -   m. Gerald Harmon
    10/5 Gary C. Kimmel (4/18/1958 -   m. Cindy S. Sterling
    10/6 Randy K. Kimmel (4/14/1959 -   m. Betty J. Long
    10/7 Lori A. Kimmel (3/18/1962 -   m. Donald W. Stutzman
        11/1 Jason D. Stutzman (6/14/1983 -
    10/8 Scott A. Kimmel (6/26/1963 -
    10/9 Lisa M. Kimmel (7/22/1965 -

SOUTHEASTERN PA 18?
7 JUL
1998

Katie Rothermel
1365 Nevarc Rd
Warminster, PA 18974-3639

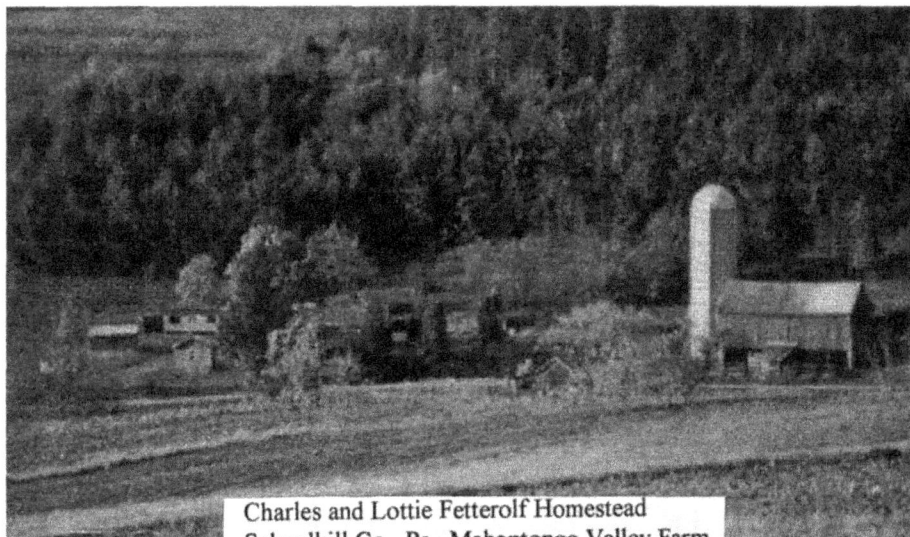

Charles and Lottie Fetterolf Homestead
Schuylkill Co., Pa., Mahantongo Valley Farm

FETTEROLF GENEALOGY

9/8 Ethel H. Fetterolf (3/4/1931 -   m. Charles J. Kimmel
                                                        (m. 7/16/1948) (b. 2/18/1926)

10/1   Ronald G. Kimmel (8/17/1948 -   m. Brenda J. Leitzel
                                                        (m. 10/10/1980)
                                                        (b. 10/8/1948)

         11/1   Erin N. Kimmel (7/16/1983 -

         11/2   Gregory Kimmel (6/26/1986 -

10/2   Linda S. Kimmel (10/31/1951 -   m. James V. Smith
                                                        (m. 11/19/1971) (b. 6/8/1945)

         11/1   Brandon J. Smith (8/1/1974 -   m. Melissa (m. 4/1/1997)
                                                        (b. 4/29/1977)

         11/2   Eric J. Smith (5/16/1979 -

10/3   Ricky C. Kimmel (7/8/1955 -

10/4   Karen L. Kimmel (5/21/1957 -   m. Gerald Harmon (m. 9/27/1985)
                                                         (b. 12/19/1953)

10/5   Gary C. Kimmel (4/18/1958 -   m. Cindy Sterling (m. 7/14/1984)
                                                        (b. 6/26/1962)

10/6   Randy K. Kimmel (4/14/1959 -   m. Betsy Long (m. 9/   /1983)
                                                        (b. 4/10/1962)

         11/1   Amanda Kimmel (9/10/1983 - 10/8/1983)

10/7   Lori A. Kimmel (3/18/1962 -   m. Donald Stutzman
                                                        (m. 11/7/1982)
                                                         (b. 5/19/1962)

         11/1   Jason D. Stutzman (6/14/1983 -

         11/2   Jeffery Stutzman (4/17/1987 -

10/8   Scott A. Kimmel (6/26/1963 -   m. Barbara Tyson (m. 9/7/1991)
                                                        (b. 11/29/1968)

         11/1   Adam Kimmel (1/3/1996 -

         11/2   Joel Miles (5/20/1999 -
                        Kimmel

10/9   Lisa M. Kimmel (7/22/1965 -

Fetterolf's School, Sawmill Road, Upper Mahantongo Twp., Schuylkill Co., Pa. Location: West side of township road between Leonard Adams and Raymond Bensinger. The school was originally built on land given by the Bensinger Family. Photo provided by Ronald Maurer, Halifax, Pa. Identification provided by Lawrence Maurer, April 2006. Grades 1-8, ca. 1930.

Front Row, left to right: Lawerence Maurer, Eugene Erdman, Harold Maurer (Lawrence's brother), Paul Martin, Bernard Adams (Leonard's brother). Second Row: Roy Erdman, Mark Fetterolf, Donald Haas, Ernest Bensinger, Jay Erdman, Guy Erdman. Third Row: Virginia Wetzel, Mae Martin (Paul's sister), Mae Fetterolf, Pauline Fetterolf, (age 12 or 13), Alma Maurer (Lawrence's sister), Arlene Zimmerman, Elda Fetterolf, Anna Fetterolf. Teacher, Clarence "Fetch" Fetterolf (Lawrence's first cousin).

Our Reiner Heritage

From Germany to Pennsylvania

The Reiner Family - from Germany to Pennsylvania.

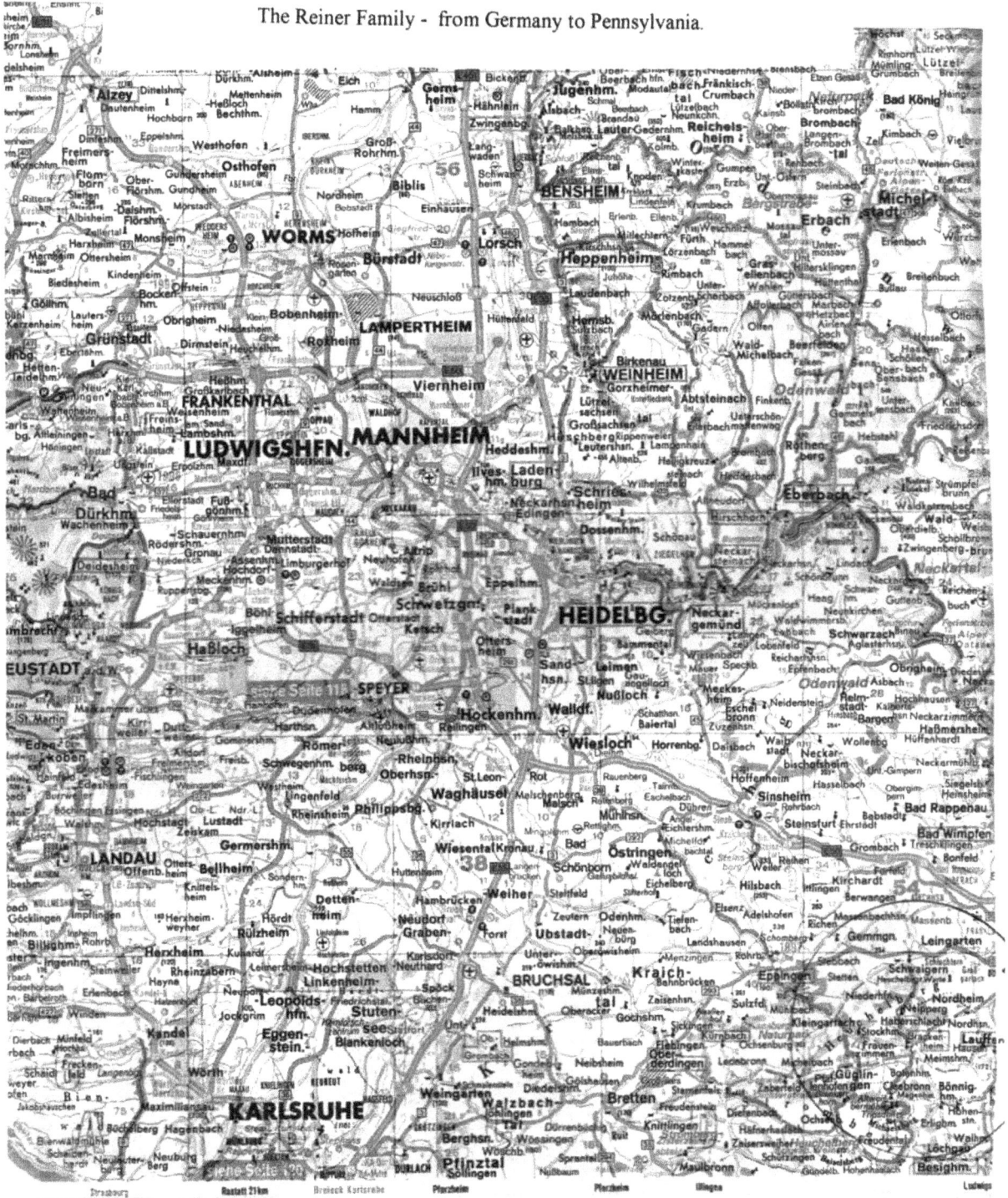

Location map showing Schwaigern and Meimsheim, Germany, the region of ancestral
Reiner homelands

The following Reiner history prepared by Rev. John L. Reiner of Latrobe, Pa., published by DocuData Associates in 1996 entitled <u>Genealogy of a Reiner Family.</u>

FOREWORD

Among the thousands of immigrants that came to the shores of America during the 18th. century was "Johann Dietrich Reiner, born in Schwaigren, Germany, under the rule of Count of Neipperg, Wuerttemberg, emigrated in April 1749 with his wife Maria Margaretha Schleicher, and six children named Johann Christian about years 30 old, Maria Magdalena 24 years old, Margaretha 22 years old, Sara 20 years old, Johannes 18 years old, Eberhardt about 16 years old, from their home to Pennsylvania. Announcement of the Council and state officials, also the Burgomaster and the court at Bonnigheim and the 'Zabergau' Wuerttemberg, 27 Oct. 1777, published OPZ 16 March 1778." The Pennsylvania Genealogical Magazine, p. 242.

"The Lutheran churchbook at the Evangelical parsonage Meimsheim contains the following: Johann Dietrich Reiner, son of Fredrich Reiner, citizen and copper at Schwaigren, was married 9 Oct. 1715 to Maria Margaretha Schleicher, daughter of the citizen cobbler Schleicher. Their children listed in the Evangelical church book were: Johann Christian, b. 10 April 1718; Maria Magdalena, b. 21 Sept. 1720; Maria Margaretha b. 12 Feb. 1723; Maria Sara, b. 2 Mai 1724; Georg Philipp, b. 30 Jan. 1727, d. 3 May 1729; Anna Maria, b. 9 June 1728, d. 8 June 1729; Johannes b. 13 July 1730; Eberharst Freidrich b. 23 March 1733." The Pennsylvania Genealogical Magazine, p. 242.

"Johann Dietrich Reiner" with his family arrived on ship FANE 17 Oct. 1749.

"Original article 'Einege Amerika Auswanderts des 18 Jarhundrets' in enftnegger Monatsblatt fuer Genealogie und Heralik, April 1958, Karl Friedrich v. Frank, editor and publisher, Schloss Senftenegg, Post Ferschmitz, Niederosterrich." The Pennsylvania Genealogy Magazine, p.242.

Johann Dietrich and his family settled in what was then known as Northampton County, now Leigh County, PA. Helen Grimes in her Reiner Genealogy p. 2 gives data items:

"Matthew & Hungerford's History of Lehigh County, printed 1884, page 372, states that the original Upper Milford Lutheran congregation at Dillingersville (now Lower Milford) listed Christian Reiner as a male communicant. In 1758 a new Lutheran congregation organized at the old Kings Highway in Zionville and Christian Reiner was a member."

"Penna. archives, 3rd. series , Vol 19, Upper Milford Twp., Northampton Co., Proprietary tax for 1772 lists:

Christian Reinard, farmer, 3 pounds, 4 shilling, 3 pence
George Reinard, farmer, 3 pounds, 4 shillings, 3 pence"

"Genealogical Society of Penna. has in their library the Zion Lutheran Church, Zionville, PA. records (UH-IL) 1757-1903 an the Evangelical Lutheran Church, Upper Milford, Northampton Co. Penna. records (NIL most records in German) page 87: Listing the children and date of birth and baptism of Christian Reinert and Catherine Reiss as follows:

1. Catherine, born August 11, 1759, baptized Sept. 14, 1757, sponsors : Joes Rohs (Ross)
   Catherine Herzog

2. Johannes, born August 23, 1759, baptized Nov.18, 1759,
   sponsors: Joes Rohs (Ross)
           Elizabeth Herzog

* see note

4. Joes Jacobus, born Sept. 12, 1761, baptized
   sponsors: Jacob Fischer
           Catharine

5. Christian, born Aug. 7, 1763, baptized Oct. 9, 1763,
   sponsors: Christian Mexter
           & wife Catherine

6. Maria Elizabeth, born Sept. 3, 1769, baptized Sept. 17, 1769,
   sponsors: Jacob Pliuginger
           & wife Maria Eli

* The third child born is Martin Reiner, born 20, 1760, as shown on
  a copy of his affidavit for a pension as a revolutionary veteran,
  dated Nov. 19, 1842." Helen Grimes, p. 2.

Johan Christian died in 1784 in Milford Twp., Northampton Co., PA. His son
[Johannes] John moved into Cumberland Co., Martin moved into Franklin Co.,
[Joes] Johan Jacob moved into Long Swamp Twp., Berks Co., Christian
remained in Upper Milford Twp., Northampton Co., PA. No data available
concerning the two daughters Catherine and Maria Elizabeth.

John Jacob Reiner married Maria Elizabeth Wagner, daughter of Jacob Wagner
and his wife Louisa Huber Wagner. John Jacob "who lived to be the last
surviving revolutionary war veteran of the entire Berks-Schuylkill area.
His tomb stone at Howerter's [St. James] Cemetery call him 'ein alter
Refulations Saldat (an old soldier of the Revolution), and his pension
papers in the National Archives furnish us with a brief autobiography:
Despont was born the 12th September 1761 in Upper Milford Township,
Northampton County, Pennsylvania-he continued to reside there in his
father's house until the year 1783- he continued to reside in Northampton
County for several years after when he removed to Berks County & resided
there for about four years-and then moved to his present neighborhood
where he has continued to reside ever since." The Northumberland County
Historical Society Proceedings Vol. XXIX p. 134.

"According to deeds in Reading he arrived in Mahantongo Valley in 1793.
Jacob Reinert was a founder and elder of the Howerter's Church, and served
also as a township commissioner for Mahantongo Township in the period of
1800-1810." The Northumberland County Historical Society Proceedings Vol.
XXIX p. 134.

A most interesting piece of folklore is told about John Jacob and his wife
Maria Elizabeth. It is said that they left their home in Long Swamp
Township, Berks County following Indian trails and paths and made their
way to the Mahantongo Valley, Berks Co., PA. (Now Eldred Twp., Schuylkill
Co., PA.) They had an ox cart that was so filled with household items plus
children that there was no room for Maria Elizabeth. She walked all the
way carrying a little baby, about 150 miles. They crossed the Hegins
mountain and came to a spring located a few hundred yards north of the
creek not far from the cross roads at the foot of the mountain. While John

Jacob went to search out the area Maria Elizabeth began to clear the areas around the spring. Here is where they settled. Here they built a log house. They cleared the land and began cultivating the land. One day as they were burning the branches and weeds the fire got away from them and the log house burned down. They built another house and lived here until both Jacob and Elizabeth died.

John Jacob died 3/8/1857. His wife Maria Elizabeth d. 3/8/1856. They are both buried in the Jacob's [Howerter's] Church Cemetery, Upper Mahanoy Township, Northumberland Co., PA. They had the following children: Johannes [John], b. 12/15/1788; John Jacob, Jr., b. 10/8/1789; Benjamin, b. 1/25/1792; Elizabeth, b. 12/14/1794; Lydia, b. / /1797; Charles b. 9/9/1799; George, b. 7/14/1802 and Sarah b. 2/26/1806.

This book is concerned with the descendants of Charles, sixth child and fourth son of John Jacob Reiner and Maria Elizabeth Wagner. It with sincere regret that it is not as complete as it might be. The reason for it is that some data cannot be found of the folks in the genealogy. Another reason is that some folks just did not respond to the request for data concerning themsevles. Others just could not be reached. One did respond by saying it "is none of your damm business". Another said she was more concerned "where she was going then where she came from".

In the "New Dictionary of American Family Names" by Elson C. Smith, published by Harper and Row the following is given for the meaning of the name Reiner:

Reinard [Eng.] variant of Reiner; Reiner [Ger.] descendants of Raginhari, [Counsel, Army]; Reinert [Ger.] Descendant of Raginhart [Counsel, Strong].

Others say that the name Reiner comes from the German word REIN which means clean. Thus it may speak of one who is REIN, clean, or one who cleans.

The name **REINER** has different variants such as Reinert, Reinard, Riner, Rynard, Reinerd, Reinhart and Reinhardt.

Daniel Mosser Reiner
(11/19/1842)-(5/5/1919)

M.Elmira (Yoder) Reiner
2nd wife of Daniel
(9/4/1856)-(7/25/1908)

Ansicht von Schwaigern um 1680 (aus dem Forstkartenwerk "Stromberg" von Andreas Kieser).

Johann Dietrich Reiner's baptism took place in Meimsheim, Germany near the larger city of Schwaigern. The Evangelical Church in Meimsheim is located in an area surrounded by grape vineyards and farm fields. The ancient building is made of stone and wood with a large steeple at one end. A sign posted recalls a lightning strike which the church survived. The church is the most prominent building in the small town of Meimsheim.

421. REINER, JOH. DIETERICH   7103 Schwaigern
     REINER, CHRISTIAN

Fane, 1749
S-H, 425

SCHWAIGERN LUTHERAN KB:
Friderich Reiner, baker and wife Barbara had:
    Hans Diter bp. 2 Mar. 1696
Joh. Dieter Reiner and wife Maria Margaretha had:
    1. Johann Frederich b. 24 Aug. 1715
    2. Hans Dieterich b. 2 Sept. 1716
    3. Johann Christian b. 10 Apr. 1718
    4. Maria Magdalena b. 21 Sept. 1720
    5. Maria Margaretha b. 12 Feb. 1723
    6. Maria Sara b. 2 May 1724
    7. Georg Philipp b. 30 Jan. 1727; d. 31 May 1729
    8. Anna Maria b. 9 June 1728; d. 8 June 1729
    9. Johannes b. 13 July 1730
    10. Eberhard Frederich b. 23 Mar. 1733
    11. Johann Georg b. 20 Apr. 1736
    12. Maria Barbara b. 3 Dec. 1738

Pennsylvania records:

For additional details concerning the emigration of this family, see Friedrich Krebs' "Annotations to Strassburger and Hinke's Pennsylvania German Pioneers", *The Pennsylvania Genealogical Magazine*, 21 (1960): 235-248; reprinted in: Carl Boyer. *Ship Passenger Lists, Pennsylvania and Delaware* (1980), 106, 107.

The following is a Reiner Family genealogy by Rev. John L. Reiner, D.D. as found in Genealogy of the Reiner Family Descendants of Charles Reiner and Maria Margaret Mosser, May 1966.

Heinrich Reiner, b. before 1600, Wuerttemberg, Germany. d. 9/11/1638 Wuerttemberg md. Anna Kneer, b. before 1600, Wuerttemberg, Germany.

Hans Dietrich Reiner, b. 8/24/1626, Wuerttemberg, Germany. md. Anna Christina Rosa, b. 8/24/1625, Wuerttemberg, Germany.

Frederick Dietrich Reinter, b. 5/9/1655, Wuerttemberg, Germany. d. 8/9/1739 Germany, md. Barbara Reiner, b. Meimsheim, Krs. Heilbrun, Germany, d. 9/10/1700

(Hans) Dietrich Reiner, b. 2/3/1690, Wuerttemberg, Germany. d. 1784 Northampton County, Pa. md. Maria Margaretha Schleicher
Left Schwaigren , Bavaria, in April 1749 and arrived in Philadelphia in October 17, 1749.

Hans Johann Christian Reiner, b. 4/10/1718, Wuerttemberg, Germany. d. 1784 Upper Milford Township, Northampton County, Pa. md. Catherina Reus (Reiss)

John Jacob Reiner, b. 9/12/1761, Upper Milford Township, Northampton County, Pa., d. 3/8/1857, Eldred Twp., Schuylkill Co., Pa. md. Maria Elizabeth Wagner, b. 2/21/1765, Macungie Twp., Northampton County, Pa., d. 3/8/1856 Eldred Twp., Schuylkill Co., Pa. These are the Mahantongo Valley pioneers.

Charles Reiner, Sr., b. 9/14/1799, Mahantongo Twp., Berks Co., Pa. d. 7/25/1878, Upper Mahantongo Twp., Schuylkill Co., Pa. md. Maria Margaret Mosser, b. 5/7/1802, Mahantongo Twp., Berks Co. Pa., d. 3/30/1880, Upper Mahantongo Twp., Schuylkill Co., Pa.

Daniel Mosser Reiner, b. 11/19/1842, Upper Mahantongo Twp., Schuylkill Co., Pa., d. 5/5/1919, Upper Mahantongo Twp., Schuylkill Co., Pa., md. First Lucetta Christ, b. 9/5/1848, Eldred Twp., Schuylkill Co., Pa., d. 9/22/1874 Upper Mahantongo Twp., Schuylkill Co., Pa. md. second M. Elmira Yoder b. 9/4/1856, Eldred Twp., Schuylkill Co., Pa. d. 7/25/1908 Upper Mahantongo Twp., Schuylkill Co., Pa.

Lottie Edna (Reiner) Fetterolf, b. 3/24/1896, Upper Mahantongo Twp., Schuylkill Co., Pa.

LOTTIE EDNA, b. 3/24/1896, Upper Mahantongo Twp., Schuylkill Co., PA.
- Ed. Attended Karterman Elementary School, Hepler, PA.
- M. CHARLES AUGUST FETTEROLF, s/o AUGUSTUS FETTEROLF & JEMINA HODGE, on 3/4/1916, in the Reformed Parsonage, Leck Kill, PA.
- Children: PAULINE MARIE FETTEROLF, b. 3/27/1916; MAE IRENE FETTEROLF, b. 1/4/1918; ELDA EDNA FETTEROLF, b. 8/9/1923. All three were born in the home of their grandfather on the REINER homestead; MARK DANIEL FETTEROLF, b. 10/22/1921; ANNA MYA FETTEROLF, b. 8/9/1923; KATIE ARLENE FETTEROLF, b. 3/26/1925; IVA FERN FETTEROLF, b. 7/2/1927, ETHEL HILDA FETTEROLF, b. 3/4/1931. These were born in the family home R. D. #1, Klingerstown, PA.
- Occupation: housewife. Her husband, CHARLES, was a farmer. During the early 1920's, when the anthracite coal industry was booming, he also worked in the coal mines at Good Springs, PA.
- **LOTTIE** d. 8/1/1973, R. D., Klingerstown, PA. Her husband, CHARLES, d. 6/10/1972, R. D. Klingerstown, PA. Cause of his death was a heart attack. Both are buried in Jacob's Cemetery, Upper Mahanoy Twp., Northumberland Co., PA.

Daniel Reiner homestead located on a farm which is lately known as the Clark Reiner farm. This old house now removed was on the north side of township road T-242, Valley Road, between Stehr Brothers' Mill and the St. Jacob's Howerter's Cemetery. This Reiner dwelling was opposite the present tenant farmhouse owned by Clark Reiner.

These photos courtesy of Marie Reiner Gallagher as well as the photo of Elmira Reiner. The enlargement shows an old man with a beard, most likely, Daniel Reiner, himself.

CHARLES AUGUST FETTEROLF & LOTTIE EDNA REINER
b. 4/20/1897   b. 3/24/1896
    Helfenstein, PA   Upper Mahantongo Twp.
                                    Schuylkill Co., PA
d. 6/10/1972   d. 8/1/1973
    R. D. # 1,   R. D. #1, Klingerstown, PA
    Klingerstown, PA

Married < > 3/4/1916
Children

Pauline	Mae	Elda	Anna
Marie	Irene	Edna	Mya
Fetterolf	Fetterolf	Fetterolf	Fetterolf

Katie	Iva	Mark	Ethel
Arlene	Fern	Daniel	Hilda
Fetterolf	Fetterolf	Fetterolf	Fetterolf

PAULINE MARIE FETTEROLF, b. 3/27/1916, R. D. #1, Klingerstown, PA.
- Ed. Completed eighth grade in Fetterolf Elementary School, R. D. #1, Klingerstown, PA.
- M. CLEMENT LLOYD MASSER, s/o CHARLES MONROE MASSER & MARY SALOME BOHNER, on 8/3/1935, in Christ United Church of Christ, Leck Kill, PA.
- Children: JUNE MARIE MASSER, b. 5/30/1936, Ashland, PA.; MARK CLEMENT MASSER, b. 10/13/1941, Danville, PA.; DIANA GLORIA MASSER, b. 3/30/1945, Leck Kill, PA.; JOAN ELIZABETH MASSER, b. 5/20/1952, Danville, PA.
- Occupation: Housewife. Her husband, CLEMENT, was a farmer specializing in potatoes.
- PAULINE d. 3/16/1978, Pottsville, PA. Cause of death was cancer. She is buried in Jacob's Cemetery, Upper Mahanoy Twp., Northumberland Co., PA.

MAE IRENE FETTEROLF, b. 1/4/1918, Pitman, PA.
- Ed. Completed eighth grade, Fetterolf Elementary School, R. D. #1, Klingerstown, PA.
- M. RALPH LAMAR FETTEROLF, s/o JOHN WALTER FETTEROLF & KATIE AMELIA SEILER, on 8/10/1940, in the home of her uncle, VICTOR Y(ODER) REINER, Pitman, PA. by MAE'S cousin Pastor JOHN L. REINER.
- Child. ELEANOR KATHRYN FETTEROLF, b. 12/8/1940; MARY JANE FETTEROLF, b. 2/2/1949. Both were born in R. D. #1, Klingerstown, PA.
- Occupation: Housewife. For a number of years was severely handicapped with poor eye sight. Her husband, RALPH, was a farmer all his life.
- MAE d. 11/11/1987, Pottsville, PA. Cause of her death was respiratory failure. Her husband, RALPH, d. 5/29/1996, Pitman, PA. Both are buried in the Salem Church Cemetery, Rough and Ready, R. D. #1, Klingerstown, PA.

ELDA EDNA FETTEROLF, b. 8/9/1919, Pitman, PA.
- Ed. Completed eighth grade, Fetterolf Elementary School, R. D. #1 Klingerstown, PA.
- M. DWIGHT ALBERT KEHLER, s/o LAWRENCE ULYSSES KEHLER & EVA LYDIA SNYDER, on 6/20/1940, in Lutheran Parsonage, Leck Kill, PA.
- Child. JOYCE ELAINE KEHLER, b. 11/21/1942, Pitman, PA.
- Occupation: Housewife. Her husband, DWIGHT, was a machine operator, Standard Pressed Steel. He died 4/21/1982, Meadow Brook., PA. Cause of death was due to metastasis to bone marrow. He is buried in the Hillside Cemetery, Roslyn, PA.

MARK DANIEL FETTEROLF, b. 10/22/1921, R. D. #1, Klingerstown, PA.
- Ed. Completed eighth grade, Fetterolf Elementary School, R. D. #1, Klingerstown, PA.
- M. LORRAINE CLARA BERTHA REINOEHL, da/o ELMER REINOEHL & MAUDE GRACE PENNYPACKER, on 9/4/1943, in Christ United Church of Christ, Leck Kill, PA.

45

- Children: CAROL EDNA FETTEROLF, b. 3/2/1944; PEGGY GRACE FETTEROLF, b. 4/17/1946; DENNIS MARK FETTEROLF, b. 8/3/1948; CHARLES JAMES FETTEROLF, b. 4/12/1951; DAVID MERLE FETTEROLF, b. 3/24/1956. All children were born at home, R. D. #1, Klingerstown, PA.
- Occupation: Farmer and coal miner. He was last employed as a security guard at the Kocher Coal Co., Valley View, PA. until he became ill in 2/1983. His wife, LORRAINE, is a housewife.
- **MARK** d. 2/20/1985 in his home. Cause of death was cancer and heart problems. He is buried in Hepler's Church of God Cemetery, Eldred Twp., Schuylkill Co., PA.

ANNA MYA FETTEROLF, b. 8/9/1923, R. D. #1, Klingerstown, PA.
- Ed. Completed tenth grade, Hegins High School, Hegins, PA., 1939.
- 1 M. LEON CALVIN SPECHT, s/o CHARLES SPECHT & ALICE MAURER, on 6/6/1942, in her uncle VICTOR Y(ODER) REINER'S home, Pitman, PA.
- Children: FRANKLIN LEON SPECHT, b. 10/19/1942, Danville, PA; JACK LEE SPECHT, b. 5/19/1944, Pitman, PA.
- 2 M. CLINTON BAKER, s/o EDWARD GEORGE BAKER & ELIZABETH JANE FULLER, on 9/2/1992, Wellsboro, PA.
- Occupation: Housewife and factory worker. Her husband, LEON, was killed in Luxembourg during WW II on 12/16/1944. He is buried in Jacob's Cemetery Upper Mahanoy Twp., Northumberland Co., PA.

KATIE ARLENE FETTEROLF, b. 3/26/1925, R. D. #1, Klingerstown, PA.
- Ed. Hegins Twp. High School, Hegins, PA., 1943.
- M. STANLEY JUNIOR ROTHERMEL, s/o AMOS ROBERT ROTHERMEL & LAURA IRENE BUFFINGTON, on 9/28/1946 in St. Michael's Lutheran & Reformed Church, Klingerstown, PA.
- Children: RANDALL CHARLES ROTHERMEL, b. 4/20/1949, Pitman PA, d. 4/23/1949, buried in St. Michael's Cemetery, Klingerstown, PA; RHONDA ROMAINE ROTHERMEL, b. 11/27/1950, Pitman, PA; SUSAN JANE ROTHERMEL, b. 12/3/1953, Ashland, PA; KRISTINE ANN ROTHERMEL, b. 4/12/1961.
- Occupation: Housewife. Her husband, STANLEY, is a press operator at SPS Technologies, Hatfield, PA.

IVA FERN FETTEROLF, b. 7/21/1927, R. D. #1, Klingerstown, PA.
- Ed. Completed eighth grade, Fetterolf Elementary School, R. D. #1, Klingerstown, PA.
- M. GEORGE HERBERT SALTZMAN, s/o CHARLES JOHN SALTZMAN & MARGARET ANN SMITH, on 9/30/1948, in Elden, MD.
- Children: GEORGE HERBERT SALTZMAN JR., b. 9/25/1954, R. D. #1, Klingerstown, PA.
- Occupation: Housewife. Her husband, GEORGE, is a heavy equipment operator, mechanic, and truck driver.
- **IVA** d. 9/15/1982, Klingerstown, PA. Cause of her death was heart failure. She is buried in Jacob's Cemetery, Upper Mahanoy Twp., Northumberland Co., PA.

ETHEL HILDA FETTEROLF, b. 3/4/1931, R. D. #1, Klingerstown, PA.
- Ed. Hegins Twp. High School, Hegins, PA., 1948.
- M. CHARLES JUNIOR KIMMEL, s/o CHARLES FRANK KIMMEL & ANNA JOSEPHINE KIMMEL,

on 7/16/1948, in Christ United Church of Christ, Leck Kill, PA.
Child. RONALD GEORGE KIMMEL, b. 8/17/1948, R. D. #1, Klingerstown, PA.; LINDA SUE KIMMEL, b. 10/31/1952, R. D. # 1, Klingerstown, PA.; RICKY CHARLES KIMMEL, b. 7/8/1955, Ashland, PA.; KAREN LOTTIE KIMMEL, b. 5/21/1957, Ashland, PA.; GARY CHARLES KIMMEL, b. 4/18/1958, R. D. #1, Klingerstown, PA; RANDY KEITH KIMMEL, b. 4/14/1959, Klingerstown, PA.; LORI ANN KIMMEL, b. 3/18/1962, Ashland, PA.; SCOTT ALAN KIMMEL, b. 6/26/1963, Ashland, PA.
Occupation. Housewife. Her husband, CHARLES, is a laborer at a coal breaker.

Lottie Edna Reiner
(1896-1973)

Charles A. Fetterolf
(1897-1972)

Buried, Jacob's, (Howerter's) Cemetery, Upper Mahanoy Twp., Northumberland Co., Pa.

The Dennis Fetterolf Farm in 2009. It is located at 331 Creek Road, Klingerstown, Pa., in the Mahantongo Valley, Schuylkill County, Pennsylvania. It is previously the site of the homestead of Charles and Lottie Fetterolf.

MEMORIES OF MAMMY AND PAPPY FETTEROLF

Franklin L. Specht

1) At planting time, Pappy Fetterolf would take his horses, equipment and seed to the field in the morning. Before watches were popular, at lunch time, Mammy Fetterolf would hang a sheet, which was visible to most of the farm, on the front porch wash line to let Pappy know that lunch was ready. Pappy would tie the horses in the shade and walk home from the field for lunch. When he returned to the field, he'd throw a 160 pound bag of fertilizer over his shoulder and carry it back to the field.

2) Prior to combines, the grain would be put in shocks, a shock is when the grain is cut with a binder machine and tied in a bundle. When the thrashing machine came to the farms to separate the grain from the stalk and husks, the farmers would get together and help each other. The women of the farm where the thrashing was taking place would prepare elaborate lunches for the workers. The women would have a competition trying to prepare a more elaborate meal or dessert than the other one. The farmer really enjoyed the competition.

3) The last horses Pappy Fetterolf had were well trained. He had three, a big team and a third horse. The third horse was used as a backup if one of the team horses had a problem. It was also used to pull a single horse cultivator and was trained to pull the hay rope to unload the loose hay from a wagon into the barn. The rope had a hay hook in order to grab the hay. When the hay was on the hook, the horse had to walk away from the barn approx, 30' to lift the hay and then make a small circle and return to the barn. He'd have to make another small circle and do it all over again. He had to be careful so he didn't get tangled in the rope. At the start of each haying season, Pappy Fetterolf had to walk with the horse six times, but after that the horse would work on commands given by Pappy who was in the barn.

4) When Pappy Fetterolf got his first tractor, the implements, such as the reaper, hay rake, grain drill and manure spreader, were made to be horse drawn. They were fitted with wooden tongues to enable a tractor to pull the equipment. Pappy didn't get the knack of turning and turned too short with the tractor and broke several of the tongues until he became more experienced with the tractor.

5) Pappy Fetterolf was a very experienced butcher. He butchered for his family, relatives and friends. He also did some veterinary procedures for area farmers which included helping cows that were having difficulty giving birth to their calves, inserting a tube into the bloated stomach of a cow to allow the gas to escape to relieve the bloat. Pappy would also put rings in bulls noses when the bull got nasty and couldn't be controlled any other way.

6) I have no first hand knowledge of this, but Pappy Fetterolf shared some of his boyhood memories with me. One that I remember is that when he lived in Helfenstein, he and other boys would get in a box car of a train in Ashland with their guns and dogs and go to Renovo, PA to hunt rabbits. They would hunt rabbits and camp in the woods and return home on another train. He hunted rabbits after he married Mammy Fetterolf and Mammy would can the rabbits. Frank also remembers Uncle Mark, Jack and Frank shooting rabbits and Mammy canning the rabbits so they could enjoy them during the winter.

Franklin L. Specht

From: **Kris Perry** (kris.perry425@verizon.net)
Sent: Sun 1/31/10 1:03 AM

I'm Kaite the 6th child of Lottie (Reiner) and Charles Fetterolf, and the first one to graduate from High School. I walked about 1-1/2 miles to the main road (I think it's now called Ridge Road) to get the bus. I had to be at the bus stop by 7 o'clock in the morning. In the winter time I carried a lantern to see, because there were mud puddles and rocks. Mom always saw that I was up and had breakfast before I left in the morning. In very bad weather Pop would take me to the bus stop. When I got home there was always something for me to do.

Mom baked all our bread and canned vegetables for the winter. We had to watch the cows in certain fields and if it got to hot we would run in the creek to cool off. Pop took the vegetables we grew to market and people would give him their children's out grown clothes and we were glad for them. If he brought shoes home that had heels on them he would cut them off and we had to wear them to work in the fields.

We never went hungry, because we had cows, chickens and grew lots of vegetables.

re mammy and pappy Fetterolf / with Hodge / Wales

From: **Joyce Gooding** (joycegooding@gmail.com)
Sent: Tue 2/23/10 12:31 AM   2/22/2010
To: troutman425@hotmail.com

Hi Joan and Steve;
   I have a few things that I can share about Mammy and Pappy , but not actual history .
just memories from when I was young and went there for days @ a time and usually with Frank and Jack
We were young maybe in the 5 yrs span when we
 were 5 - 10 ,
I'm sure more of you will remember some things too.

Their house had low ceilings and in the winter it was so hot that you could barely breathe.
If Pappy was in the living room ,   they always kept the door shut , you'd open the door and the room was
hot as blazes and full of cigar smoke.
They never seemed to mind the heat , and we and Iva would just laugh and wonder why Mammy's plastic
living curtains never caught on fire from the heat in the room .
You could buy thin plastic printed living room drapes @ that time and that's what Mammy always bought
when I was young.
She bought regular sheer lace curtains when I was older.
Pappy loved Lipton noodle soup in a packet that you would add water to and we often had that for lunch,
Pappy would eat boiled potatoes that he mashed on his plate with a fork and pour milk and add butter and
mix it around.   He was the only one I ever knew that ate that.
Mammy often made bacon gravy that we ate for any meal and never got tired of.
Mammy also would take a piece of meat with the most fat on it , and eat that too.
We always cut the fat off our meat and she would eat it.
She made cinnamon flops too that were great and we all drank coffee with it.   Parents have fits these days if
their kid gets a sip of coffee !

I would help Mammy collect the eggs and clean them for the egg man .
She had mean , nasty chickens that always picked my hands on top .
I would get so annoyed with them when she wasn't looking , I'd grab them around the neck and throw them
out onto the floor.
They always made a racket , but I didn't care , and she never caught me.
She loved her chickens and would have been upset if she saw what I did . They never seemed to pick
her !!!!!

Mammy had a pump organ , which I bought @ their farm sale and have in my living room
That was kept in the meat room upstairs with slabs of bacon and sausage and hams hanging all around it
Mammy got it for her 16th Birthday.   It was made in Lebanon
It is the only thing in my house I could never replace . except for photos etc.
I always had a great time there , and loved my Aunt Iva who lived in the other side of the house .

There were great lightning bugs up the hill behind their house in the Pines and we would get jars and catch
them
Mammy and Pappy were always sweet and kind and we never got yelled at ,
They got mellow in their older years and just seemed to enjoy us.

We moved to Hatboro when I was 12 and then didn't get to see them very much .
We brought them down several times for a few days and I especially remember that Pappy ate hot hard
boiled eggs for breakfast while we ate soft boiled eggs .
 When I had Steve (Feb 10 1967) and we went upstate Pappy always took him for a tractor ride . Pappy
still had a red large tractor and I don't know if it was A Farmall , or an Ellis Chalmer . maybe some one
else remembers . Steve remembers the tractor rides to this day and he was about 3 when we took him for
his 1st ride .
Lara (Sept 5 , 1970) never got the tractor rides and is still envious of Steve and his good fortune .

From: **bjkimmel@comcast.net**
Sent: Wed 2/24/10 5:33 PM
To: troutman425@hotmail.com

2/25/2010

My name is Ronald Kimmel, I am the oldest child of Charles Kimmel and Ethel Fetterolf Kimmel. Ethel is the youngest child of Charles and Lottie Fetterolf. To me, they were always Mammy and Pappy. So, hensforth, I will refer to them as Mammy and Pappy.

I lived on the west side of Mammy and Pappy's house until I started second grade. At that time my parents moved to a farm house one mile west of Pappy's house. I worked on Pappy's farm until I was sixteen, at which time I started working at Spread Eagle in Klingerstown.

I have so many fond memories of my grandparents. I can't list them all in writing. Whenever I think of Mammy, I think of her as a very kind and soft spoken woman. The memories I have of Mammy are watching and helping her bake cookies, pies, and bread. I also helped her feed and water the chickens and gather the eggs. I also helped her wash and grade the eggs. I also remember the great tasting hugh meals she would prepare for the Saturday noon meal. I helped Mammy with the chickens, baking, and house work until I was about twelve. That is about the time my cousin, Jack Specht, stopped working for Pappy and started another job.

I started working with Pappy when I was about twelve. I learned so much from Pappy about carpentry, farming, and work ethics which I have carried into my retirement. I remember Pappy as a very stern person, but under the exterior laid a heart of gold. I remember pulling mustard from the fields in the spring all day long and picking stones in the fields. I swear those fields grew rocks as well as grain. I can remember bringing in the hay bales from the fields and stacking them in the barn and many times Mammy would come walking up to the barn with a glass iris print pitcher of mint tea from the tea that grew along the road west of their house.

I learned a lot about carpentry from Pappy repairing buildings around the farm. One time he built a grain house. To build the grain house we went up into the mountain to cut down trees with a two man crosscut saw. We then used his tractor to drag the trees to his field and then loaded them on his farm wagon and took them to the saw mill.

52

My least favorite job was cleaning out the steer pen in the spring of the year. That was hard work with a pitch fork because it was fairly deep and was packed down because the steers were in the barn all winter and I only weighed 119 pounds when I went into the Navy at age 18. I was a skinny bean pole!

I really enjoyed when it was time to have the corn husked because I got to stay home from school and I would sleep at Mammy and Pappy's the night before. Pappy would have Willard Dietz from up on the main road bring his corn husker. If I rememer correctly, it was a red Farmall tractor with two four wheel trailers hooked behind, one red and one green. I can still remember bouncing on the back of the trailer as Mr. Dietz was husking the corn and I shoveled the corn to the back of the trailer.

Pappy got peeps every spring to replace the laying hens in the fall and along with the peeps some were always roosters. So in the fall of the year many a Saturday evening after the chores were done, Pappy would catch a rooster and put it in a burlap bag and say this is Sunday dinner for your family. I would pedal my bicycle home with this live rooster in my bicycle basket. My mother was always glad to get the rooster, but then we had to chop off its head, feather and clean it that Saturday night.

I also enjoyed butchering time. I can't remember if it was either December or January when Pappy normally butchered one steer and two or three pigs. On the second day of butchering, I would pedal my bicycle up to my Pappy's before daybreak because Mammy would always make steak and eggs for breakfast before we started cutting up the meat and grinding meat to make bologna, sausage, and ponhaus (scrapple).

Looking back, farm work was hard back then, but I know I am a better person to have known and to have learned work ethics from my Mammy and Pappy.

May God Bless them and may they rest in peace.

Dennis Fetterolf and George Saltzman recall the following story as told to them by their parents, Mark Fetterolf and Iva Saltzman: Our grandfather, Charles Fetterolf, was at home on his farm working. Raymond, (Bink), Bensinger stopped by, and told Charles that he had heard there was a meeting that night at the Hepler Hotel that they did not want to miss. Charles asked what it was about, and Bensinger said that he didn't know exactly what it was about, except that it was a big event. Later that evening, Charles and Bink Bensinger drove up to the Hepler Hotel. The hotel at this time was the focal point for community entertainment and official business. The post office was located here. The two men walked into a crowded room and found seats. Shortly afterward, the entry doors were closed, and the speaker rose and walked to the front of the room. He began his speech, the subject of which was to promote the Klu Klux Klan. At this time in the 1920's there were crosses being burned in the valley by the Klu Klux Klan in protest of minority ethnic families and individuals in the local area of Pitman and Franklin Square. Some of these events were directed toward Catholics who were viewed as outsiders at that time. After hearing the subject material of the program, Charles and Bink decided that they had heard enough. They got up to leave and went to the back doors. There a large fellow blocked their exit and told Charles and Bink to go sit down again, that nobody was allowed to leave until the speaker was finished. Charles was a big fellow, accustomed to working hard on the farm and in the coal mines. He picked up the doorman, stood him roughly aside, and said, "Come on Bink. We're going home", and so they did. No doubt this disturbance soon ended this Klu Klux Klan meeting in Hepler, Pa.

Dennis Fetterolf recalls: My grandfather Charles Fetterolf, came to the Mahantongo Valley from Helfenstein. He worked as a hired man for farmers in the valley. Eventually, he was able to buy a farm for himself along the Mahantongo Creek. He never forgot his coalmining heritage. Charles worked two jobs. He mined coal in the earlier part of the day, and farmed his land in the later part of the day. In the 1920's and 1930's there were many men from the valley who would walk across the mountain to the coalfields for a better paying job. Many of these men walked home in the early afternoon to their farms where they labored the rest of the day until sunset. Charles Fetterolf would get up very early and ride his horse to cross Mahantongo Mountain and Hegins Mountain to the coal mine where he worked near the village of Good Spring. After arrival at the mine, he would send the horse home again. This horse knew the way back to his stable. Charles sent the horse home to be used for the farm work that needed to be done by others in the family. Joan recalls that her mother Pauline told her that she would use this horse to plow the fields after returning home from the coal mine. It is difficult to imagine an event like this in consideration of traffic on the roads today. However, in those days, automobiles and trucks were rarely seen, the roads were of ground and packed dirt which became a muddy path in wet weather. The walking mine workers had footpaths over the mountains which followed the shortest routes. These paths were passable only by foot. No doubt, Charles and his horse followed some of these paths over the mountain.

George Saltzman recalls: Pappy Fetterolf grew corn on his farm in the lowlands along the Mahantongo Creek. At harvest time this corn crop was cut by hand. At this time there were no mechanical corn huskers or combines. Corn was cut by hand and put on shocks in the fields to dry. The stalks were cut with a sickle like tool often homemade of sharpened tin, lashed to a wooden handle. Some corn chopping tools were of better quality and were able to be sharpened with a whet stone by rubbing the edge of the blade. A sharp corn chopper made this hard work somewhat easier. George would crank the whet stone which turned in a water trough. The water trough was a piece of a tire. As the stone turned the water and the stone sharpened the steel. The next step in the sharpening process was the oil stone which was kept in the tractor shed. It had a coarse side and a fine side. This flat stone was laid on the workbench, squirted with oil, and then the steel blade was rubbed and rubbed until Pappy could cut a paper or shave the hair off his arm. George remembers his grandfather preparing to cut corn the next day, and sitting on the front porch, in the evening, rubbing and sharpening the corn choppers until they were very sharp with his pocket whet stone. This stone was also kept in Pappy's pocket while working in the fields, for a quick touch up of the blade. Even in the 1950's, some farmers continued to cut some corn by hand for animal feed as needed, especially if the end rows were not fully developed.

George Saltzman recalls: Pappy Fetterolf talked a bit about his childhood in Helfenstein. Charles did not talk much about his time of youth growing up across the Line Mountain in the Mahanoy Valley. He did say that his mother had borne a set of twins. They were delivered by the doctor in their home. Pappy was outside during the delivery, and when he came indoors, the babies were wrapped up, placed on the open oven door to keep them warm. The doctor told his mother that he had done all he could, and that they should keep the tiny babies near the stove to keep them warm. These newborn babies did not survive. Perhaps they were premature and little medical assistance was available.

Charles worked at the Locust Gap Colliery when he was 12 or 13 years old. The miners' paths from Helfenstein and Doutyville can still be seen today when snow is on the ground on a bright sunny day. These paths led up Mahanoy Mountain, through the ravines, across the ridge to the deep mine known as Locust Gap. Charles worked with the carpenter crew in the breaker. Here he learned how to use a hatchet and he became very skilled. Charles learned to make beams from sawed boards, splicing them together for great strength and notching them to fit as needed.

Dennis recalls after the death of Pappy's mother and father, Charles was legal guardian for some of the younger family members. George recalls after Jemima and August died, Pappy told him that he was "batter up!". About this time, Daniel Reiner came to Helfenstein on his weekly farmer's market route. Through this acquaintance Charles learned of Daniel's daughter, Lottie. Soon Charles was spending time across the mountain and "got hooked up" with Lottie Reiner. Mark told his son Dennis that after Pappy's parents died, Charles and some of his brothers stayed at the Harvey Hepler farm. This was in the Mahantongo Valley on the road between Haas and the Helfenstein Mountain, near the base of the Helfenstein Mountain. These boys were unmarried.

Dennis at the young age of 7 or 8, asked his daddy Mark, where he, (Mark) was at this time. Being a tricky fellow, Mark told Dennis that he was "sitting on the wagon seat". Of course, Mark was not yet born, but this explanation satisfied young Dennis!

Pauline, the oldest of Charles and Lottie's children was born at the Reiner homestead, and perhaps some of the older children, also. Joan has her mother's baptism record which states the event took place at St. Paul's Church in Gowen City, Pa. In 1921 Pappy bought a farm. Some of Charles's brothers lived there on the farm with them as Charles looked after them and kept them in line. Sometimes he had to go the extra mile to get them out of a troubled situation.

Dennis and George recall that Mammy always had pies in the cellar way. There were two shelves there, usually full of baked pies. She kept the empty crusts in the cupboard. Mark told his mother when it was time to bake again. One time, Pappy wanted pie and there were none there, so Pappy ate the crusts unfilled. Mammy was loved by all, and no one ever said a bad word to her. She spent a lot of time in the wash house. This was a small separate building above the farmhouse. Here was a bathtub and a shower, as well as the washer, and in later years an electric dryer. Everyone remembers the washlines stretched everywhere inside this little wash house, and the large amounts of clothes drying there during the winter months. There was a "bucket a day" stove in here, which gave a great amount of heat, ideal for drying clothes. In summer time the outside washline was used. This building was also used for other chores like at butchering time when casings were cleaned and sausage was stuffed.

There were many other buildings on the farm. Many were chicken houses of all shapes and sizes. Eggs were sold to Eshelman's from Hegins or Shade's from Spring Glen. There were tractor sheds where tools were kept. The pig stable was below the road, as well as another chicken house. Horses, mules, and milk cows were in the barn. Guinea hens ran about making great noise when anyone was near. There is a story told that they are not always good to eat. Their meat turns blue if they are scared at butchering time.

In the house Mammy and Pappy's bedroom was downstairs. Their children slept upstairs and later on the grandchildren slept upstairs, also. Charles's brothers would visit Mammy and Pappy sometimes. They came to talk, but most often they ended up listening to Charles, and not talking too much. Ray Dietz recalls that Charles helped his younger brothers. Charles's uncle Jack W. Hodge sometimes worked for Charles, as well as doing work for other local folks. He had a small cabin built in a woodlot where George Saltzman's house is now located. George and Dennis remember evidence of the foundation slab of this cabin which was only a temporary residence for Jack when working in the area. While working for Charles, he carved his initials on a stone. Dennis found this stone when excavating for an addition to the barn. These initials, J.W.H. represent Jemima's brother, Jack W. Hodge.

In the 1920's Charles was a coalminer as well as a farmer. Charles worked at the Good Spring Colliery. This was a large coalbreaker and deep mine located northwest of Good Spring. There is a railroad crossing approximately one mile west of Good Spring on the

56

road to Rauch Gap. The Good Spring Colliery was served by this railroad track which leads north toward the mountain crest. Here 900 men worked, mining and processing coal. The miners' path leading from Hegins to this colliery can be seen from Route 125 today. This is the path that Charles took for work. The path is located west of Route 125, and goes straight up the mountain, bypassing the Village of Lamberson . Good Spring Colliery foundations remain and the PP&L plant ruins are nearby where electricity was generated.

The men from Good Spring soon learned of Charles Fetterolf's daughters and so it was that Iva Fetterolf met George Saltzman from Good Spring and Ethel Fetterolf met Charles Kimmel from the Village of Keffers, near Joliet. George said that the boys met the Fetterolf girls at the picnic bush near Franklin Square.

This coal mining tradition has survived to the third generation. Dennis worked above ground at Kocher's Coal Breaker and Meadow Brook Coal Breaker and today farms the homestead. Grandson of Charles, George, works in the coal industry also with Lindemuth Company doing strip mine and coal bank reclamation work. Dennis's father Mark, worked at Locust Gap when he was 16 years old. He also worked coal mines at Good Spring and Rauch Gap, while he farmed his own farm. Mark Fetterolf's farm is now operated by his son Charlie and wife Linda Fetterolf. Mark told his son Dennis to keep out of the deep mines, unless he absolutely needed the work. The pay was good, but the work was dangerous and bad for your health.

George was told that during World War II, Anna's husband Lee Specht went into the army. Their sons, Frank and Jack were very young at this time and Anna and the boys lived at home with Mammy and Pappy. Lee was killed in the service in Europe. He was buried at Howerter's Cemetery.

George went with his Pappy quite often. Trips to the livestock market in Danville were fun. They also made trips for supplies. Typically, they would get gas, and then stop at Soll Snyder's at Franklin Square for Pappy's supply of King Edward cigars. Charles had a shot of Kessler's whiskey, and young George drank an orange soda and then they were on their way again. This box of 50 cigars only lasted one month. He always had a cigar lit, and had "parking places" for his cigar as he went around the farm buildings. He never took his cigar in the building or barn, and had a special place on the outside foundation stones where he rested his cigar until he returned to retrieve it.

There was a wagon shed near the walnut tree on the farm. Charles was not having a good day. He was a bit cranky. He and his son Mark were working on a broken cultivator in the shade of this tree. There were several large birds in the upper branches. Unfortunately Charles was hit on the head by some bird droppings. Charles looked up at the birds, and then he looked at Mark, and said, "Go get my gun"! Mark immediately left for the shotgun, kept in the house. He returned and gave the gun and shells to his father who promptly shot the bird as well as any others he could see.

Dennis's father in law, Leonard Adams, recently deceased, told Dennis this story. Leonard was helping Charles on the farm. The men stopped work at noontime and sat at the table. They began to eat, and Charles shook the salt shaker. It was empty. Charles didn't say anything. He opened the kitchen door, and threw the salt shaker out. He said, "If it's on the table, it shouldn't be empty". According to Dennis, dinnertime at Pappy's was a "Holy big huarrah"! Leonard just sat quietly and watched the events. Dennis remembers dinnertime at Mammy's. They had to wash in a basin outside. The water hydrant was at the back porch and a towel hung nearby.

The last year of thrashing the grain crop was in 1948, the year Dennis was born. The next year Charles and his son Mark bought a combine. It was an International machine. Mark drove the tractor that pulled the combine and Pappy bagged the grain in burlap bags and tied them. This was a dusty, dirty job, and the grain chaff stuck to the perspiring men covering their arms and faces with the dust. Dennis, age 6 or 7, sat on the platform with his Pappy in the dust.

Another memorable event on the farm, was the time Charles unloaded the manure spreader on the highway. Dennis and Mark came up to visit and they saw the trail of manure leading all the way past the barn toward the bridge crossing the creek. Charles had loaded the manure on the spreader to take it to a distant field near the edge of the farm at the mountain. One of the levers on the spreader fell down, and engaged the unloading chain which emptied the spreader as he drove. Charles did not look back very much when he was operating farm equipment as he had an injury preventing him from turning his head. He had been hit by a branch while working for the Hepler's in the timber business. When he arrived at the field to be fertilized, he saw the empty spreader. He returned to the barn and saw Dennis and Mark laughing. They helped him sweep and shovel up the manure, and even Charles laughed about it!

Charles was asked to put a ring in a bull's nose. A mad bull was in the barn on the Valentine Farm, where David Rothermel lives today. Charles pointed to the hay manger, and Jack and Frank Specht knew exactly where to go, even though no words were spoken. This was a safe place above the bull. Charles lassoed the bull with a rope around his neck and circled the rope around a metal pipe at the feed trough. He slowly drew the rope in as the animal bucked and gave slack in the rope. Eventually the bull's head was against the feeder. The bull bellowed and kicked but the rope around the pipe held him, separated in the bull pen, from the men and boys in the feed entry way. Charles fitted the hinged brass ring in the nose of the bull. This required setting and turning two screws which kept the ring closed. He calmly and surely secured the ring and gave it a good pull to let the animal know its purpose. He was a fearless man.

George was told by his mother Iva, that when she was 14, she needed a medical operation. She needed to have her lung removed and had to travel to a Philadelphia hospital for the operation. Pappy accompanied her to the train station in Ashland. The train station in Ashland was located where Boyer's IGA is located. At that time there were three tracks there, the passenger station, and a water tower. This was quite a notable trip in those days. Charles and Iva fared well. It was a serious medical operation, but it was successful.

Addendum S.E.T.   Perhaps this is the same train station where the Joseph and Sarah Hodge family disembarked from a passenger train car originating at the port city of New York.   Ashland was probably the Hodge family's last stop on their route to their new home in Helfenstein in 1870.

Joan Troutman recalls: Whenever visiting Grammie and Pop Fetterolf, one would encounter a blue haze upon walking into their living room.   This haze was a result of Pop's cigar smoking regiment.   He sat on his chair smoking his cigar, while watching television.   This tv had a blue-gray plastic veil over the screen to eliminate the fuzzy images that were received with the poor reception.   Needless to say, this was not the best method to enhance reception, but he continued to smoke and watch television as we visited.   Also, I remember, Grammy always had the best coffee to dip cookies in.   She had "cooked" coffee, not instant, and it was her custom to use "canned" milk to put in the coffee.   This gave the coffee a good, rich taste.

Robert Zimmerman recalls: Robert is 84 years old at the time of this interview in 2009.   He resides in Helfenstein and recalls working with Charles Fetterolf for the Pennsylvania Department of Highways.   Charles was his foreman and Robert and the rest of his crew helped rebuild the highway along Mahantongo Mountain now known as Vista Road.   They put in stone for a road base and pipes for drainage.   Charles must have liked Robert Zimmerman as he was allowed to visit with his younger daughters.   Robert remembers the girls were attractive to him.

Diana Klinger recalls: I remember going to Grammy and Pop's for "vacation".   When it was time for bed, I got ready and just laid on the edge of the bed, barely under the covers.   Grammy came in to say goodnight and said I should get in bed a little farther.   I told her that I always sleep on the edge.   But needless to say, about a half hour later they took me home.....I had a "terrible" belly ache!

I also recall that we had family reunions at Grammy and Pop's.   They would set up tables in the grass driveway above the house in front of the shanty.   Later on the reunions were held at Pauline and Clement's in the potato storage and also at Uncle Mark's and Lorraine's in one of their open sheds.   Dennis Fetterolf remembers that Floyd Hodge, a cousisn, attended some of these reunions.   He usually had a fancier car than most of the other local farmers!   A highlight of the reunion was trying to ride Uncle Mark's donkey.   Today the reunions are held at the Klingerstown Carnival Ground picnic pavilions.

Mark C. Masser recalls: What I remember most about Pop Fetterolf was his terrific temper.   When he spoke he got action.   He barked to his kids, but he was nice to his wife Lottie.   The kids had better have their work done, or else!   Pop was a butcher for everyone, including the Clement Masser family.   He killed the animals, cut and cooked the meat, and processed the sausage.   He was also the "cow doctor".   Sometimes the milk cows would get a bloated stomach which could be fatal.   Pop would come and stick the cow belly so the gas could work its way out.   He usually saved the cow's life.   I remember one time he had to go down to Harold Wehry to sew up a cow that had pushed its innards out. When Pop arrived at the cow in distress, he laid his cigar on the barn wall, pushed the innards back in place, and sewed her up. He was cigar powered! He also castrated the pigs. This is a necessary procedure to raise hogs for butchering. When Pop visited us, he would always drive in by the back road, and park the car in the direction to drive home. He dropped Grammy off at the top of the walk to our house, and he headed to the barn, or wherever he was needed. I could always tell if Pop and Grammy were visiting when I was not at home. The cigar smoke smell lingered.

Charles and Lottie were a hard working young family. Grammy, Lottie, would hang a cloth on the washline as a signal to the field workers that dinner was ready. They also had the tradition of having a coffee break in mid-morning. This was unusual, as most other farmers worked from breakfast until noon. Most of the fields to Pop's farm were south of the house and barn, toward the Mahantongo Mountain. When Charles returned to his fieldwork after break, he would throw a bag of fertilizer over his shoulder. These bags weighed 160 pounds. He carried it back to the spreader where he had stopped working. Some of the farmland was wooded on the mountain. To get to the farm fields it was necessary to cross a small wooden bridge over Mahantongo Creek. Horse drawn implements could easily cross it, but some tractor drawn equipment was too wide to cross. Pop, made a special plate to attach to the hillside hitch on the back of the tractor. This enabled the combine to cross the bridge. It was a grain harvesting combine that put the grain into burlap bags.

When I was quite young, my father, Clement, asked Pop to build us a rabbit pen. This was used by both Mark and Diana. Clement took wood over to Pop's to build the pen. He had to take additional wood the second time, because Pop was building an "extra heavy duty" pen. That rabbit stable lasted for years and years. I guess he figured that this would be the last one that he had to build. It was heavy to move, but they did get it loaded on Clement's flat bed truck and pushed it to the front. I remember later that same day, we had to dig potatoes for market and put the potatoes in bags on the truck, too. This was about the year 1950, when I was 8 or 9 years old. The placement of the rabbit pen in the front of the truck worked out well for me, as it was my job to drag the potatoes to the back of the truck and empty them onto the potato grader. This time, I didn't have to drag the bags nearly as far. I did have success raising rabbits. We had lots of rabbits! Eventually, I sold many of them to Marlin Kieffer.

Pop Fetterolf's farm was old fashioned. He used his horses longer than some of the other farmers who bought tractors. After his son Mark bought a tractor, then Pop Fetterolf got a tractor, also. They were some of the last to get electricity in the house. There was a good grapevine near the house for eating grapes. As a youngster, I liked to pick them. I was swallowing only the skins, and spitting out the grape centers which had the seeds. Pop corrected me and told me the proper way to eat grapes! Pop was a potato grower also. He had an unusual machine. It was a potato duster. Many modern farmers now spray their potato crops for insects and blight. Pop's duster did the job, but was pulled by a horse or a tractor.

When Pop was a young man, he worked in the coal mine near Good Spring. He would leave on a Sunday night with his horse, and stay over several days for several shifts of work. But...by Monday, the horse was home. The family needed the horse to do the farm work, and Pop sent the horse home alone from Good Spring. He and the horse walked to work over the wooden bridge, near his farm, and over the next two mountains. Dennis Fetterolf was told that Charles stayed the week in a miner's shanty.

Grammy had a stroke in mid-life. After this event she developed some idiosyncrasies. When she and Pop would go shopping to Romberger's Store in Pitman, Grammy stayed on the car. She did not like the knotty pine paneling inside the store, so Pop bought the groceries. On some occasions, she refused to answer the telephone, causing concern among her family. When asked why she didn't answer the phone she replied, "I didn't want to." Although Lottie was a hard working farm wife, and raised a large family, she was never known to be a robust woman.

In 1967, when Ralph Masser got a new Emeryville International truck, Pop wanted to go along with me to Milton, Pa. The local farmers grew tomatoes for the cannery. This new truck cost $15,000, and had a cab over the engine. This was a new design. The flat bed trailer was 32 feet long and carried the tomatoes in large wooden bins stacked 3 high. By today's truck standards, this was a short trailer and the truck was underpowered. They picked up the load south of Pitman near the Zimmerman farms and went to "Chef Boy ar dee" tomato cannery in Milton. I remember Pop enjoyed the trip.

Pop also worked for the Department of Transportation. He did mellow after he got the job as foreman with the Pennsylvania Department of Highways. He had a state pick up truck that had chains on the rear drive wheels, almost all winter long. He must have worn out many sets of chains because it seemed in those years, there was a lot of snow on the roads. Pop was one of the first foreman to put calcium chloride on the roads. Previous to the use of "road salt" only cinders were used and they were spread mostly on hills and at intersections. One of the first roads to receive the calcium chloride was in Frackville where Pop Fetterolf tried out the new anti-skid material.

After Pop died, Lottie did not want to stay alone. Her daughter, Iva Saltzman, lived on the other side of the farm house. To lessen the burden on Iva, Iva's sister Pauline, asked Grammy to come to stay with her in Leck Kill for awhile. This did not go over well. She stayed one night, and the next day, said "I want to go home".

Grammy wanted a cat, so since Clement's had plenty of cats around the barn, Pauline picked one, and drove it over to Grammy's. Shortly afterward, the cat came back! He wasn't staying either.

I remember that Pop Fetterolf was proud of his grandchildren. He built a new cement walk from the house to the outside toilet. Some of the grandsons helped. The initials of all the grandchildren at that time, were inscribed in the new cement walkway.

Our English and Welsh Heritage

From South Wales to Pennsylvania

England, Scotland, and Wales from the United Kingdom. In the 1800's Wales was the largest coal exporting country in the world. The capital city of Cardiff and the port of Newport on the Usk River were the ports of coal export.

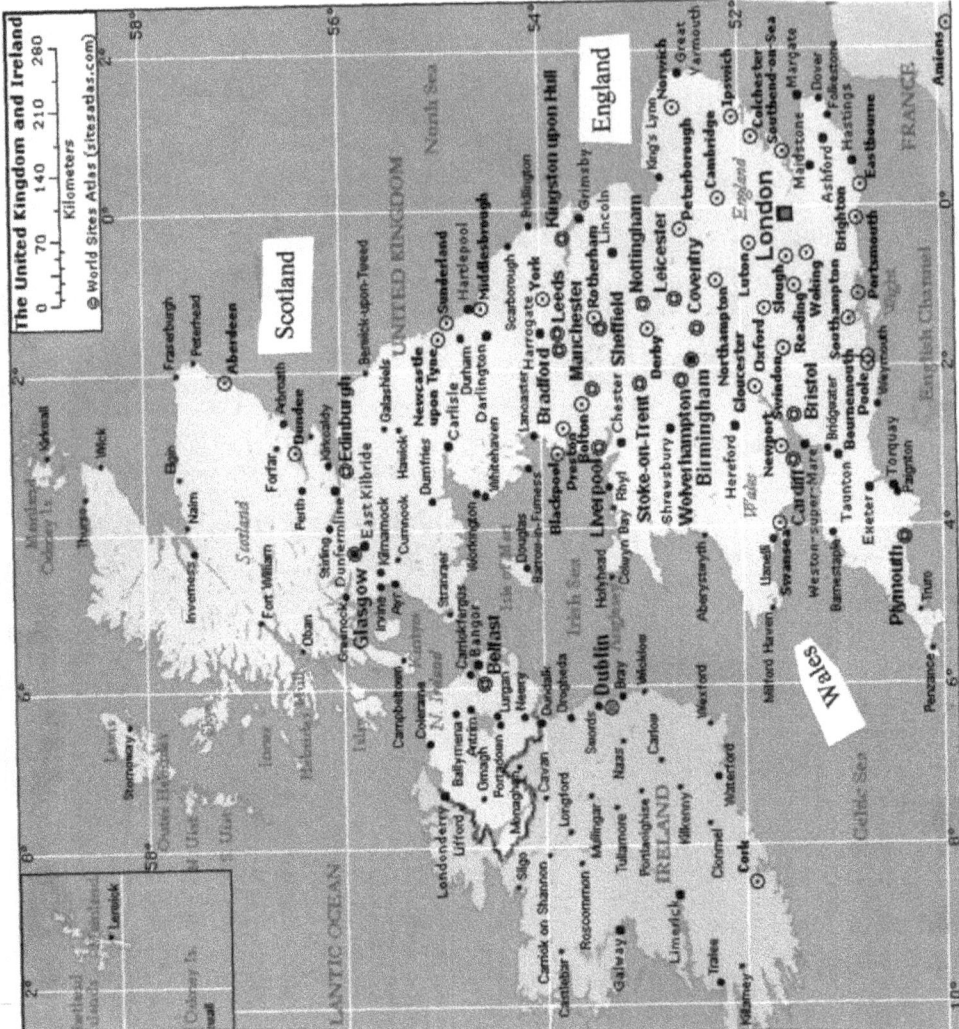

The United Kingdom and Ireland

Kilometers
0 70 140 210 280
© World Sites Atlas (sitesatlas.com)

Scotland

England

Wales

SOUTH AND MID-WALES

CARDIFF, SWANSEA & ENVIRONS · CARDIGANSHIRE
CARMARTHENSHIRE · MONMOUTHSHIRE · POWYS · PEMBROKESHIRE

South and mid-Wales are less homogeneous regions than North Wales. Most of the population lives in the southeast corner. To the west is Pembrokeshire, the loveliest stretch of Welsh coastline. To the north the industrial valleys give way to the wide hills of the Brecon Beacons and the rural heartlands of central Wales.

South Wales's coastal strip has been settled for many centuries. There are prehistoric sites in the Vale of Glamorgan and Pembrokeshire. The Romans established a major base at Caerleon, and the Normans built castles all the way from Chepstow to Pembroke. In the 18th and 19th centuries, coal mines and ironworks opened in the valleys of South Wales, attracting immigrants from all over Europe. Close communities developed here, focused on the coal trade, which turned Cardiff from a sleepy coastal town into the world's busiest coal-exporting port.

The declining coal industry has again changed the face of this area: slag heaps have become green hills, and the valley towns struggle to find alternative forms of employment. Coal mines such as Blaenafon's Big Pit are now tourist attractions; today, many of the tour guides were ex-miners, who can offer a first-hand glimpse of the hard life found in mining communities before the pits closed.

The southern boundary of the Brecon Beacons National Park marks the beginning of rural Wales. With a population sparser than anywhere in England, this is an area of small country towns, hillsheep farms, forestry plantations and spectacular man-made lakes.

The number of Welsh-speakers increases and the sense of Welsh culture becomes stronger as you travel further from the border with England, with the exception of an English enclave in south Pembrokeshire.

The changing face of the coal industry: former miners take visitors down the Big Pit in Blaenafon

Introduction to Our Welsh and English Heritage

We can now compose a record of the Welsh and English heritage for the descendants of Charles and Lottie Fetterolf. Researchers in Wales have contributed greatly to this family history and much praise and gratitude is due to them. Their e-mail communications are included in this book so that all who study this family tree may discern for themselves the excitement of each new discovery as records of birth, marriage and local history were found.

The story will begin with the parents of Joseph Hodge and Sarah Marsh. Joseph and Sarah's family left Brynmawr, South Wales to come to Helfenstein, Pennsylvania, ca. 1869-1870.

Joseph's father, Thomas Hodges is listed on the 1841 Census as living and working in Cwm Sychan, a village within the Parish of Trevethan, Monmouthshire County, Wales. This was an industrial area with canals, collieries, lime pits, and iron works. See map in this book. Cym Sychan is near the larger town of Abersychan.

Thomas was born in Somersetshire, a county in England not far from the Welsh border. His wife Ann was born in Blaenavon, Monmouthshire County, Wales, not far from Cwm Sychan. Thomas worked at the British Iron Works as a "Coker" and is listed on the 1841 Census with Joseph (8 years old), Charlotte (6 years old), Edward (4 years old), and Mary Ann (1 year old), all born in Monmouthshire County, Wales.

Thomas is listed on the 1851 Census as living and working in Llanelly Parish, Breconshire County, Wales. We know the local village name as Clydach. The location Francis Row seems to be their address, which would denote a row of identical dwellings, all under the same roof. Each home was similarly constructed to include a fireplace cooking area, and perhaps two rooms downstairs, and two rooms upstairs. Many of these row houses were built of stone by the iron and coal industry to house their workmen. Thomas is listed as an "iron miner", Ann is listed "at home", Joseph (age 11) is listed as "iron miner", Ann (age 18) is listed as "iron miner", and baby Sarah is "at home". All children listed as born in Llanelly. The birth place listed is unusual, as in the 1841 Census, ten years earlier, some were listed as born in Monmouthshire and here the children are listed as born in Breconshire. But this is not a problem as these counties lie next to each other and Clydach is near the border.

At this time in 1851, the Clydach Iron Works was a huge industry employing hundreds of workers. Men were mining iron on top of Llanelly Hill near Brynmawr, mining coal underneath Llanelly Hill, and quarrying limestone at the outcrops on the edge of Llanelly Hill. The Clydach River flowing down from Brynmawr at the top of Llanelly Hill, through the Clydach gorge to the village of Clydach below, served the iron industry with water power. Railroads and canals provided transportation of the raw materials and the iron produced. Joseph Hodge (the 11 year old iron miner) has a birth certificate which states he was born at Cym Nant Gam. This is a small hamlet between Clydach and Brynmawr. The name means "valley by the crooked stream". This community exists today and we have an acquaintance Joyce (Thomas) Scurr, who can see from her home across the valley a row house named "Long Row" on the hillside. The row is made of stone.

In 1862 Thomas Hodge is named as a miner on his son's marriage record. Thomas married Ann James. Her place of birth is in Blanavon, Monmouthshire County, Wales. Today this small city is known as World Heritage Site. Early coal industry and iron foundries and iron forges made this area famous as the largest iron industry in the world in the early to mid 1800's. Tourists can see the restored coal mines and foundry monuments which remain impressive as ruins today.

We have examined Joseph Hodges family and now we will consider Sarah Marsh's family. Joseph Hodge married Sarah Marsh on the 19th of August, 1862. The name Marsh has been noted on many certificates and other occasions, but the names Mass, and Moss have also been noted in British records. The inability of Sarah and her father to write their names themselves prompted the registrar to write the names as spoken. The most accepted form, "Marsh", is recalled in Pennsylvania by family members.

James Marsh, (the father of Sarah), married Louisa Dainty on the 4th of July, 1837 at Tipton, Staffordshire County, England. Louisa was baptized on the 12th of January, 1817 at Weston Under Lizzard, Staffordshire, England. Her father was James Dainty, and her mother was Elizabeth.

In the 1851 Census, Parish St. Mary's, Bridge North, we find the names James and Louisa Marsh have daughters Jane, Sarah, and and a son James. All the children were born in Sedgley, Staffordshire which is about 4 miles from Tipton, Staffordshire.

In the 1861 Census we find the James Marsh family has migrated across the English-Welsh border to Clydach in South Wales. James is listed as a miner. Wife Louisa is listed as born in Tipton, England, and Sarah (age 19), is listed as born in Sedgley, England.

In the book Destination America, the author Maldwyn A. Jones, describes the conditions which affected the Marsh family. In the last quarter of the 19th Century, witnessed a severe agricultural depression. All over Britain farmers were compelled to return plough land to grass, adopt labor saving machinery, and dispense with a large portion of their laborers. The main cause of this agricultural depression was the flood of American grain that began to arrive in Britain in the 1870's. Many of the disposed farm laborers gravitated to the industrial districts of Britain. The uprooted people of the country side were absorbed by the mines, mills, and factories of South Wales and nearby England.

The result was that in 1861 we have the young English born girl Sarah Marsh, living with her parents in their new home at Clydach, South Wales, near Clydach Bridge. Joseph Hodge, as a young boy, had previously lived between Clydach Bridge and Station Road in 1851, ten years prior.

In 1861 we find Joseph living with his mother Ann now the wife of Charles Sykes. No doubt, Thomas has died and Ann soon remarried as was the necessity in those days. Joseph Hodge is listed as a stepson in the James Sykes household now being age 21. He would not remain in this household very much longer.

Joseph Hodge, age 21, occupation collier, married Sarah Marsh, age 19, in Tabor Chapel in Brynmawr on the 19th of August, 1862. Both signed with a cross, as they could not write their names.

Joseph and Sarah's marriage proved fruitful. A son, Joseph Thomas Hodge was born on the 7th of February, 1864, at Baily Street, near the center of Brynmawr. Son James William, (later known as William) Hodges was born on the 15th of November, 1865, at King Street in Brynmawr. Mary Ann Hodges was born on the 20th of May, 1869 at King Street, Brynmawr, South Wales. Sometime after her birth, Joseph and Sarah emigrated to Helfenstein, Pennsylvania. Mary Ann died in Helfenstein on the 15th of July, 1870. She was just over 1 year old and is buried at Taylorsville in the Pioneer Cemetery, on Mahanoy Creek. Mary Ann's short life documents the time frame that Joseph and Sarah emigrated to America. Her birth is recorded in Brywnmar, Wales, and her death is recorded in Schuylkill County, Pa.

Included in this book is a History of Brynmawr by Hilda Jennings, which describes the life and times of the people of this era, where only the privileged were educated.
According to Hilda Jennings, there was a large scale movement of people away from South Wales in the 1860's and 1870's because of a depression in the coal and iron industry.

M.A. Jones described immigration to the United States between 1866 to 1875 when 729,600 persons emigrated from England, Wales, and Scotland. This nine year period records the largest group to have come to America from the United Kingdom. The immigrants left from the port city of Liverpool, England, located north of Wales. By 1870 railroads were well established in Wales and carried passengers to the ships in the harbor of Liverpool, England. Sailings from Liverpool were frequent and the ships were large and seaworthy. By the 1870's the westbound crossing was taking less than 14 days. Iron and steel were a good deal safer than the old wooden sailing ships. Fire was less of a hazard and ship wrecks became less common, too. The transition from sail to steam, did not however entirely mean the end of Sterrage passenger class epidemics. Outbreaks of typhus, small pox, and cholera proved to be the last cause of serious loss of life during the Atlantic crossing. Perhaps young Mary Ann was a victim of one of these scourges.

The bulk of the immigrants landed at New York City, America's largest city and greatest port. In the harbor off the tip of Manhattan Island a Landing Depot was established for the immigrants in 1855. This large circular building, shaped like a wedding cake was named Castle Garden. Joseph and Sarah Hodge, their three young children, and perhaps Sarah's mother Louisa, would have entered through these doors. Ellis Island, which succeeded Castle Garden, was later established in 1892. The famous Statue of Liberty was not seen by the Joseph Hodge family, as it was first unveiled in 1886.

Historian, M.A. Jones, writes that by the time steam had supplanted sail, the expansion of trans-Atlantic commerce had reduced the price of passage to a level that all but the very poorest could afford. By 1860 it was possible to reach New York from Liverpool for 3 or 4 British pounds, which would have equaled approximately $15 in that era. A British migration of skill across the Atlantic set in, who were supervising and instructing Americans in new manufacturing techniques. Welsh miners came to Pennsylvania. From the valleys of South Wales they flocked to the anthracite regions of northeastern Pennsylvania, especially around Scranton and Wilkes-Barre. By the end of the 19th Century, British immigration dramatically reduced as mechanization improved production methods. Many English and Welshmen in American industry moved upwards from laborers to supervisory and managerial positions.

Perhaps Joseph Hodge was encouraged to emigrate by other family members in Pennsylvania. There were other Hodges living in Schuylkill County at least one generation previous to our Joseph Hodge. The name of Archibald Hodge is mentioned in Northumberland and Schuylkill County Court Records, as owner of coal lands in Pennsylvania in 1850. In 1850, our Joseph Hodge would have been a lad of 10 years old in Clydach, South Wales. The repetition of the names in old Archibald's family including Jemima and James strongly suggest they are related to our Joseph, but so far the connection remains elusive. Our Joseph later had a grandson born in Pennsylvania with the name of Archibald born to Jemima Hodge Fetterolf.

We have not found any family tradition or story of the Joseph and Sarah Hodge Atlantic crossing other than that stated by Charles Fetterolf that "his grandmother came over on a boat from Wales".

Our research gives compelling evidence that the emigration event would have begun in Brynmawr, Wales, on a train to Liverpool, England and by steamship to the port of New York City. The American railroad system could have brought them from New York City to the Schuylkill County coalfields. We can only suggest Pottsville or Ashland as their destination on the train. Question? Did anyone meet them at the station? Remember that Sarah's mother Louisa probably accompanied them. She was the one who purchased the early home on Mahanoy Creek in Helfenstein. Louisa's daughters Sarah Hodge and Mary Skelding soon occupied homes nearby on High Street above the Mahanoy Creek homestead. Pennsylvania records also name Louisa's son George of Helfenstein and Shamokin, Pa. Some Pennsylvania records state Louisa's married name as Kidson. Louisa must have married a Kidson after James Marsh.

Question? Did the Skeldings emigrate with the Hodges, before the Hodges, or soon after? We do know of the strong family ties between Louisa and her daughters. There is a happy ending to this emigration story. They all settled together in Helfenstein, Pennsylvania and prospered as some of the earliest pioneers in that vicinity.

Map showing the industrial valleys of South Wales – the iron manufacturing and coal mining districts

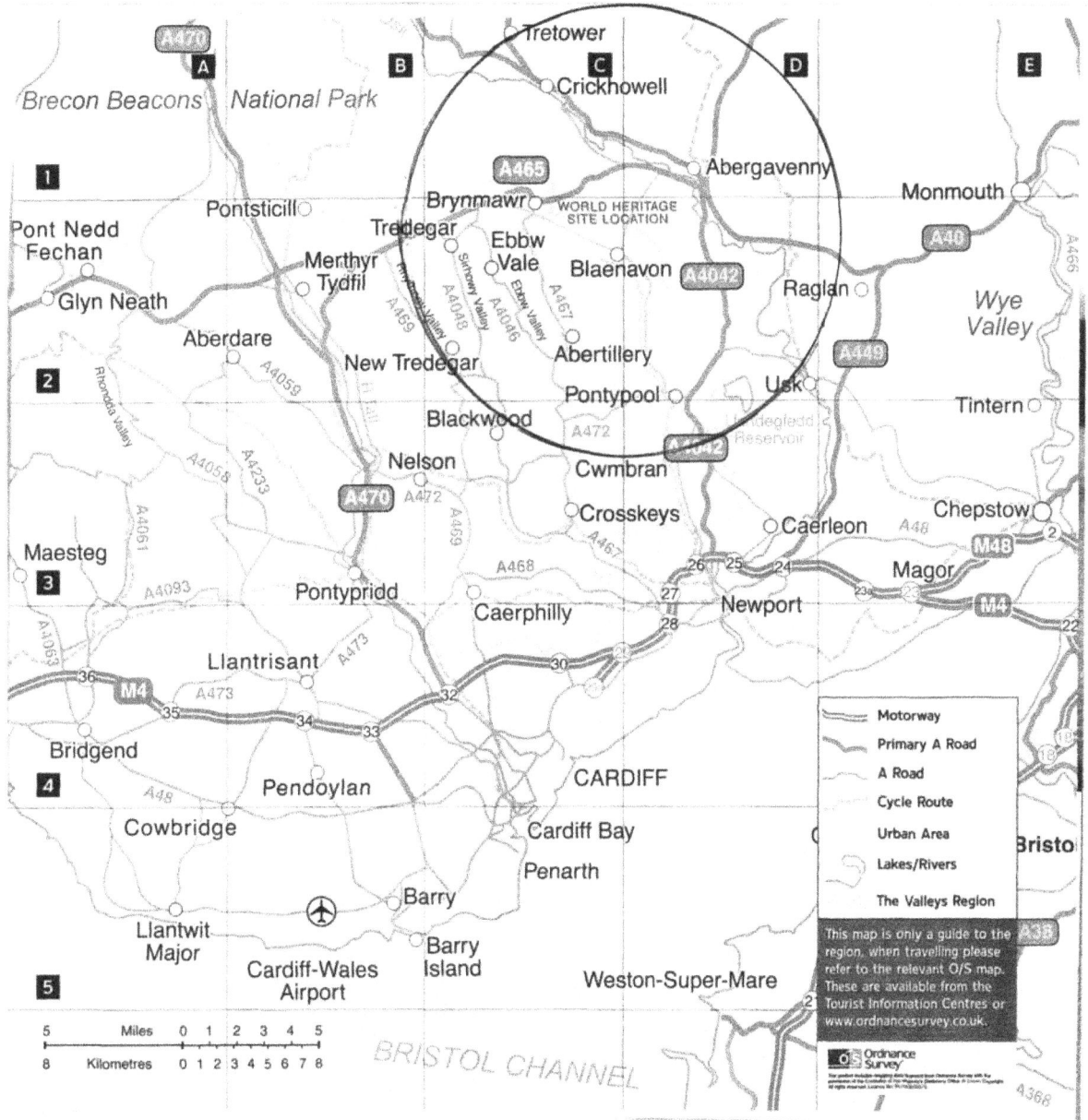

Joseph Hodges family records are found in the areas encircled here

Re: Family Research

From: **Matthews, Hywel** (Hywel.W.Matthews@rhondda-cynon-taff.gov.uk)

Sent: Wed 8/12/09 11:01 AM

To: troutman425@hotmail.com

Hello Joan and Steve Troutman,

Thank you for your enquiry.
I was wondering which source gave you Joseph Hodges date of birth. When I looked at the birth index of births registered in England and Wales between 1837 and 2005 I was only able to find one Joseph Hodges whose birth was registered in the first six months of 1840. His birth was registered in the registration district of Crickhowell. Is he the Joseph Hodges that is of interest to you?
I found no Sarah Kidson or Sarah Marsh whose births were registered in Wales during April, May and June 1843 on the birth index for the second and third quarter of 1843.
I noticed on the US census for 1900 that Joseph Hodge states that he was born in Wales in February 1864. Interestingly I found the registration of a birth of a Joseph Thomas Hodges in the first quarter of 1864 in the Crickhowell registration district.

Regards
Hywel Matthews Reference and Local Studies Assistant Librarian
Pontypridd Library

RE: Family Research

From: **Joan Troutman** (troutman425@hotmail.com)

Sent: Fri 8/14/09 1:38 AM

To: hywel.w.matthews@rhondda-cynon-taff.gov.uk

Dear Mr. Matthews,
What great news you have for us! We say thank you from our hearts. There are many descendants of Joseph and Sarah Hodge. Joan is descended from Jemima Jane Hodge, (sister of Joseph T. Hodge), and married August Fetterolf. This year's Fetterolf reunion held locally here in Klingerstown was well attended. Perhaps 75 people were there, and most were very interested in their new found Welsh heritage. We have only recently found the gravestone of Joseph and Sarah Hodge in Mt. Carmel cemetery near Mt. Carmel, Pa. The monument has their birth and death dates. Jemima died young of a dosmestic injury, and her husband August was killed at a young age in a mine accident. The orphaned youngest children were raised by other family and friends. There was not much family history handed down to these children. Your discovery of Crickhowell, as the birthplace of both the immigrant father, Joseph Hodge and his first born son, Joseph T. Hodge is an earth shaking discovery for us!!
It is late tonight but we wanted to reply immediately. Our daughter will scan and email some documents in the morning.
We will be in South Wales September 25, 26, and 27. Could we meet with you to personally thank you?
Sincerely, Steve and Joan Troutman

RE: Hello

From: **Matthews, Hywel** (Hywel.W.Matthews@rhondda-cynon-taff.gov.uk)

Sent: Fri 8/21/09 2:58 PM

To: Joan Troutman (troutman425@hotmail.com)

Hello Steve and Joan,

I have found a marriage between a Joseph Hodges and a Sarah Moss/Mass that was registered at Crickhowell in July/August/September 1862. Hopefully the certificate of Joseph Thomas Hodges birth in Jan/Feb/March 1864 would show that the maiden name of his mother was Moss/Mass. You would know then whether you had the correct marriage. I also may have found Joseph Hodges on the 1851 census living at a village called Llanelly only a few miles from Crickhowell. (Not to be confused with the much more well known Llanelli on the Welsh coast in Carmarthenshire) The 1851 census list his parents and siblings. The marriage certificate of Joseph Hodges and Sarah Moss would give their fathers' names. Hopefully it would match up with the father's name on the 1851 census. Perhaps you have already have a copy of the 1851 census. Feel free to let me know whether you want a copy of the 1851 census.

All certificates (Joseph Thomas Hodges birth 1864 , Joseph Hodges & Sarah Moss/Mass marriage 1862 and Joseph Hodges birth Jan/Feb/March 1840) would be available from the registry office at Llandrindod Wells. The following website give the registry office postal and email addresses and information about obtaining certificates.
http://www.powys.gov.uk/index.php?id=5528&L=0

Regards
Hywel Matthews
Pontypridd Library

-----Original Message-----
From: Joan Troutman
[mailto:troutman425@hotmail.com]
Sent: 20 August 2009 22:05
To: Matthews, Hywel
Subject: Hello

Dear Sir:

How wonderful it was to be able to talk with you on Wed. Aug 19, 2009! We look forward to visiting you at the Pontypridd Library. We will be in South Wales Sept 25, 26, and 27. Do any of these dates fit your schedule?

Joseph Hodges certificates request

From: **Joan Troutman** (troutman425@hotmail.com)

Sent: Fri 8/21/09 11:50 PM

To: family.history@powys.gov.uk

Dear Sirs: Hywel Matthews at Pontypridd Library has suggested that we write to you. 1.We request a birth certificate for Joseph Hodges born in 1840 near Crickhowell. 2. We also request a marriage certificate for Joseph Hodges who married Sarah Moss/Mass, registered at Crickhowell in July/Aug/Sept/ of 1862. 3.We also request a birth certificate of their son, Joseph Thomas Hodge, birth in Jan/Feb/March of 1864. It would show the maiden name of his mother, hopefully it being Moss or Mass. 4. In addition, do you have a birth certificate for William Hodges, born ca. 1865, the second son of Joseph and Sarah? If so, we request a copy also. (4 Copies in total, if available)

We will visit Crickhowell on Sept. 27 in search of Joseph Hodges ancestral home which Hywell Matthews suggested possibly as Llanelli. We hope to publish a Hodges Family History Book and are excited about this new-found information. Here In pennsylvania Joseph Hodges and sons Joseph T. Hodges and William Hodges were pioneer coal miners in Schuylkill County, near the town of Ashland, Pa.

Home telephone #   570-425-3485   United States
Home address: Joan and Steve Troutman
                1442 Ridge Road
                Klingerstown, Pa. 17941   USA

We will pay any fees you incur. Please let us know how we should handle this transaction.

Re: Joseph Hodges certificates request

From: **Crickhowell Library** (crickhowell.library@powys.gov.uk)
Sent: Tue 9/08/09 4:44 PM
To: troutman425@hotmail.com
Cc: ystrad.library@messaging.powys.gov.uk; chris.price@messaging.powys.gov.uk

Dear Joan and Steve Troutman,

I am sorry that you did not receive a reply from family.history@powys.gov.uk. That address is handled by the county registration office, which has been undergoing some re-organisation so I guess the service has been disrupted. I would add that the certificate service provided by the county office is prioritised for requirements such as the obtaining of passports.

As an alternative I suggest you try the UK General Register Office (GRO), which is the central national body responsible for registration of births, marriages and deaths and which operates a semi-automated online service. I have used it for my own family research and found it very efficient. Certificates (more accurately described as copies of entries in registers) can be ordered from the GRO website at http://www.gro.gov.uk. There is a charge for this service but I do not know what it will cost to get certificates posted to the USA.

It will help you greatly if, before using the GRO website, you can find out the registration district, volume and page number for each certificate. The best way to do that is to search the indexes to the registers, which you can do online through various websites. I suggest Free BMD (accessesd at http://www.freebmd.org.uk/), which is a voluntary project and is, as its name suggests, free. The database at Free BMD is the source of UK birth, marriage and death information offered by some commercial sites (such as ancestry.com)

I would also suggest that you double-check the name Llanelli, as this spelling generally refers to a place in Carmarthenshire, which is some distance from Crickhowell. There is a place near Crickhowell called Llanelly (sometimes Llanelly Hill). It may help you to know that Llanelly is currently in the county of Monmouthshire and Crickhowell is in the county of Powys, but both places were once within the former county of Brecknockshire (sometimes referred to as Breconshire).

If you need to do more research when you visit later this month then we will be happy to try to assist, however we only have a very small local history section at this branch. You might also like to contact the Crickhowell District Archive Centre, which is a small charity staffed by volunteers. It has some quite useful material and also provides a research service for £10 per hour. You can find more about it at: http://www.crickhowellinfo.org.uk/communitygroup/CDAC (note that their office is generally only staffed in the mornings).

I hope this is of help.

Mark Cottle
Library Assistant
Crickhowell

Re: Joseph Hodges certificates request

From: **Christian Phillips-Gunter** (findmyancestors@btinternet.com)

Sent: Mon 9/14/09 11:16 AM

To: Joan Troutman (troutman425@hotmail.com)

Hi there

Apologies for the delay in getting back to you.

OK - I have located 3 of the certificates you require

Birth - Joseph Hodges - March quarter 1840 - Volume 26 Page 274
Marriage - Joseph Hodges to a Sarah Mass or Moss - September quarter - Volume 11b Page 179
Birth - Joseph Thomas Hodges - March quarter 1864 - Volume 11b Page 133

All of the above were registered in Crickhowell.

FY1 - I can find no record of a birth for a William Hodges, born in Crickhowell - searched from 1860 through to 1870 just in case. However there are records of births of;

Charlotte Ann - June quarter 1865 Volume 11b Page 143
James Hodges - December quarter 1865 Vilume 11b Page 123
Charles Hodges - March quarter 1866 Volume 11b Page 125
Mary E Hodges - June quarter 1866 Volume 11b Page 150
Mary Ann Hodges - June quarter 1869 Volume 11b Page 127

Might one of the highlighted registrations be for William? Maybe he was registered as James or Charles but in later life used William as a name?

Anyhow - to obtain certificates for Crickhowell, you would have to go to

**The Register Office, Powys County Council, The Gwalia, Ithon Road, Llandrindod Wells, LD1 6AA
Tel: 01597 826020. Fax: 01597 826220.

E-mail: registrar@powys.gov.uk

FW: Joseph Hodges certificates request

From: **Joan Troutman** (troutman425@hotmail.com)

Sent: Fri 9/11/09 12:41 AM

To: findmyancestors@btinternet.com; troutman425@hotmail.com

2 attachments
joseph ho...doc (22.1 KB), hewel mat...jpg (174.7 KB)

Dear Christian Phillips-Gunter, We anxiously request your assistance in securing for us the certificates listed below. We will gladly forward you any fees involved. We feel this is easier for us than doing this work ourselves on line. See 2 attachments, one from Hewel Matthews, 8/21, and the second one from Crickhowell Library, 9/08. Please advise us as to the next step in this process. Sincerely, Steve and Joan Troutman

From: troutman425@hotmail.com
To: family.history@powys.gov.uk; hywel.w.matthews@rhondda-cynon-taff.gov.uk
Subject: FW: Joseph Hodges certificates request
Date: Fri, 28 Aug 2009 23:53:29 +0000

Addendum: Joseph Hodges birthdate is March 20, 1840, which corresponds to what is recorded in the Welsh records in the first 6 months of 1840.

Addendum, 9/10/09 Per recent info we know the birth place of Joseph Hodge to be Llanelly, sometimes Llanelly Hill in the county of Monmouthshire. Crickhowell, the registration district is in the county of Powys but both places were once were within the former county of Brecknockshire.

72

To: christian phillips gunter
Sent: Thursday, September 17, 2009 1:55 AM
Subject: Frances Road?

Dear Christian, What are the possibilities of locating this place named on the 1851 census? We have contacted Crickhowell but have not received definite location. See follow up email to Mark Cottle at Crickhowell Library which I will forward to you after this email.

Also see http://www.genuki.org.uk/big/wal/BRE/Llanelli/index.html for more info.

I searched on the 1841 census and found the following family at the British Works at Trevethan. It looks like your family but the children's names and ages are a bit "off". OVER →
1841 image attached.

TREVETHAN, a parish in the upper division of Abergavenny hundred, county Monmouth, 7 miles from Usk, and 1 mile from Pontypool. It is situated near the Brecon and Monmouthshire canals and the river Afon Llwyd. The parish contains the townships of Aberyschan, Pontnewydd, and Pont-y-pool, the last being a polling place for the county and a petty sessions town. Many of the inhabitants are employed in the collieries, lime-pits, and extensive iron-works, chiefly at Pont-y-pool."

See http://www.genuki.org.uk/big/wal/MON/Trevethan/index.html

The address on the 1841 census image is stated as Cwm Sychan - not a house name as such but an area within Trevethin so it would be difficult to pinpoint any specific dwelling unfortunately.

Looking back at the 1851 census, Thomas Hodges' birthplace is given as Backley, Somersetshire (England). I cannot locate a "Backley" but there is a Brookley and a Berkley in Somersetshire. I know very little about that area and for further clarification I would advise contacting Somerset Archive and Record Service

(details - at this link)

http://www.genuki.org.uk/big/eng/SOM/index.html

His wife Ann's place of birth is written as Blaenafon, Monmouthshire but it is in fact Blaenavon (nr Llanover). See here

http://www.genuki.org.uk/big/wal/MON/Llanover/

FYI, my home address is 13 Hampton Street, Twynyrodyn, Merthyr Tydfil, CF47 0RR

I'll carry on digging around. Quick question though - when did the Hodges family move from Wales and when did they arrive in the US?

Catch up later

Christian :)

Re: Frances Road?

From: **Christian Phillips-Gunter** (findmyancestors@btinternet.com)
Sent: Thu 9/17/09 1:20 PM
To: Joan Troutman (troutman425@hotmail.com)

2 attachments
Thomas Ho...jpg (409.2 KB), Trevethan...gif (15.8 KB)

Hi there

What I have done is trace the addresses either side of the 1851 image you sent to me for Joseph Hodges. As the librarian at Crickhowell stated, it does look as if the address is based near Clydach. If you click the below link

http://freespace.virgin.net/paul.benham/aber/clydach.htm

This will give you an idea as to the location and how to get there.

Judging by the addresses - it looks to me as if a lot of these houses were roughly made dwellings, some in stone and others possibly in wood. There's even an address that simply states "house in field". The immediate address (but 1 dwelling) after what I think is Frances Row or Road is Clydach Bridge (see above link) and after Clydach Bridge comes Station Road, so your realtives must have lived very near to the bridge and Station Road.

Sadly, it does not look as if there are any houses remaining in that area as it is/was quite a remote location that relied on the Llanelly Quarry and Clydach Ironworks which were closed many years ago.

http://www.breconbeacons.org/visit-us/easy-access/places-to-visit-with-easier-and-disabled-access/clydach-ironworks

I would assume that your ancestors all worked either at this ironworks or Llanelly Quarry.

1841 Census, City or Borough British Works, Parish or Township of Trevethin Trevethin is between Blaenavon and Pontypool, closest to Abersychan.

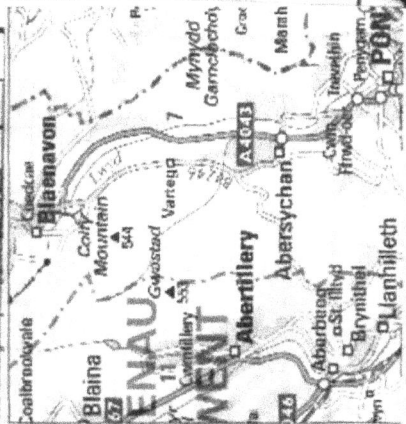

Thomas Hodges, age 35, profession –coker. Ann Hodge, age 30. Joseph Hodges, age 8. Charlott Hodges, age 6. Edward Hodges, age 6. Mary Ann Hodges, age 1. (Listed as born in the same county.)

1851 Census, Parish or Parish or Township of Llanelly, Brecon (Breconshire). Name of place Francis Road or Row.

Thomas Hodge, head of family, age 37, occupation iron miner, born Backley, Somersetshire, (England). Ann Hodges, wife, at home, age 36, born Blanafon, Monmothshire, (Wales). Ann, daughter, age 15, iron miner, born Llanelly. Joseph, son, age 11, iron miner, born Llanelly. Sarah, daughter, age nine months, at home, born Llanelly, Brecon.

1861 Census, Parish of Llanelly, town of Brynmawr, hamlet of Aberbaidan, Llanelly

House number 81, Worcester Street, Charles Sykes, head of household, age 42, laborer, born York, Leeds, (England). Ann, wife, age 40, born Monmouthshire, Blenavon. Joseph Hodge, step son, age 21, coal miner, born Breconshire, Llanelly. William Sykes, son, age 5, born Breconshire, Llanelly. James Sykes, son, age 4, born Breconshire, Llanelly. It is interesting to note that on this page of the census, a total of 26 people lived in 3 houses on Worcester Street. House number 79 is a lodging house.

76

2nd batch

From: **Christian Phillips-Gunter** (findmyancestors@btinternet.com)

Sent: Fri 10/09/09 12:30 PM

To: Joan Troutman (troutman425@hotmail.com)

📎 3 attachments | Download all attachments (9.4 MB)
James Hod...jpg (3.0 MB), Joseph Th...jpg (3.2 MB), Mary Ann ...jpg (3.2 MB)

a. **Joseph Thomas Hodges - March quarter 1864 - Volume 11b Page 133**

Joseph Thomas born 7th February 1864 at Bailey Street, Brynmawr. Bailey Street is in the centre of Brynmawr and still exists today. Thought this may be of help.

http://www.thomasgenweb.com/brynmawr_photos.html

b. **James Hodges - December quarter 1865 Volume 11b Page 123**

James was born 15th November 1865 at King Street, Brynmawr (see above link). Could this be the William Hodges that you mentioned in earlier emails?

c. **Mary Ann Hodges - June quarter 1869 Volume 11b Page 127**

Mary Ann was born 20th May 1869 at King Street, Brynmawr. This must be the daughter you mentioned that is buried in the US which means the family must have emigrated *after* the date of her birth.

Email 1 - Joseph Hodges

From: **Christian Phillips-Gunter** (findmyancestors@btinternet.com)

Sent: Fri 10/09/09 11:42 AM

To: Joan Troutman (troutman425@hotmail.com)

📎 1 attachment
Joseph Ho...jpg (3.0 MB)

Hi there

First of all glad you had a great time. I've found it very rewarding and somewhat emotional walking in the same footsteps as my ancestors. Really pleased you had a warm welcome!

OK - re Marriage Certificate

- Joseph Hodges to a Sarah Mass or Moss - September quarter - Volume 11b Page 179

I just need to pick that up (hopefully by Monday) but I now have all the birth certificates - 7 in total. A mixed bag of results!! I will send an email re each batch & attach a scanned copy. Once I have all the certs, I will post them onto you :0)

1. Birth - **Joseph Hodges - March quarter 1840 - Volume 26 Page 274**

Image attached - this essentially tells us that Joseph Hodges was born on the 1st of February 1840 at a location named Cwm Nant Gam. His father was Thomas Hodges, a Miner and his mother was Ann Hodges nee James. Joseph's father, Thomas registered the birth on the 16th of February 1840 and signed with a cross as he presumably was illiterate.

If you go to Google and enter Cwm Nant Gam in the search box and search for maps, the location is recorded as Cwm-Nant-Gam, Llanelly, Monmouthshire NP7. Its just up the Llanelly Hill - outside Brynmawr.

I couldn't find much out about Cwm-Nant-Gam but came across this snippet

"HOUSE OF THE LAWS 149

district of Cwm-nant-gam, Llanelly Hill near Bryn-mawr, in that county 'is quite a solidly-built terrace of houses on the hillside and two of these, to my certain knowledge, have wells inside and I rather think that the whole terrace is similarly built. . . . .

CRICKHOWELL

| REGISTRATION DISTRICT |
| DOSBARTH COFRESTRU |
BIRTH in the Sub-district of	Llanelly
GENEDIGAETH yn Is-ddosbarth	in the County of Brecon
	yn

1840

Columns:	1	2	3	4	5	6	7	8	9	10
Colofnau										
No. Rhif	When and where born Pryd a He'r ganwyd	Name, if any Enw os oes un	Sex Rhyw	Name and surname of father Enw a chyfenw'r tad	Name, surname and maiden surname of mother Enw, cyfenw a chyfenw morwynol y fam	Occupation of father Gwaith y tad	Signature, description and residence of informant Llofnod, disgrifiad a chyfeiriad yr hysbysydd	When registered Pryd y cofrestrwyd	Signature of registrar Llofnod y cofrestrydd	Name entered after registration Enw a gofnodwyd wedi'r cofrestriad
143	First of February 1840 at Cwm Nant Gam	Joseph	Boy	Thomas Hodges	Ann Hodges formerly James	Miner	The mark of × Thomas Hodges Father Cwm Nant Gam	Sixteenth of February 1840	Wm Thomas Registrar	

WBXZ 338728

78

REGISTRATION DISTRICT
DOSBARTH COFRESTRU } CRICKHOWELL

BIRTH in the Sub-district of
GENEDIGAETH yn Is-ddosbarth } Llanelly in the County of Brecon
yn

Columns:	1	2	3	4	5	6	7	8	9	10
1864	When and where born	Name, if any	Sex	Name and surname of father	Name, surname and maiden surname of mother	Occupation of father	Signature, description and residence of informant	When registered	Signature of registrar	Name entered after registration
Colofau Rhif	Pryd a lle y ganwyd	Enw, os oes un	Rhyw	Enw a chyfenw'r tad	Enw cyfenw a chyfenw morwynol y fam	Gwaith y tad	Llofnod, disgrifiad a chyfeiriad yr hysbysydd	Pryd y cofrestrwyd	Llofnod y cofrestrydd	Enw a adnablwyd wedi'r cofrestru
79	Seventh February 1864 Body West Breem	Joseph	Boy	Joseph Thomas	Sarah Thomas formerly Morris	Coal miner	X The mark of Sarah Thomas Body West Breem	Fourteenth February 1864	Sinton Roberts Registrar	

CRICKHOWELL

| REGISTRATION DISTRICT DOSBARTH COFRESTRU } | Llanelly | | | | | in the County of Brecon | | | | |

BIRTH in the Sub-district of
GENEDIGAETH yn Is-ddosbarth

1865

Columns:– Colofnau Rhif No.	1	2	3	4	5	6	7	8	9	10
	When and where born	Name, if any	Sex	Name and surname of father	Name, surname and maiden surname of mother	Occupation of father	Signature, description and residence of informant	When registered	Signature of registrar	Name entered after registration
	Pryd a'r lle y ganwyd	Enw os oes un	Rhyw	Enw a chyfenw'r tad	Enw, cyfenw a chyfenw morwynol y fam	Gwaith y tad	Llofnod disgrifiad a chyfeiriad yr hysbysydd	Pryd y cofrestrwyd	Llofnod y cofrestrydd	Enw a gofnodwyd wedi cofrestru
90	Fifteenth November 1865 King Street Brynmawr	James	Boy	Joseph Hodges	Sarah Hodges formerly Marsh	Coal Miner	X The mark of Sarah Hodges Mother King Street Brynmawr Llanelly	Ninth December 1865	John Thomas Registrar	

APJ

80

Application Number \ 1685797-8
Rhif y Cais

| REGISTRATION DISTRICT | CRICKHOWELL | | | | | | | | |
| DOSBARTH COFRESTRU | | | | | | | | | |

BIRTH in the Sub-district of **Llangattock** in the **County of Brecon**
GENEDIGAETH yn Is-ddosbarth yn

1869

Columns- Colofnau No.	1	2	3	4	5	6	7	8	9	10
	When and where born	Name, if any	Sex	Name and surname of father	Name, surname and maiden surname of mother	Occupation of father	Signature, description and residence of informant	When registered	Signature of registrar	Name entered after registration
Rhif	Pryd a lle y ganwyd	Enw os oes un	Rhyw	Enw a chyfenw'r tad	Enw, cyfenw a chyfenw morwynol y fam	Gwaith y tad	Llofnod, disgrifiad a chyfeiriad yr hysbysydd	Pryd y cofrestrwyd	Llofnod y cofrestrydd	Enw a gofnodwyd wedi'r cofrestru
229										

81

Additional Hodge Birth and Marriage Records of Interest

Here we have recorded William and Charles Hodges birth records and marriage records. The birth and marriages seem so similar in time and place in association with our Thomas and Ann Hodges from Llanelly, S. Wales. We must assume they are relatives of Thomas's son Joseph who emigrated to Pennsylvania.

Batch 3

From: **Christian Phillips** (cphillips10@btinternet.com)
Sent: Fri 10/09/09 12:51 PM
To: Joan Troutman (troutman425@hotmail.com)

3 attachments | Download all attachments (9.0 MB)
Charles H...jpg (3.0 MB), Mary Eliz...jpg (3.0 MB), Charlotte...jpg (3.0 MB)

The next batch could be related - the fathers of the children being the brothers or cousins of Joseph (b1840)??

a. Charlotte Ann - June quarter 1865 Volume 11b Page 143

Charlotte Ann was born 20th March 1865 at Graig Arlwydd, Llanelley Forge, Llanelly. Her father was William Hodges, an Iron
Hammerman & her mother was Mary Hodges formally Powell.

b. Mary E Hodges - June quarter 1866 Volume 11b Page 150

Mary E was born 5th June 1866 at Graig Vaughan, Llanelley. Her father was William Hodges, an Iron Hammerman & her mother was Mary Hodges formally Powell.

c. Charles Hodges - March quarter 1866 Volume 11b Page 125

Charles was born 17th February 1866 at Beaufort Hill, Llangattock. His father was Charles Hodges, an Iron Miner & his mother
was (what looks like) Eavis Hodges formally Nash.

In case it helps - I have located a marriage for

a William Hodges to a Mary Powell - March quarter 1865 at Crickhowell &

a Charles Hodges to an Alice Naish - December quarter 1861 at Bradford upon Avon which spans the boundaries of the counties
of Somerset and Wiltshire. Information about it can be found here.

http://www.ukbmd.org.uk/genuki/reg/districts/bradford%20on%20avon.html

Hope this helps. I'll be in touch when I have the marriage certificate details.

Cheers for now

Chris :0)

Re: Last cerificate

From:
    Christian Phillips (cphillips10@btinternet.com)
Sent: Sun 10/11/09 10:36 AM
To: Joan Troutman (troutman425@hotmail.com)

I now have Joseph and Sarah's marriage certificate. It shows us that Joseph Hodges, age 21, Bachelor, Collier by occupation of Brynmawr, Llanelly, married Sarah Mafs, (see 1), age 19, Spinster also of Brynmawr, Llanelly. The marriage took place on the 19th of August 1862 at Tabor Chapel, Brynmawr in the presence of the Registrar, Thomas Jones. Joseph's father was Thomas Hodges, a Miner, and Sarah's father was James Mafs, (see 1), a Collier. Witnesses were Roger Edwards and Hannah Davies. Both bride and groom signed with a cross. (See 2).

1. Confusingly, words with a double "s" - like Mass, moss, pass - were often written as Maf, Mof, Paf. The double "s" was abbreviated in written text with an "f". This seems to be the case here, so the bride's maiden name would appear to be Mass or Moss.

However, as the bride and her father could not write, the Registrar would write down the surname phonetically - as it sounded. We know from subsequent birth certificates that Sarah's maiden name was written as Marsh on 3 separate occasions, so Sarah's family name could be Moss, Mass or Marsh!

To add further confusion we also have the court records that give her maiden name as Kidson!

2. At this timeframe in the Welsh Valleys most children/adults who had attended formal schooling were able at the very least to sign their own name. The fact that both bride & groom (& for that matter Joseph's parents as well from the birth certificates) sign with a cross indicates that it was unlikely that any of them had any form of formal schooling.

Hi there - did a bit of further digging and I think I've found Louisa (aka Susan) Dainty's christening

12th January 1817 at Weston Under Lizard, Staffordshire, England

Father James Dainty - mother Elizabeth

C

Just in case, I also checked for marriages of a James Marsh to a Louisa and found the following.

James Marsh married a Louisa Dainty on the 4th July 1837 at *****Tipton, Staffordshire*****, England.

Re: Last cerificate

From:
Christian Phillips (cphillips10@btinternet.com)
Sent: Sun 10/11/09 10:36 AM
To: Joan Troutman (troutman425@hotmail.com)

I now have Joseph and Sarah's marriage certificate. It shows us that Joseph Hodges, age 21, Bachelor, Collier by occupation of Brynmawr, Llanelly, married Sarah Mafs, (see 1), age 19, Spinster also of Brynmawr, Llanelly. The marriage took place on the 19th of August 1862 at Tabor Chapel, Brynmawr in the presence of the Registrar, Thomas Jones. Joseph's father was Thomas Hodges, a Miner, and Sarah's father was James Mafs, (see 1), a Collier. Witnesses were Roger Edwards and Hannah Davies. Both bride and groom signed with a cross. (See 2).

1. Confusingly, words with a double "s" - like Mass, moss, pass - were often written as Maf, Mof, Paf. The double "s" was abbreviated in written text with an "f". This seems to be the case here, so the bride's maiden name would appear to be Mass or Moss.

However, as the bride and her father could not write, the Registrar would write down the surname phonetically - as it sounded. We know from subsequent birth certificates that Sarah's maiden name was written as Marsh on 3 separate occasions, so Sarah's family name could be Moss, Mass or Marsh!

To add further confusion we also have the court records that give her maiden name as Kidson!

2. At this timeframe in the Welsh Valleys most children/adults who had attended formal schooling were able at the very least to sign their own name. The fact that both bride & groom (& for that matter Joseph's parents as well from the birth certificates) sign with a cross indicates that it was unlikely that any of them had any form of formal schooling.

Hi there - did a bit of further digging and I think I've found Louisa (aka Susan) Dainty's christening

12th January 1817 at Weston Under Lizard, Staffordshire, England

Father James Dainty - mother Elizabeth

C

Just in case, I also checked for marriages of a James Marsh to a Louisa and found the following.

James Marsh married a Louisa Dainty on the 4th July 1837 at ***Tipton, Staffordshire***, England.

1851 Census, Parish St. Marys, Bridge North, Shropshire, England

I have a found a possibility for the family in 1851 (as attached), living in Bridgnorth St Mary, Shropshire. They do have a daughter Sarah (age 3 or so it seems - arrgghh!!) as well as a son James (age 1) and another daughter called Jane (who be 3 or 9!). Father is James, age 32 (approx 1819), a Miner & his wife is Louisa, also 32 - all born in Sedgley, Staffordshire (which is about 4 miles from Tipton, Staffordshire).

1842. Marriage solemnized at Llan Chapel Bryn mawr in the District of Crickhowell in the County of Brecon

No.	When Married	Name and Surname	Age	Condition	Rank or Profession	Residence at the time of Marriage	Father's Name and Surname	Rank or Profession of Father
189	Nineteenth August 1842	Joseph Hodges	21 years	Bachelor	Collier	Brynmawr Llanelly	Thomas Hodges	Miner
		Sarah Wolf	19 years	Spinster		Bryn mawr Llanelly	James Wolf	Collier

Married in the Ebin Chapel according to the Rites and Ceremonies of the

This Marriage was solemnized between us
{ Joseph Hodges
{ X the mark of Sarah Wolf

in the Presence of us,
{ Robin Edwards
{ X the mark of David

before

Christopher Jenkins

86

United Kingdom, Wales researcher, Christian Phillips-Gunter
(find my ancestors@btinternet.com)
13 Hampton Street, Twynyrodyn, Merthyr Tydfill, CF47 ORR

1.<u>Do you have any idea, at all, where Sarah was born. From the information you sent me earlier, her birth place is just recorded as England.</u>

Reply: PA. records do not list Sarah's birthplace other than "England".

2. Did Sarah's parent/s move to the USA with them? If so have you found them on the US census - any details??

Reply: Yes, Sarah's mother Louisa came to Helfenstein, Pa. with her daughters Sarah and Mary Ellen, and an older step son, George Kidson. In 1869, Louisa (first married Marsh, second married Kidson), purchased land along the Mahanoy Creek.

3. Do you know if Sarah had any siblings?

Reply: Yes, Sarah married Joseph Hodge, Mary Ellen married Jonathan Skelding, and no evidence of a marriage naming George Kidson has been found. The Hodges, Skeldings, and Kidsons all lived in Helfenstein.

I have searched the English & Welsh census for Sarah but without having an idea of her birthplace (& different maiden names!), its difficult to pinpoint the right record. The only *near* possibility (& its a highly likely one) is as attached - a Sarah Marsh.

If you look at the census image - she is living at Clydach Bridge - ring any bells?? Yup - a few houses away from where Joseph Hodges was recorded living at on the 1851 census. Only fly in the ointment is the fact that Sarah is recorded as being 14. I think this could be a mis-transcription as if you look at the image, her age could be 19 which would tie in with her approx age on the marriage certificate.

Her place of birth is given as ***Tipton*** in Staffordshire.

Father James Marsh, a Miner, age 39 (B c1822) POB, Tipton, Staffs

Mother Susan Marsh, a Miner's wife, age 39 (B c1822) POB, Tipton, Staffs

I have a found a possibility for the family in 1851 (as attached), living in Bridgnorth St Mary, Shropshire. They do have a daughter Sarah (age 3 or so it seems - arrrgghh!!) as well as a son James (age 1) and another daughter called Jane (who be 3 or 9!). Father is James, age 32 (approx 1819), a Miner & his wife is Louisa, also 32 - all born in Sedgley, Staffordshire (which is about 4 miles from Tipton, Staffordshire).

Could Louisa have been known as Susan? Could the marriage I found - James Marsh married a Louisa Dainty on the 4th July 1837 at ***Tipton, Staffordshire*** - be the right one??

Reply: Yes, and yes again. You have completed a masterful genealogical search and reached reasonable and convincing conclusions. Thank you so much. Steve and Joan.

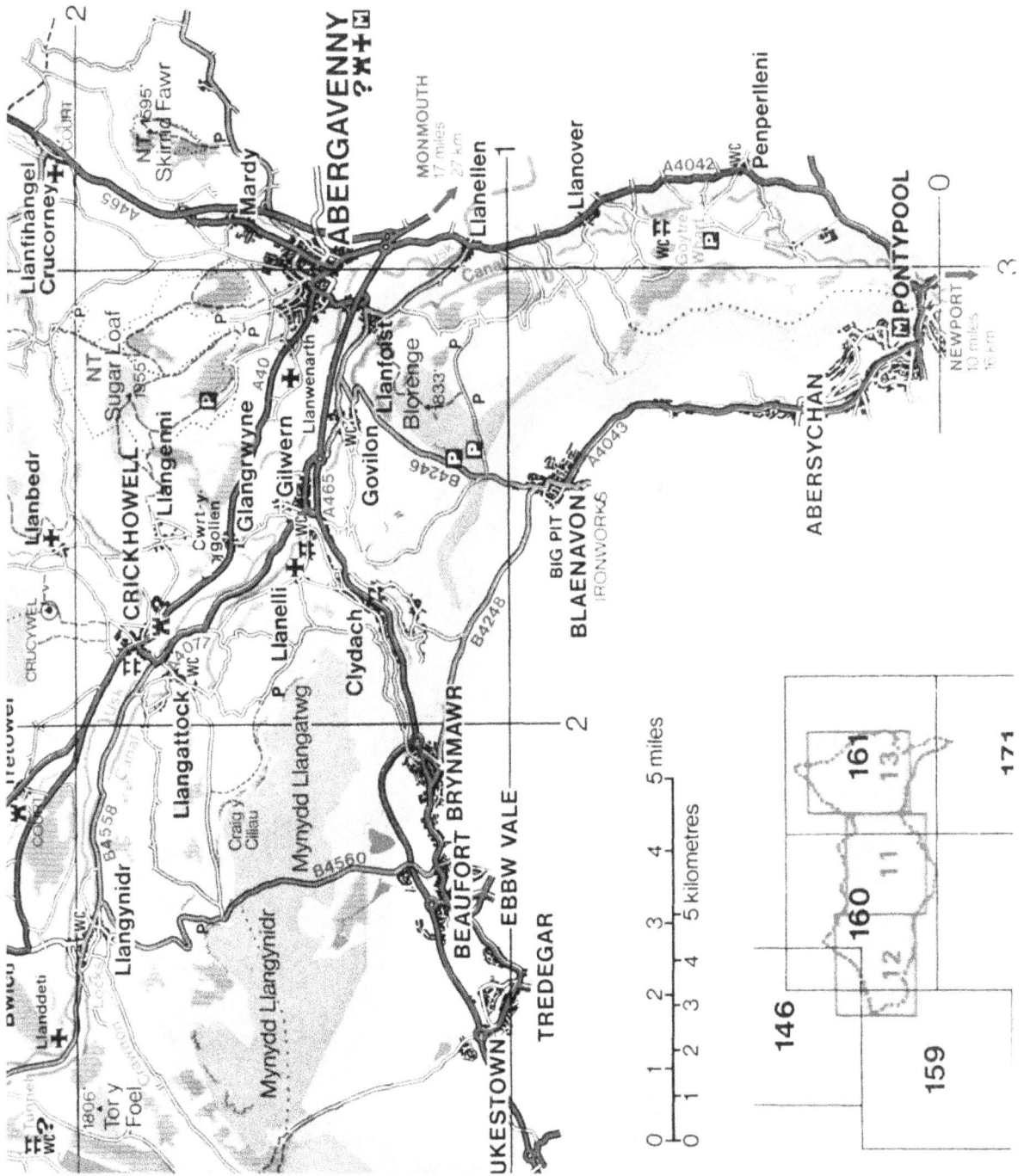

Blaenavon and the James Family

Blaenavon was once the most important mining town of Britain, located in South Wales. The Blaenavon Iron Works was built in 1789 and was the largest in the world at that time. A method to produce steel was first discovered at these iron works which remain today as a World Heritage Site. This World Heritage Site includes a coal mine named "Big Pit", now a visitor's center.

Ann James, the wife of Thomas Hodge was born in Blaenavon, Monmouthshire County. The James Family could have lived in a company row house, similar as pictured below. Thomas and Ann married. They are recorded in 1841 as living at Cwm Sychan, British Works, Parish Trevethin, near Abersychan as a coke worker. By 1851 Thomas and Ann relocated across the mountain to the Clydach Gorge near Llanelly. Here, Joseph Hodge, their son, was listed as an iron miner 11 years old in the 1851 Census.

The rear of Staffordshire Row with the former general offices of the Blaenavon Company perched on the high ground above

Visitors can go down this coalmine (called Big Pit) for free.

89

These illustrations of iron mining techniques and coal mining show how these occupations employed the entire family. Illustrations by Michael Blackmore from the book *Exploring Blaenavon Industrial Landscape*, by Chris Barber, 2002

Ironstone deposits were once removed by 'scouring'. This involved extracting the minerals (which fortunately lay close to the surface) by first removing the turf and then clearing away the top soil by releasing water from above. A lake was formed by constructing a simple dam and when this was breached, the water surged down and scoured the soil away to reveal the iron ore.

A large pond or reservoir is dug on the Common, divers channels are dug along the Commons to catch the water and convey it to this pond or reservoir, from thence is another channel leading to the mine pits. When a considerable quantity of ore is dug the pond sluice is taken up and the water running from thence with great force on the dug oare in the pits scoures and washes away the clay.

Early 19th century account

Breaking up the ironstone was strenuous work, yet this task was undertaken by young girls using picks and heavy hammers. They worked shifts of 12 hours (6am to 6pm), with only a short break for lunch and earned 7 shillings a week. A visitor to Blaenavon in the early years of the 19th century described how the girls wore hobnailed boots with 'toecaps that would pull the legs off some of the ploughmen!'

The overlooker, a Welshman named Powell showed me round... Some women were filling and wheeling barrows of ironstone: but most were engaged inside certain wooden sheds in breaking the big lumps of iron- stone... Lifting the hammer over their heads and bringing it down with manly skill and force... They were all well grown lasses, aged from 15 to 21... Mr Powell said, 'they are the finest women of this kind anywhere, and if it wasn't for the girls here I don't know what the ironworks would do.'

Arthur Munby 1865

When William Lloyd the Furnace Manager at Blaenavon Ironworks was interviewed he commented:-

I have about 37 children working about the furnaces under my charge; the youngest are about seven years of age. I think I only have one so young as seven years; he clears the tramroad and is paid by the company five shillings per week. I have some boys from eight to twelve years old helping the 'fillers' at the furnace top, they fill the limestone barrow and assist the filler in pushing it from the yard to the furnace; they do not go into any heat or danger. There are 14 girls from ten to sixteen years of age on the coal and coke yard, they are paid by the Cokers from six shillings to nine shillings per week. There are six boys in the cast-house and refinery from ten to fourteen years. The refinery boys work in some heat in the summer time and sometimes get burned, but not very bad. There are few girls at the mines working below. They all work twelve hours and the furnaces and refineries work all night. There are only four boys and two girls working at night, they change every other week and they all take an hour for dinner and half an hour for breakfast.

The boys called carters are employed in narrow seams of coal in parts of Monmouthshire. Their occupation is to drag the carts or skips of coal from the working place to the main road. In this mode of labour the leather girdle passes round the body and the chain is between the legs, attached to the cart, and the lads drag on all fours.

Report of the Childrens' Employment Commission 1842

Of the children employed at the Blaenavon Ironworks in 1841, it was reported that 21 could read and 4 could write. In the forges there were 70 boys between the ages of thirteen and eighteen. Of these 44 could read and 24 could write. This undoubtedly showed the results of the school established in 1816 at Blaenavon by Sarah Hopkins. It had become the aim of the Blaenavon Ironworks Company that their workers' children should have a good enough education to enable them to read the Bible and newspapers.

The report revealed that a quarter of the Blaenavon boys between the ages of five and thirteen were working in the coal and iron industries. Only a few of the girls of this age group worked in the mines, where both boys and girls below the age of ten, were employed to look after the air doors.

Children as young as five or six would sit 12 hours in the dark, opening and closing air-doors at the approach of men, horses and trams moving to and from the coalface. These youngsters had to start work at the same time as the hewers and remain at their positions until the last tram of coal had been cleared from the colliery. The Blaenavon door boys earned from 10s to 12s a month, which was the amount that they would earn in a week when they progressed to becoming hauliers.

Mary Davies, near seven years old, a very pretty girl, was fast asleep under a piece of rock near the air-door below ground. Her lamp had gone out for want of oil. Upon wakening her, she said the rats, or someone, had run away with her bread and cheese, so she went to sleep. The overman thought she was not so old, although he was sure that she had been below for fifteen months.

Report of the Childrens' Employment Commission 1842

Llanelly Church of Breconshire
South Wales

Baptism Location of Joseph Hodge

LLANELLY - Extract from National Gazetteer, 1868

[Description(s) from *The National Gazetteer* (1868)]

"LLANELLY, a parochial chapelry in the hundred of Crickhowell, county Brecon, 2 miles S. of Crickhowell, and 5 W. of Abergavenny, its post town. It is situated on the rivers Clydach and Usk, and the Brecon canal passes through it. It includes the parcels of Aberbaidan and Maesgwartha, and two waterfalls. Coal and lime are obtained, and iron ore is smelted at the Clydach and Llyndach iron-works. A tram road passes by the side of the river, under the canal aqueduct to the Beaufort works. The tithes were commuted in 1839. The living is a perpetual curacy* The church is dedicated to St. Ellyw. The parochial charities amount to about £30 per annum. The Independents, Wesleyans, and Primitive Methodists have chapels."

Back to index

St Elli's Church, Llanelly, Breconshire

Denomination: Anglican

Dedication: St Elli

Built: Medieval

There were two building periods in the history of the church; to the first, 1175-1250, belong the font, the south aisle, and the tower. The north aisle was added in 1626, possibly through the influx of wealth following the foundation of the nearby Clydach Iron Works. The west tower, of early English style, is of the fortified type, of which many specimens remain along the Welsh Border. It contains a ring of six bells. There is a low 13th century priests' door in the south wall, opposite the chancel arch.
[Adapted from description in the church guide]

An ancient circle of Yews surrounds this church. There are wide views across the valley. There are two naves, the South part probably of Norman date, with a second 'nave' added in the 15th century. The 20th century stained glass includes scenes of iron making and coal mining associated with the area. Outside the churchyards are maintained as managed wild life areas.
[Extracted from entry on the *Church in Wales* website]

For further details and photographs, see:
Jeffrey L. Thomas's website

Photography: John Ball
Date: 5 June 1998
Camera: *Agfa ePhoto307* digital

Back to index

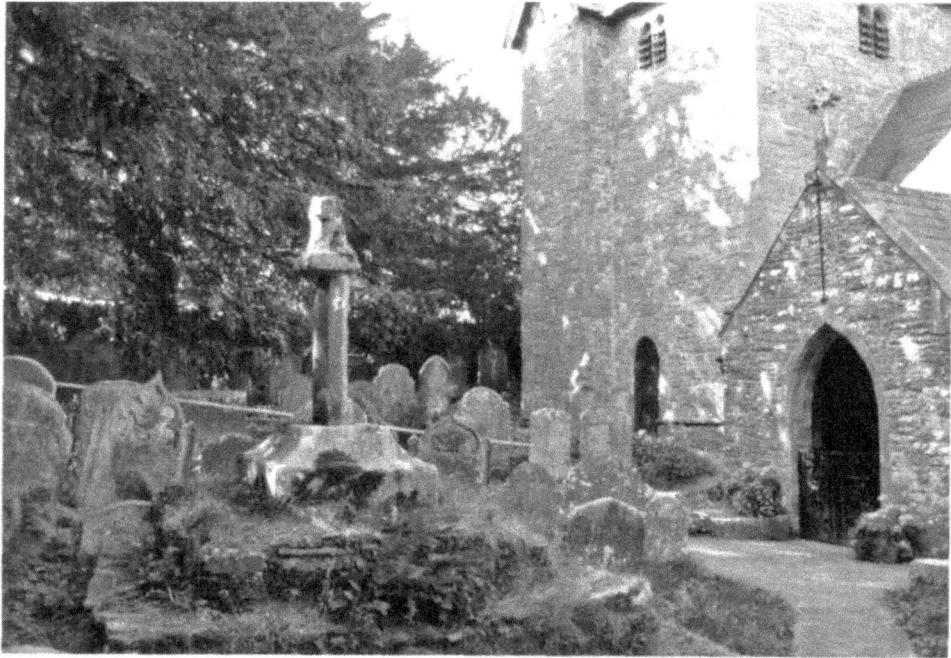

One of the walk ways leading to the doors of the Llanelly Parish Church. The oldest part of the church is the tower with the smaller door which was built from 1175-1250. In the foreground is a broken cross set upon a circle of stone which pre dates the stone church building. Llanelly Hill has been a spiritual center for nearly 1000 years. An ancient circle of yew trees surrounds the church.

The entrance doors open with a large iron key about 12 inches long. The welcome sign reads, "The Diocese of Swansea and Brecon (Church of Wales). Parish Church of ST. ELLI. Rector Rev. A. Francis. Weekly Services, Parish Church of Llanelly. Marriages and Baptisims by arrangement with the Rector. Everybody welcome. The Rectory, Abergavenny Road, Gilwern, S. Wales."

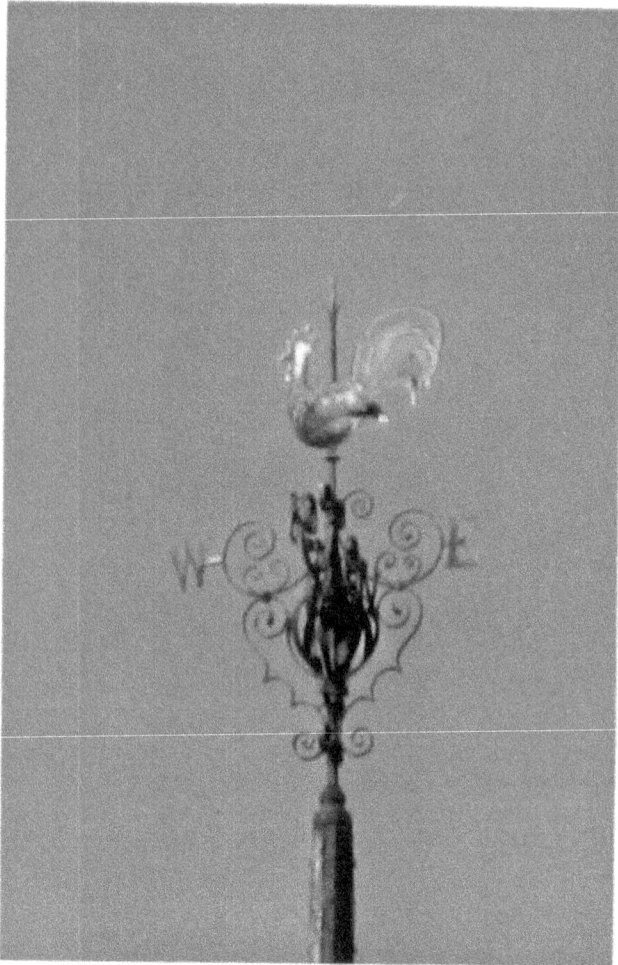

A golden rooster crests a weather vane
on top of the old tower steeple.
In the grave yard below, are many
obelisk style markers, similar to
Joseph Hodge's marker at
Mt. Carmel Cemetery, Pa.

The building is surrounded by grave markers
crowded together, close by the ancient stone
walls of the sanctuary. The grass is not cut and
grows several feet high in sunny areas.
The large markers are high and stand
above the grass.

Llanelly Church was enlarged in 1626. Here we see the north aisle and the earlier south aisle with the cross on top. The stained glass windows are dedicated to coal miners, iron workers, and St. Elli. The figures are all beautifully depicted in vivid colored glass.

A northerly view from the Llanelly Church toward the town of Crickhowell. Here we see a Rose of Sharon in full bloom in late September.

Scenic westerly view toward Gilwern and Abergavenny in the Usk River Valley below. Clydach is in the valley toward the right edge of the photo, which is south. "Ll", as in Llanelly, is pronounced "sch" as in the word schell. Therefore "Llanelly" is spoken as "Schlaneschy". The "sch" sound for "ll" is standard pronunciation for Welch vocabulary.

Sugar Loaf Mountain as seen from Llanelly Hill, looking northwest from the parish house. Sheep roam the green countryside in Wales.

The ancient baptisimal font dating back to 1175-1250 A.D. Presently the font is located near the main entry doors to the church and is at the back of the sanctuary. The font is near the north tower which is the oldest part of the building. Joseph Hodge was baptized here on 16th of February, 1840. Parents were Thomas and Ann Hodges.

Communion table made of carved wood located in the south aisle of the sanctuary. This Tudor period altar dates from the early 1600's.

The old church tower has six bells, dating from 1908, 1620, and 1440. The ancient bells are some of the oldest in Wales. They are marked as cast in Bristol. Here are the colorful ropes to pull that swing the ringing bells.

Mr. Russell, Joan Troutman, and the Pastor at Llanelly Church, 27th of September, 2009. The sermon was about the signs of the end of time. Mr. Russell, who lives in the village of Gilwern, told Joan that he recalled his parents speaking of Hodge people as well as Moss (Marsh) people from Gilwern. None are living in the area today. The Hodges had Llanelly Church connections.

Clydach Gorge of Monmouthshire South Wales

The Iron and Coal Industry and the Hodge Family

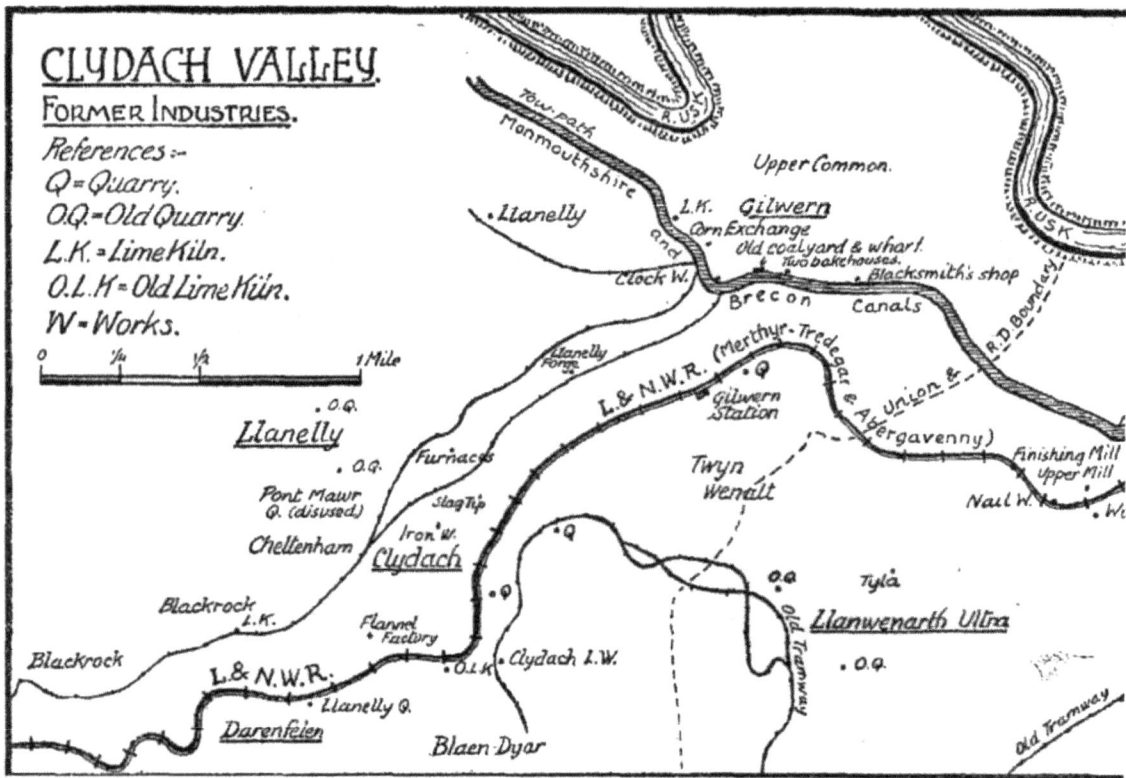

CLYDACH VALLEY.
FORMER INDUSTRIES.

References:—
Q = Quarry.
O.Q. = Old Quarry.
L.K. = Lime Kiln.
O.L.K = Old Lime Kiln.
W = Works.

Clydach, Monmouthshire

From Wikipedia, the free encyclopedia

Clydach is a village in Monmouthshire, Wales. Its nearest neighbours are the towns of Gilwern and Abergavenny.

Contents

- 1 Heads of the Valleys
- 2 Industrial Heritage
- 3 Primary School Closure 2006
- 4 Local Walks
- 5 External links

Heads of the Valleys

It is split by the A465 road (the 'Heads of the Valleys') into North Clydach and South Clydach.

Industrial Heritage

Coordinates: 51.8086°N 3.1255°W

Clydach

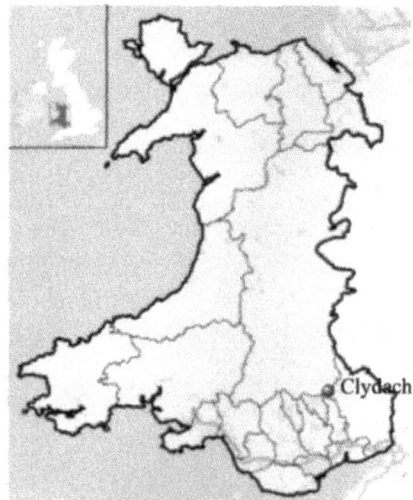

Clydach shown within Wales

Historic Landscape Characterisation

Clydach Gorge

The short but spectacular Clydach Gorge cuts through the extreme north east corner of the South Wales coalfield, between the North Gwent uplands to the south and Llangattock Mountain to the north. The floor of the gorge drops steeply down from Bryn-mawr in the west at 350m above OD, to Gilwern in the east at 100ln above OD, in a distance of just over 5km. The gorge is seldom more than 0.5km wide and its sides rise extremely steeply, precipitously in places, to gentler slopes on either side above about 350m above OD. The River Clydach plummets and cascades its way through the gorge to join the River Usk at Gilwern where the gorge dramatically opens out into the Usk valley.

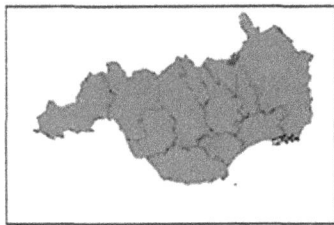

Character Areas
of Clydach Gorge
Historic Landscape

Use the map to select your area of interest or go directly to character area summaries.

As the gorge cuts the South Wales coalfield, it exposes stratified seams of coal, clay and ironstone and then cuts deeply into the Carboniferous Limestone. This geological structure, together with the resource and power of the River Clydach, has ensured that the area was exploited at least from the prehistoric period as evidenced by Craig y Gaer, an Iron' Age fort occupying the top of a natural bluff overlooking the north side of the gorge. The presence of woodland, to provide timber and charcoal for firing furnaces, must also have been a key factor in attracting early industry to the gorge.

Geomorphologically, the steepness of the terrain was an advantage to the early ironworking and lime-burning industries, where the blast furnaces and lime kilns could be strategically built into the valley sides, facilitating the charging of materials from above and their withdrawal from below.

The dramatic landscape and scenery of the Clydach Gorge is supplemented by its diverse historical and archaeological associations, and the variety of communication systems that have utilized the natural communication route of the gorge, which links the inhospitable uplands of Glamorgan with the fertile valley of the River Usk. However, most of the communications systems primarily served the industries that sprang up in the gorge, which from historical documentary evidence were first introduced into it in the 17th century, though medieval exploitation, albeit undocumented, should be expected. It was at this time that the Hanbury family of Pontypool established the Llanelly furnace and forge on the north bank of the river. By 1684, these works were producing large quantities of iron and charcoal, which ensured that the early exploitation and settlement of Clydach Gorge rapidly developed. Clydach House, situated nearby and built in 1693 by Francis Lewis, clerk to the furnace, ostentatiously displays his family arms above the main entrance to the property. Elsewhere in the valley, and in social contrast, are the visible remains of the former workers' houses, including the iron workers' terraces in Clydach South.

The Clydach Ironworks, founded before 1795, was established to exploit the recent introduction of coke as the fuel for blast furnaces. The site of the works lies alongside the modern A465(T) Heads of the Valleys road, with the surviving remains including two large masonry furnaces, together with the foundations of their casting houses, a cupola and other related buildings. The site is approached over a cast iron bridge, Smart's Bridge, dated to 1824. Production at the works continued until about 1860, up to which time it had become the focal point for activity in the gorge. By 1841, over 1350 people, including 133 children under the age of 13, were employed, of whom about two-thirds were engaged in extracting the required iron ore and coal higher up the valley. In its early years, the works were closely associated with the Frere family, which was to gain notoriety for a different reason when Sir Bartle Frere, born in 1815 in Clydach House, became High Commissioner of South Africa, and unwittingly helped to start the Zulu War.

The major industry of the late 19th and early 20th centuries in the gorge was stone quarrying and the manufacture of lime for agricultural and building purposes. The first lime works had started production in 1795, at Blackrock, but numerous other quarries were opened throughout the next century. Llanelly Quarry supplied the Clydach Ironworks with limestone, and subsequently lime for farming and building mortars. It closed finally in 1962. The surviving Clydach Limeworks was built in 1877 to provide lime for building the railway viaduct. Its large kilns, with double draw arches for each shaft, are particularly fine surviving examples.

Communications and transport have also clearly played a fundamental part in the development of the gorge. In the 1790s, railroads and tram roads, both initially horse-drawn, were being built to link mines and quarries with works. In 1793,permission was granted by Parliament for the construction of the Brecknok and Abergavenny Canal, together with a connecting tramway system, the first line of which ran through the gorge. The canal traverses the floor of the gorge near Gilwern on a huge earthen embankment, 25m high, with the river running in a tunnel at its base. The canal between Gilwern and Brecon opened in 1801, but the final connection with Pontymoile to the south was not made until 1812.

Other tramways and inclines to serve specific mines were lad in the gorge, with the consequence that the area now has the densest network of surviving early tram road routes anywhere in Wales. These were supplemented in 1862 by the single track Merthyr, Tredegar and Abergavenny Railway. This was absorbed Into the London and North Western Railway in 1866 and converted to a double track system eleven years later. The precipitous slopes meant that the route could be negotiated only with a series of tunnels, cuttings and viaducts. The route, now dismantled, remains a prominent and spectacular linear feature which can be seen on the south side of the gorge. The present A465(T) Heads of the Valleys road, built in the 1960s, is the latest in a series of road systems that have, from the 18th century, traversed the gorge as important connecting routes.

Today, all mineral and limestone extraction has ceased, leaving little employment within the gorge; nevertheless, the old-established communities still thrive. Vestiges of past industries and communications systems are plentiful, as is the evidence of former social conditions, including not only housing, but also surviving chapels and public houses. The dense and varied industrial sites and successive transport systems in the gorge represent a compact and integrated microcosm of the Welsh industrial past; this, in turn, depended on the remarkable geology and topography of this inspiringly visual historic landscape area.

Francis Lewis, Clerk to the iron furnace at Clydach, is named within this document. The 1851 census for the Parish Llanelly, names the Thomas and Ann Hodge family dwelling as Francis Row. Joseph Hodge, age 11, is listed as an iron miner in this family. The row of iron workers houses must have been named after this Francis Lewis and were no doubt located nearby Clydach House, built by Francis Lewis. S.E.T. Jan. 2010

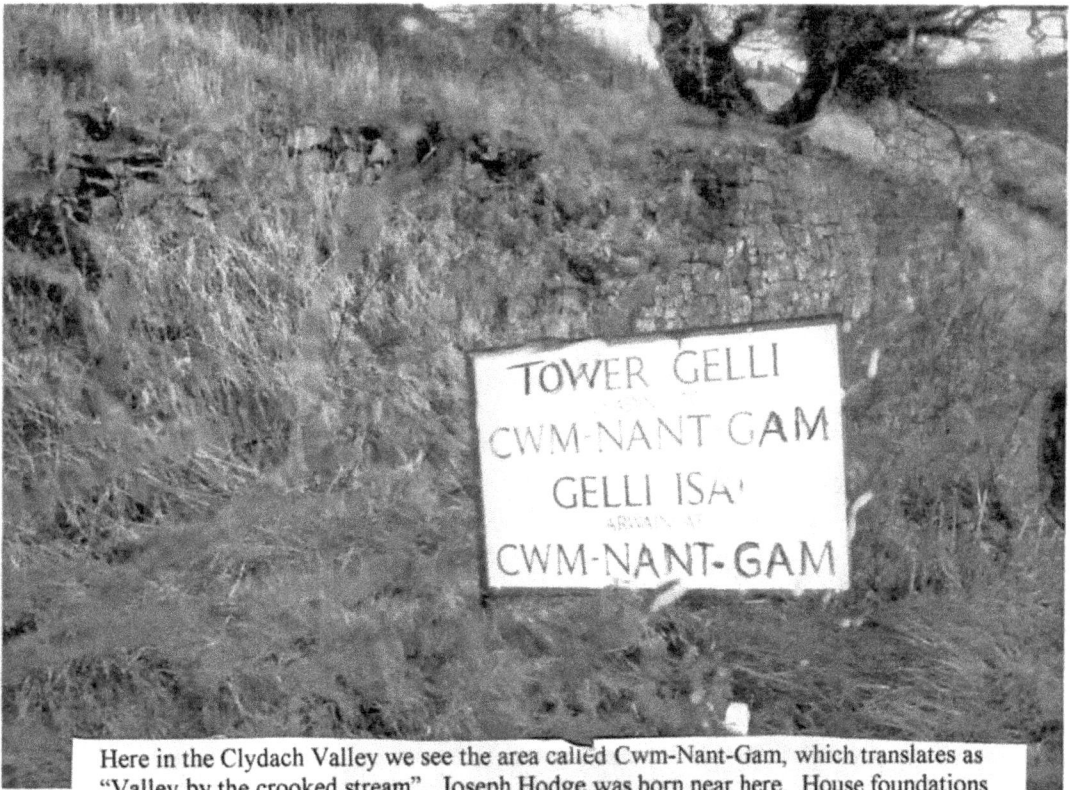

Here in the Clydach Valley we see the area called Cwm-Nant-Gam, which translates as "Valley by the crooked stream". Joseph Hodge was born near here. House foundations of the miners' cottages and mine scars remain along the old railroad grade presently used as an access road to power lines. Photo by joyce@jljm.co.uk on a rainy day, 12/06/09.

The Clydach Valley industry was served by a canal before the railroads were developed.
   At Gilwern, a wharf was established for the Monmouthshire and Brecon Canal.
This canal carried coal, iron, and limestone from the mountainous interior of South Wales
to the coastal city of Newport, located where the River Usk meets the Bristol Channel.

The Clydach Gorge

INDUSTRIAL ARCHAEOLOGICAL TRAILS

John van Laun

BLORENGE BOOKS

Introduction

Only 5.7km long by less than 1km wide, the gorge cuts downwards from 335m above sea level in the west at Brynmawr, to 121m in the east at Gilwern. Thereafter the valley opens out as the river Clydach reaches the Usk around 2km below, at Glangrwyney.

Geologically, this cut is made through most of the rocks of the South Wales Coalfield: coal measures, millstone grit and limestones of the Carboniferous period (about 300 million years old) down to the Old Red Sandstone of the preceding Devonian period.

North Side of the Clydach Gorge
(upper section)
from Llanelly Quarry

The valley had the natural assets to invite early industrial exploitation: iron ores; woodlands to provide timber for charcoal furnaces; and fast streams to supply power for simple mechanisation. In fact the Hanbury family of Pontypool became involved in ironmaking here from as early as the 17th century onwards.

But if their activities started as a rural enterprise, ironmaking in the Clydach Gorge became an industry when new men introduced the use of coke as a fuel, and steam to supplement waterpower. Coal for coke was available from drift-mines (tunnelled into the hillsides to meet coal seams). Though charcoal continued in use at one forge for some years, it was the building of coke-fired blast furnaces that enabled the Clydach to withstand for the time being growing competition from more recently established ironmaking centres in the main coalfields of South Wales.

Although all the required raw materials and sources of energy for ironmaking were to be found within the valley, they had to be brought together for processing. Much ingenuity and almost incalculable human labour were needed to create well-graded routes for the transport of materials along the steep, gullied sides of the valley. And the area's industrial potential could only be realised as systems were developed to take its heavy products to markets outside the immediate locality.

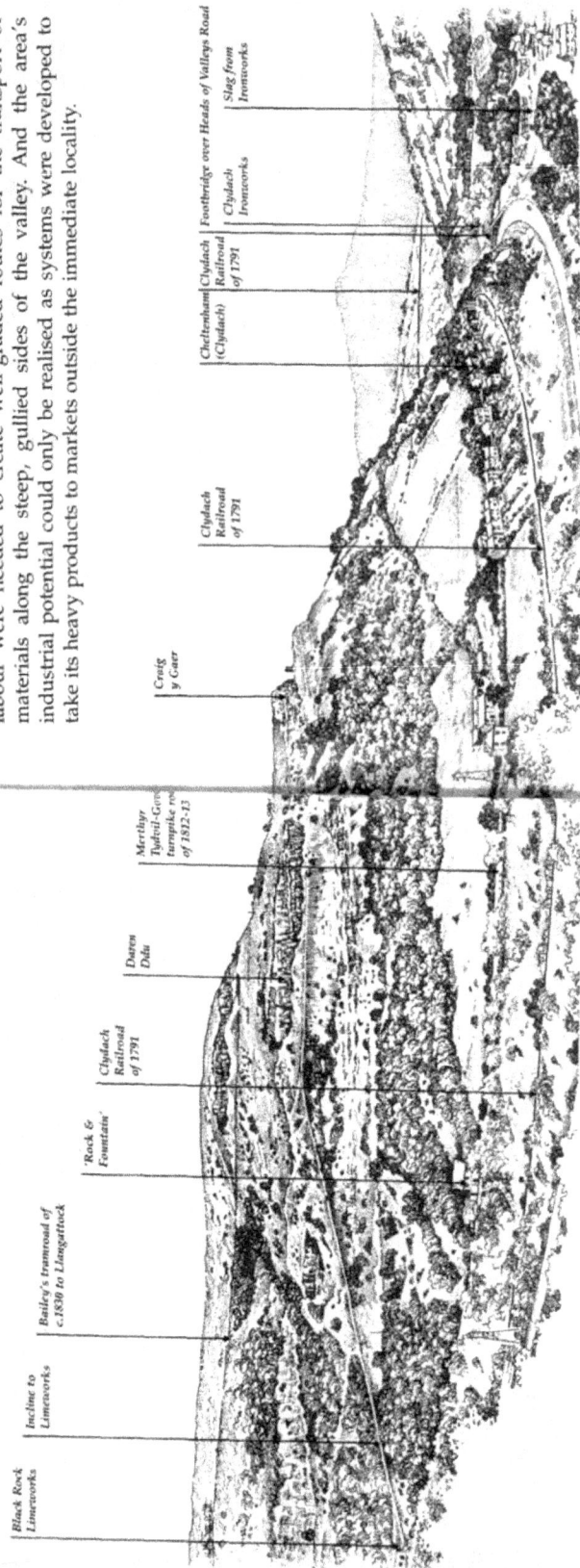

Black Rock Limeworks

Incline to Limeworks

Bailey's tramroad of c.1830 to Llangattock

'Rock & Fountain'

Clydach Railroad of 1791

Daren Ddu

Merthyr Tydvil-Gove turnpike ro of 1812-13

Craig y Garr

Clydach Railroad of 1791

Cheltenham (Clydach)

Clydach Railroad of 1791

Footbridge over Heads of Valleys Road

Clydach Ironworks

Slag from Ironworks

South side of the Clydach Gorge
viewed from Bailey's Tramroad to Llangattock

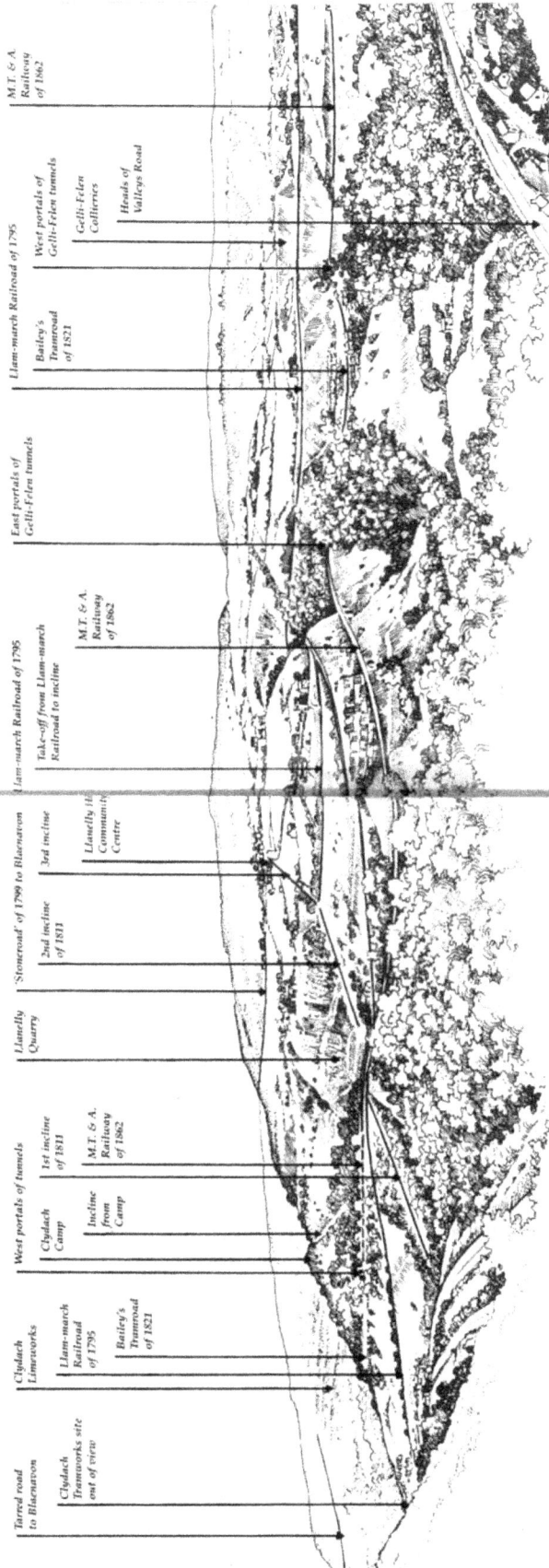

Tarred road to Blaenavon

Clydach Tramworks site out of view

Clydach Limeworks

Llam-march Railroad of 1795

Bailey's Tramroad of 1821

West portals of tunnels

Clydach Camp

1st incline of 1811

M.T. & A. Railway of 1862

Incline from Camp

Llanelly Quarry

'Stoneroad' of 1790 to Blaenavon

2nd incline of 1811

3rd incline

Llanelly Hill Community Centre

Llam-march Railroad of 1795

Take-off from Llam-march Railroad to incline

M.T. & A. Railway of 1862

East portals of Gelli-Felen tunnels

Llam-march Railroad of 1795

Bailey's Tramroad of 1821

West portals of Gelli-Felen tunnels

Gelli-Felen Collieries

Heads of Valleys Road

M.T. & A. Railway of 1862

South side of the Clydach Gorge from Bailey's Llangattock Tramroad (SO 197123 - 201159). The tramroad was built around 1830 to bring limestone to Nantyglo Ironworks from Llangattock Quarries and for the export of iron at Llangattock village beyond which it met the Brecknock & Abergavenny Canal.

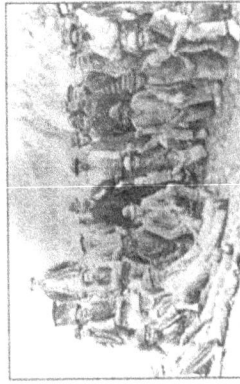

Quarrymen at Gilwern Hill, 1888

Social Conditions

The social consequences of industrialisation of the area were immense. Many more people found work here than ever can have won a living by farming such difficult terrain – and some who had small farms supplemented their meagre income by quarrying. Workers came into the area from Cardigan, Radnor, Hereford, Shropshire, Gloucester and Somerset, as well as from Monmouthshire and rural Breconshire.[1]

The population growth in the early part of the 19th century is indicated by the five chapels which were built in the valley between 1829 and 1836.

There was much discontent with conditions in such areas. 'What the men had to complain of,' it was reported in 1830, 'was chiefly the Truck System of paying in goods instead of money, particularly articles of food, for which it is said they were made to pay from 20 to 30 per cent dearer …'[2]

Even six-year olds were employed at Clydach Ironworks in 1841 – when output was about at its highest – and the harshness of the working week is indicated by the management's statement that 'We find our workpeople derive comfort and moral advantage from the suspension of their labours for a certain number of hours on the Sundays.[3]

But closure of the works in the 1860s brought great distress when people were forced to look for jobs elsewhere, leaving many cottages to become ruinous. A similar sequence of events followed the decline of mining in the area many years later.

'Muck' may have brought money to some here, but even for them prosperity was often brief. For most it was an incredibly hard and insecure life. The graveyard of the parish church (at Llanelly, high above the gorge to the north-west) still bears testimony to the lives and deaths of some of those involved with local industry of the period.

1 Source: 7
2 Source: 12
3 Source: 34

With the development of the motor vehicle in the 20th century, **roads** were progressively improved, some tramroads being tarred over to take the new traffic. Since the closure of the railway in 1958, the most dramatic change in regional communications took place when the Heads of the Valleys Road (A465) was cut through the valley in the early 1960s. This is now the dominant man-made feature of the Clydach Gorge, though the 400 kv electricity pylons, erected at about the same time, also dwarf most of the buildings scattered along its sides.

The A465 was constructed through the Clydach Gorge in the early 1960s

Clydach Ironworks

O.S. map reference SO 229132

The importance of Clydach Ironworks in the valley's exploitation is still conveyed by the impressive remains, dominated by the large archway of a charging house, high on the bank above a furnace on the right. In 1986 the area had become covered by dense vegetation and trees. Then a programme of excavation and restoration was started. The scheme was funded by Blaenau Gwent Borough Council and Cadw (Welsh Historic Monuments), with labour supported by the Manpower Services Commission. Subsequently the owner of the site, Mrs. C. S. Chivers, generously gave the property to the Borough Council.[1]

Clydach Ironworks in about 1823 when the furnaces were out of blast (sepia wash by Peter Richard Hoare (1803-1877)).[2] In the foreground is the bridge you have crossed (page 22) and the Llam-march Tramroad linking the ironworks to the canal. On the left is the launder carried on stilts which brought water from higher up the Clydach to supply the 42-ft waterwheel. This lay between the two charging houses with the furnaces to their fronts at a lower level. A casting house lies to the right. The waterwheel at the side of No 2 furnace is, no doubt, related to the second of 'Two capital [blowing] Machines worked by water' referred to in 1813.[3] There is a very similar illustration by John George Wood dated 1811. [4]

112

At the heart of the operations were the furnaces, producing 'grey forge iron'. In front of you, built into the bank, stood two furnaces which were fed from the charging houses above.

Little of the furnaces now remains except their bases. You can see remnants of the insides glazed as far up as the 'boshes' and the 'white work' of refractory brick. The splayed 'forepart' indicates the path which the molten iron would have followed.

Most of the stone cladding has been robbed for other building purposes, but this has revealed the vaulted gallery which allowed access for maintenance of the blast main and the 'tuyeres' (the ends of the pipes through which air was blasted into the furnaces).

A third, rather later furnace was probably sited well to the left; then in about 1844 a fourth, free-standing furnace was built, served by a steam-driven blowing engine.

Beyond the remaining charging house was the coke yard where coal was burnt in heaps or ovens (of which there were 26 in 1833) to produce the coke.

The coke, iron ore and limestone were assembled near the coke yard; then 'fillers' loaded them into two-wheeled barrows for tipping into the open tops of the furnaces.

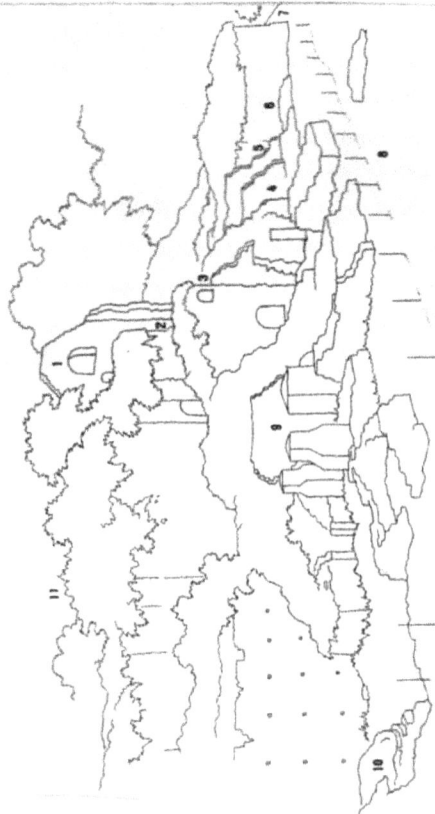

1. Charging house for furnace No 1
2. Site of waterwheel
3. Wheel pit
4. Furnace No 1
5. Hot blast stove foundation
6. Air furnace
7. Incline
8. Casting area
9. Furnace No 2
10. Furnace No 3 (freestanding)
11. Charging area (football field)

Clydach Ironworks as it might have appeared in the mid-1840s

Incline to slag dumping area (now culverted area around Danycoed bungalows)

No. 1 furnace (1793)

No. 2 furnace (1797)

Charging house (arch still standing) where raw materials were assembled in correct mixes

Barrow material from charging house

Casting house with men stacking 'pigs' of iron

No. 4 furnace (1842–44) free standing circular structure built where large waterwheel had earlier powered blast for No. 3 furnace

Launder carrying water from river to high-level wheel between No. 1 and No. 2 furnaces

Wrought iron air reservoir for blast for No. 4 furnace

No. 3 furnace (c.1826) probably sited out of picture to left

Engine house containing blowing engine for No. 4 furnace

114

Clydach Valley.

With the ironworks in full production and the Clydach Gorge echoing to the noise of the iron forges, many men were required to work on the sites. This not only included the men of Clydach and Gilwern but also men from Brynmawr. Here we see a view of the Clydach Valley from Clydach South side.

The Tunnels—under The Dinas, Clydach Station. 1602.

Above and below: Clydach Station and the viaduct can be seen in the first of these photographs. The curvature of the viaduct is a fine testament to the Victorian engineers and navvies who built the line. Both photographs show how the line clings to the side of the hill as it twists and turns on the steep climb towards Brynmawr. The final section of the route to Merthyr was opened on 4 June 1879.

The curvature of the viaduct is a fine testament to the Victorian engineers and navvies who built the line. Both photographs show how the line clings to the side of the hill as it twists and turns on the steep climb towards Brynmawr. The final section of the route to Merthyr was opened on 4 June 1879.

Brynmawr, South Wales
On the border of Breconshire and Monmouthshire

Joseph and Sarah Hodges last home in Wales and their Emigration to America

History of Brynmawr, Wales

Excerpts from the Book *"Brynmawr: A Study of a Distressed Area,"*
by Hilda Jennings

Photographs   2004 by Jeffrey L. Thomas

Above: A modern view of Brynmawr in a photograph taken from King Street just above Well Street. Although the houses here have changed over the decades, the hills seen in the distance would have been familiar to the town's early 19th-century residents.

History of Brynmawr, Wales

Brynmawr, a town that lies on the northern fringe of the south Wales coalfield in what was formerly Breconshire, was one of dozens of communities that was irrevocably transformed in the 19th century by the region's iron and coal industries. According to most sources, in 1800 the village that was once know as *Waun-y-Helegyn* was little more than a collection of farm cottages, yet by the early 1830s this small village had exploded into a thriving industrial community due to the nearby ironworks at Nantyglo, Clydach and Beaufort.

In her book, *Brynmawr: A Study of a Distressed Area*, Allenson & Co., London, 1934, Hilda Jennings provides an in depth examination of Brynmawr's social and economic history. Jennings analyzes the development of the town using a combination of standard texts and personal memories from some of the town's older residents, who at the time were only a generation or two removed from Brynmawr's early 19th-century roots. Most importantly, the book gives readers a good idea of what life was like in Brynmawr, particularly for the countless families employed by the region's iron and coal industries.

Below you will find a collection of excerpts from the book concentrating on the town's development in the early to mid 19th century, supplemented by photographs that were taken when my wife and I visited the area in April of 2004. The excerpts are presented here in the same order as found in the book.

Brynmawr: A Study of a Distressed Area,
by Hilda Jennings,
Allenson & Co., London, 1934.

II. The Growth of the Community of Brynmawr

Brynmawr stands at the extreme northern edge of the South Wales Coalfield on the border of Brecknockshire and Monmouthshire. A few miles to the north lie the fertile valleys of the Usk, while in the more immediate vicinity coal and iron outcrop on the mountain side. Up to 1800 it was practically uninhabited. The great hill fringed on one side by the long line of willows gave it its early name of Waun-y-Helegyn, or the field of the willows, remained for centuries untenanted except by the inhabitants of two or three farm-houses and shepherds' cottages. The turnpike road running from Abergavenny to Merthyr passed through the little village of Clydach two miles away through the turnpike gate up the steep rock to the bleak upland plateau, which is now Brynmawr, and where stage and later a coaching-inn provided a change of horses.

The new settlement, in which lived some of the workers at the iron works and the men, women and children who were engaged in the extraction of iron-ore, were thus ringed round by a mile or two of uninhabited ground which divided it from the earlier settlements of Clydach, Beaufort and Nantyglo. At first the focus of social interests was in these settlements. A newcomer to Brynmawr in 1820 might have found work locally in the iron-ore gathering grounds, or have walked daily to one of the Iron Works. For his chapel, for his shopping at the Company Shop and even for his children's school, if they were privileged to attend one, he would have been forced to go to Nantyglo. There he would have learnt history and gossip about local personalities and have taken part in the building up of the workers' organisations and in the religious meetings and services of the Independents or Baptists. Insensibly, too, he would acquire the prevalent attitude, half admiring and half satirical, to the employers and their doings, expressed in the doggerel English song set to an old Welsh tune which told of the doings of Crawshay Bailey, who with his brother had purchased the <u>Nantyglo Iron Works</u> in 1813,

Yet the fact that the worker had his home and family at Brynmawr would have introduced him to a new set of interests. As the congested streets in the older part of the town sprang up, the neighbourhood would play an ever increasing part in his thoughts and conversation and those of his family. The children playing together in the narrow roads or on the mountain-sides, the women meeting at the wells from which they daily drew their water, he himself talking with his fellows in the public-house, would evolve new human interests as they grew to know each other in daily intercourse. Births, deaths and marriages would be made known, friendships and antagonisms would spring up, and in a very short time the fabric of thought and conversation would be tinged by the common knowledge and assumptions of the growing settlement.

Into the little community came a constant flow of newcomers from Wales and England, each the subject of speculation, and each adding some new ingredient to the common life. Difficulties in providing houses and house-furnishings, added hardships owing to the severity of climate and the poorness of roads would be common to all; all too, would have a tale of past history and their reasons for and difficulties in migrating to this isolated spot, which would provide the material of romance and adventure to be imagined and talked over in the home and public-house. Gradually the cleavage between English and Welsh was overcome as the English language gained ground and the habit of living together as pioneers in a strange place affected the customs of immigrants whatever their place of origin.

Owing to the geographical position of the town at the head of the mining valleys, it was a natural meeting place of bands of workers, who were combining in the attempt to extort better wages and freedom from the Truck system. Since, whatever their place of work, almost all the inhabitants of Brynmawr were in some way dependent on the iron industry, these meeting and processions would be deemed of great importance and would help to relate the common interests of Brynmawr to those of the place of occupation. The workers living in the town soon found the need for a permanent local meeting-place, and the Brynmawr public-houses became the centres of local lodges and branches of the Secret Union Clubs.

In other ways also the centre of social interests and activities shifted from Nantyglo. The march of men, women and children bearing the chapel furniture from the Mother Church at Nantyglo to a separate chapel at Brynmawr in 1828 was symbolic of the inevitable transfer of interests to the home town and of the process of building up a body for the life of the new community. Buildings and organisations as well as social groupings were bound to spring up to provide a mode of expression for the common life. Thus chapel after chapel was built; little schools were held in chapels and cottages; the few shops in private houses were added to by a line of shops in what was to be the main street in the centre of the town, even if the Company Shop established a Branch in Brynmawr itself.

Moreover, common needs which could not be provided for individually began to make themselves felt. Cholera visited the town, and could not be stayed by either the precautions of individual families or the ministrations of the churches, to which new converts rushed in terror; the water supplies were polluted and insufficient; the chapel burial grounds became overcrowded. Thus, in 1851, a Board of Health was elected, and discussion of its doings, of the services which it instituted and the rates it imposed became a standing feature of the life of Brynmawr. To the social and industrial organisations was added the machinery of government, and thus on all sides the common life, which at first had been fluid and shapeless, acquired fixed methods of expression; groupings and activities were no longer altogether shifting and spasmodic but were stabilised in social institutions.

The many-sided expressions of community life touched the individual at so many points, that even when one bond was snapped, there were other close ties which bound him to the place. Thus, in the period when depression in the iron industry had not yet been counterbalanced by the growth of coal production for export, the community of Brynmawr showed a surprising stability, and civic pride and optimism even gave rise to new developments and experiments. Some workers left the town, but many were kept there by the fact that they had built or bought their houses, by family ties, attachments to a chapel, and by the more intangible attachments to place and people which played so large a part in their lives.

Closely related to the quality of social life and the generally accepted standards of family and neighbourhood relationships was the growing up of a conception of leadership. First the old Ironmasters assumed supreme power over the lives of their workers. Then leaders sprang up from diverse sections, exerting an influence sometimes over the lives of one or other of the various groups of citizens only, but in some cases guiding the aspirations of the community and influencing its fortunes at many points. From the workers sprang leaders in revolt, nameless leaders of the terrorist body known as "Scotch Cattle" and "King Crispin," the Chartist shoe-maker; later Mr. Hicks, shopkeeper from Bristol and founder of the Boot Factory, known as the

King of Brynmawr, and Chairman of its Board of Health, held sway for many years, while for nearly half a century John Thomas, the "stern, unbending Calvinist" and capable Town Clerk, combined leadership in religious and social movements with enthusiastic membership of the Abergavenny Cymreigyddion, the pioneer of the modern Welsh Renaissance. Towards the end of the nineteenth century workers, who not only influenced their fellow wage earners but took their share in guiding the fortunes of the town, came to the front. Such was William Davies (Bricks) who worked in the mines from the age of eight, and could neither read nor write, yet by force of character came to serve as a member of the local Council and even of a deputation to the House of Lords, which urged extension of the railway from Nantyglo to Brynmawr.

Old-standing religious ideals remain a force in some sections of the community and decline in others; new political ideas such as Communism are preached unremittingly by a few enthusiasts. Coal is slowly being dethroned in men's minds as ten years' mining depression in South Wales is recognised to be due to more than temporary causes; persistent unemployment since 1921 has altered standards of living and caused a heavier migration from the district than ever before. Yet the life of Brynmawr is still shaped by the dynamic force of nature, race, common traditions and common history. It remains a community and still exerts its power over individuals through community attachments. We cannot "pluck out the heart of the mystery" of Brynmawr, but it is well that we should study its history if we wish to plan a future for it instead of drifting down the stream of declining prosperity and disillusionment.

III. The Development of Natural Resources

☞ Follow this link for a map of coal and iron mines/works in the vicinity of Brynmawr.

Right: A section of tramroad near Brynmawr

Iron-ore was the first mineral, the value of which was recognized in the district, and the Clydach Valley leading up to Brynmawr is still made beautiful by the thick line of beech trees planted to serve as charcoal for the Iron Works. With the discovery of the use of coal for smelting and its general adoption towards the end of the eighteenth century came the opening out of small coal levels by the ironmasters The coal produced was both used in the iron works and taken on the backs of mules and later by canal for sale as house-coal in Brecon and Abergavenny.

Many workers at the Clydach, Nantyglo and Beaufort Iron Works made their homes at Brynmawr, but the industry of the town itself was the gathering of the raw materials, iron-ore, blackband and coal. Clydach Dingle on the northern outskirts of the town was the first scene of this industry. Here the earth was "patched," or its surface removed, in order to reach the ironstone strata. Iron-ore and blackband was collected and stacked in great heaps which were burned to remove the grossest impurities before the minerals were sent to the furnaces. Streams were plentiful and sometimes the ironstone was scoured by rushing water.

At the same time levels were driven into the hillside and the hill gradually became honeycombed with subterranean passages. At first most of the work was above ground, and the little community of workers must have been well inured to the hardships of climate, torrential rains, piercing winds and falls of snow, as well as to the heavy manual labour. From Clydach and Llangattock would come the sound of blasting of limestone, while at night not only the fires of the burning stacks of mineral along the outcrop, but the greater glow from the furnaces would light up the sky.

122

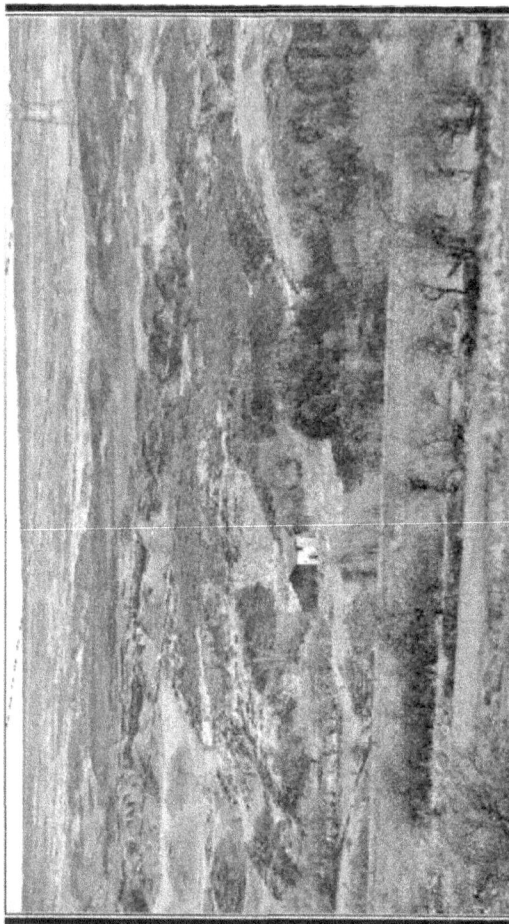

Below: Two views of the "The Patches" above the town. Some of Brynmawr's earliest mining activity was concentrated here in the hills behind the town, where the earth was "patched" (the top layer of soil removed), and shafts were dug into the sides of the hills to extract coal and iron ore near the surface. Today this area stands as a stark reminder of Brynmawr's industrial past.

Unlike the industrial settlements of Nantyglo, Beaufort, Blaenavon, and to a lesser degree Clydach, where the iron works were actually situated, the dormitory town of Brynmawr owed little in the way of building enterprise to the great employers. Individual workers built their own cottages here and there along the tramroads in the very early days, and shortly afterwards tradesmen who, like the workers, were attracted by the central position of the town, began to build courts and rows of houses as a commercial speculation. Later still, thrifty workers, who built their own cottages, invested what was left of their savings in the building of an additional cottage which was inhabited by a married member of their family or let to a fellow worker, and speculative builders put up rows of houses. Thus the tied cottage belonging to the employers has never been a feature of Brynmawr life, and in consequence of this labour has been mobile and workers have been able to move from one colliery to another within traveling distance from Brynmawr in the search for work in bad times.

As usual in a rapidly expanding mining district the younger men came in greatest numbers; hence the tendency to impulsive action and the desire for excitement of whatever nature were greater than in the well established communities, where older and more experienced men formed a greater proportion of the population. Many of the newcomers were single men or had left their wives and families behind until they should have an assured living and a settled home to offer them. Males were thus in excess of females and this again influenced the social habits of the community and their reactions to the outward circumstances of their lives.

The women, whether married or single, took their share in the work of gathering iron-ore and in the coal levels. Often they took their babies to work with them and from an early age children were employed in the less skilled operations, such as turning over the rubbish and picking out the nodules of ironstone. Even today a local coal-level is known as "Peggy's Pit," the name being derived from that of a woman driver of outstanding personality who was employed as a haulier in the mine.

Early life in Brynmawr must have been both simple and lacking in comfort and security, and the iron-workers of the district seem to have experienced considerable difficulty in obtaining even the bare means of livelihood. Thus in 1800 two hundred men, women and children congregated along the Beaufort road, stopped the horses and mules which were being led to the Dowlais Company Shop, drove them into the Beaufort works and declared that the barley meal and bran which they carried should not be taken out of the county.

While the Ironmasters and Colliery Owners were transforming the once quiet hills and valleys and communities were being evolved by the joint influences of nature and man, the development of steamship and rail transport was bringing rival raw materials within the scope of South Wales Iron Works. By the middle of the nineteenth century it was found that iron-ore of superior quality could be brought in from England or even imported profitably from Spain. The local blackband contained only 37.8 per cent of metallic iron as compared with 55 and 60.3 per cent in the various iron-ores of Spain. In addition the working of the mines by the patchwork process was prohibitively expensive in view of the thinness of the veins and the thickness of the burden to be removed before they were reached. Already, by 1865 imports were one third of local products; by 1878 they were four times and in 1890 a hundred times the local product.

Difficulties with regard to the quality and cost of extraction of local ores, together with the gradual superseding of iron by steel, led to a decline in the iron trade which culminated in the closing down of the Clydach and Beaufort Iron Works in 1861, and the sale of the Nantyglo Iron Works by the Baileys in 1870, followed by the end of their activities shortly afterwards. The neighbouring works at Ebbw Vale and Blaenavon were converted into steel works.

The communities which had grown up around the Iron Works were by this time not entirely dependent on them, but the demand for coal was also diminished temporarily by the closing of the works, and for the twenty years between 1860 and 1880 there was great distress in Brynmawr. Thus, while in 1821 males between the ages of twenty and forty constituted .3 of the total male population of the Crickhowell district, after the twenty years' depression due to the closing of the Iron Works in 1861, only .13 of the male population of Brynmawr Urban Sanitary District were in this age group. On the other hand, by 1891, when the coal mines were beginning to call for more men, the proportion had already risen to .16.

IV. Origins and Nationalities

It is not generally realised in England how great has been the admixture of peoples in the South Wales Coalfield, nor how cosmopolitan is the present population. The ports of Cardiff, Swansea and Newport are understood to contain foreign seamen and other immigrants; Pembrokeshire is known to include the curious phenomenon of "Little England," but the Coalfield generally is assumed to be almost entirely populated by persons of Welsh stock. No assumption could be more mistaken. In the early-developed districts on the northern borders of South Wales the mixture of peoples has persisted for over a century and a quarter. The extent to which persons of various origins and nationalities have immigrated into these districts can be judged by the example of Brynmawr.

Surrounded on three sides as the place was by swiftly developing iron works and itself possessing supplies of iron-ore on its northern slopes, it was almost inevitable that it should be used both as the home of some of the workers who were crowding into the works in the narrow valleys near by, and as the gathering ground of the raw material.

The first workers at the Iron Works were drawn from the surrounding agricultural districts and were of Welsh nationality. The distress which was present among agricultural labourers in Breconshire and Monmouthshire between 1795 and 1801 made them glad to exchange their average weekly wage of 6s. to 9s. a week for the 2s. 6d. or 3s. a day which they could earn at mining collieries or in lime kilns.

Something of their mode of life, interests and characteristics is revealed in the accounts of Monmouthshire and Breconshire written by Archdeacon Coxe and Theophilus Jones in the early years of the nineteenth century. A simple diet, to a great extent produced by their own exertions, pride in the appearance of house and garden, a love of poetry, story and music, and a cheerful sociability, are portrayed by both writers. The Welsh language was predominant and Archdeacon Coxe says that when he visited Blaina, two miles from the site of Brynmawr, the English language was so little known that without assistance the Parish Clerk could scarcely understand or answer his questions intelligibly.

As early as 1801 there were as many as 937 people living in Llanelly Parish, and 1,000 in Llangattock Parish. During the next thirty years the growth of the settlement of Brynmawr accounted for part of the increase in population in the two parishes in which it was included. This increase averaged 1,000 for each decade in Llanelly and over 500 in each decade in Llangattock, and was largely due to immigration. The immigrants came not only from Breconshire and Monmouthshire, but from more distant Welsh Counties such as Carmarthenshire and Cardiganshire, and both worked in the Iron Works and crossed the mountains for purposes of trade. In this way the preponderance of the Welsh workers was maintained, and their racial characteristics can be seen in the history of the early chapels of Brynmawr. The devotion of the ministers shown in their long and lonely journeys over the mountains with utter disregard of wintry weather, scanty clothing and poor food, was equaled by the self-sacrifice of the scattered congregations which at first met in cottages but whose zeal soon found the means to build little chapels. Perhaps the very repression of the natural lighter interests and the degradation of enjoyment of a secular nature, intensified the force of emotion in its narrow channel; at any rate, religious fervour rose periodically to a high pitch of intensity. A typical Welsh "Revival" took place immediately after the building of the first Brynmawr chapel in 1827, when "an indefinable wave of feeling swept over the place and scenes of hysterical ecstasy were witnessed." By 1832 the membership of the chapel, which was entirely Welsh, had risen to 250, and, with industrial prosperity, religion also seemed to prosper, new members constantly flowing in at the rate of 20 or 30 a month.

Jeff's Note: The church being referred to here is Rehoboth, the first non-conforming chapel built in Brynmawr in 1827 (shown below). Follow this link to learn more about the early history of this important church.

Even before 1830 some English workers had entered the district, and at Clydach a purely English Wesleyan Sunday School was opened in 1807 in what had been a roadside inn called the "Trap," and a chapel was built for the joint use of English and Welsh Wesleyans in 1822. In Brynmawr itself, an English and Baptist Church was built in 1836. There are no records available to show the places of origin of the early English immigrants into the Brynmawr district, but references to workers from Staffordshire and other industrial areas in neighbouring iron works, such as those at Merthyr, seem to indicate that the English pioneer immigrants into South Wales were not drawn direct from the land as in the case of the Welsh immigrants to the iron-ore districts. In any event, they must have brought with them very different traditions and habits of life, influenced not only by their different racial characteristics but by the different nature of the country from which they came. The wild and rugged mountain scenery, great, lonely spaces, and poor roads may well have affected the imaginations and courage of all but the more hardy newcomers. Again, the difference in language must have been a bar to speedy assimilation, and to the growth of understanding and unity between the two racially divided sections of the population of Brynmawr.

V. Industrial Relationships and Community Life

As has been said, the early iron workers and collieries in the Brynmawr district, as elsewhere in Monmouthshire, were almost all owned and developed by English or Scotch employers, while the first workers were mainly Welsh. Strikes over the truck system arose as early as 1801, 1810 and 1816, and in 1830 all the collieries in the Western Valleys of Monmouthshire struck. A chain of "Union Clubs" was established from Swansea and Neath in the West to Pontypool and Brynmawr in the East.

It does not appear, however, that the original Welsh workers initiated the movement of industrial revolt. Probably the difference in outlook between the Ironmasters and the English immigrants was as marked in some ways as was the difference between them and the Welsh workers from the moorlands. Richard Crawshay, the "Iron King," complained that "inflammatory tracts" were circulating among the workers from Derbyshire and Staffordshire, who had already known Unions in their native places, and there are other indications of the active part played by the English workers in the early attempts at combination against the masters.

The struggle was a violent one; the military was called in again and again by the employers, and the workers in their turn, with the law and organised religion both against them, resorted more and more to secret terrorist methods. The ardent sprits of the movement organised themselves as "Scotch Cattle" and disguised with blackened faces, sallied forth at night to paint the sign of the red Bull's Head on the doors of blacklegs, and sometimes, as at Nantyglo during the strike of 1832, to raid their houses, destroy their furniture and beat the inhabitants. Even the house of the manager who had introduced the blacklegs was stoned, and neither military nor the heavy rewards offered for information as to the identity of the ringleaders sufficed to quell the workers.

The far-reaching nature of the employers' power over the lives and intimate concerns of the workers made the issue of the struggle of direct importance to their families and to all in the community. To be forced to procure goods at the Company Shop at prices 20 to 30 per cent dearer than those charged by the private tradesman was a grievance which the women as well as the men understood. Moreover, in those early days women and children took a large share in the actual work of the mines. In other ways the employers allowed their workers little personal freedom. Even such children as attended the Works Schools at Nantyglo found that their parents' Nonconformist views did not prevent their being beaten if they failed to learn the catechism or attend the Parish Church at Blaina on Sunday mornings. Yet, the Sunday School children of Brynmawr went annually for an outing in Crawshay Bailey's trams drawn by one of his famous engines and in an autocratic fashion the employees were ready to work for the well-being of the community, as was shown by Henry Bailey's energy in agitating for a Board of Health for Brynmawr after the cholera outbreak of 1847.

Note from S.E.T.: Here is mention of the town of Staffordshire, England. We now know that the James Marsh family originated in Staffordshire and migrated to Clydach, Wales. Joseph Hodge met Sarah Marsh in Clydach where they lived as neighbors. They married in Brynmawr and emigrated to Helfenstein, Pa., about 1870.

Seen from the orthodox point of view of the surrounding clergy and magistrates, the town "presented a frightful picture." In evidence given before the Hilly Royal Commission of Enquiry into the State of Education in Wales, in 1847, the "immoral and corrupt state of what is generally termed the Hilly District, more especially the locality designated as Brynmawr" was described with horror by more than one witness. "The elements necessary to produce a contented, well-disposed and orderly community" were said not to be in Brynmawr, with all its "dense population" and many licensed public-houses and beer houses. Bouts of drunkenness lasting from Saturday to Monday or even Tuesday night as long as wages were high, "strife, jealousy, bickerings, assaults, grumblings, oaths and profane language," characterised the town. On the other hand, "Disaffection and sedition" were said to have subsided since the last Chartist movement, since the people "Have seen the error of their ways and felt the effects of insubordination."

Probably the violent character of the struggle with the masters as well as the secret conspiracies, terrorism and suspicions of spies and blacklegs, and the constant incoming of new workers, had all conduced to bring about this state of affairs. Yet, the picture must have been one-sided; the habit of mutual loyalty, the pursuit of common interests, the contact with the industrial and political movements in the wider world, even the discussions in the public houses, centring round the personalities of the masters, and the struggles of workers in other parts, and the fact that the geographical position of Brynmawr made it a meeting place for the workers of the district, must have provided some education in affairs and in social life.

VI. Local Administration And The Political Movement

The local gentry who gave evidence of the "frightful state" of the morals of Brynmawr in 1847 made no mention of the probable connection between this and the lack of the elementary conditions of decency, comfort and good health from which many workers suffered. The town had sprung up haphazard at the bidding of the industry; it was perhaps less fortunate than Clydach and Nantyglo in that the employers did not live within its bounds and had therefore less personal knowledge of its condition and needs and less incentive to remedy obvious evils. The workers coming in from different areas with different traditions had no common ideal of what was desirable or even essential for the purpose of public health.

There was no town sewerage, scavenging or water system, but the inhabitants drew their water from numerous wells, some of which were seriously polluted. Under such primitive conditions, outbreaks of disease were to be expected, and in 1847 there was a bad epidemic of cholera. In 1849, an "Enquiry into the Sewerage, Drainage, Supply of Water, and the Sanitary Conditions of the Town of Brynmawr in the County of Brecon;: was made by a Superintending Inspector to the Board of Health. Even in those days of primitive ideas of the requisites of public health, conditions in Brynmawr seem to have been exceptionally bad, since the inspector wrote:-

"It is scarcely within the power of pen or pencil to convey to the apprehension of those who are dependent upon such sources of information, an adequate idea of the condition of the cottage tenements which constitute the town, as they presented themselves to my examination during the visit."

The inspector recommended that a Board of Health should be formed to remedy these evils and, owing largely to the initiative and organising ability of Mr. Henry Bailey, this was done in 1851. The Board was one of the first twenty-one in England and Wales and the first three in Wales to be elected. Brynmawr thus owed its position as a pioneer town in public health administration to one of the industrialists who had helped bring it into being.

The Board set to work with great energy. It found that most of the wells could not profitably be put into a state of repair. A water system was therefore devised, although from that time until now the problem of securing an adequate and pure supply has never been wholly solved, and in exceptionally dry weather people still "Besiege the springs and wells all day long." The condition of the town was improved by the employment of a man to sweep the main streets, requiring the owners of property to put roads and highways in repair, by "street-leveling" at the public expense, by penalising persons who deposited "filth or rubbish" in the roads, and by efforts to educate the public generally in town cleanliness. Permission was sought from the Duke of Beaufort as ground landlord to tip rubbish at suitable spots, street lighting was attempted, a cemetery was formed and steps were taken to restrict and finally prohibit in the old and overcrowded chapel burial grounds. A sewerage system was installed, and, here perhaps, the early start made by the Board of Health was not altogether an advantage, as the science of sanitary engineering had not yet made great strides, and complaints were constantly received from persons who stated that sewers leaked or discharged near their houses or polluted their water supply.

The establishment in 1894 of the Urban District Council in the place of the Board of Health coincided with the beginning of the direct influence of the workers on town affairs, and in that year a miner was for the first time elected as a member of the local Government body. The point of view of the organised workers began to come to the fore in Council meetings from that time onwards. In the following year it was resolved as a result of a letter from the Secretary of the Tin plate Workers' Association that as far as possible hands thrown out of employment in consequence of the stoppage of the Tin Plate Mills at Nantyglo and Blaina should be employed on works of improvement in the district. In the same year the Trade Union rate of wages of

3s. 4d. per day for a week of fifty-four hours was adopted by the Council for its able-bodied labourers. Trade Union influence thus began to play an increasing part directly and indirectly in town administration.

VII. Housing

☞ Follow this link for a map showing the growth of the town, 1800-1930.

The rapid growth of population owing to successive influxes of workers from outside Brynmawr meant that houses also sprang up rapidly and without any conscious planning. Fortunately the intersecting tramroads built for industrial purposes provided a skeleton town-plan, as the worker's dwellings, apart from those in outlying districts such as Clydach Dingle, where the iron-ore industry of the town was concentrated, naturally grew up along the existing tracks. The streets tended, therefore, to be at right angles to one another, and the town escaped the monotony and congestion of the ribbon-like neighbouring settlements along the narrow valleys to the south and west. The situation on a spacious plateau allowed of subsequent expansion on all sides and of a central square, as well as of the use of outlying land for gardens, allotments and recreation grounds. Hence a centre for community life as well as means of outdoor recreation and spare time occupation were available.

Joseph Hodge
and
Sarah Marsh
married here in
Brynmawr, S. Wales

Tabor Church on Davies Street is a non-conformist chapel built in 1835. The church was rebuilt in 1857.

Below: 19th century map of central Brynmawr showing the layout of the streets.

A: Tabor Welsh Chapel
    Davies Street
    Joseph and Sarah md.
    here in 1862

B: Bailey Street
    Joseph and Sarah's first residence in 1864

C: King Street
    Joseph and Sarah's second residence in 1865-1869

: The ruins of the Clydach Iron Works near Brynmawr are the closest surviving iron works to the town, and can be seen as part of the   Clydach Gorge walk.

Building in Brynmawr seems to have kept pace with the growth of population throughout the nineteenth century. Both in 1811, 1821 and 1831 the houses of Llanelly Parish were almost equal to the number of resident families, while between 1831 and 1841, when the population of the Parish increased by an amount exceeding the whole increase in the previous thirty years, the number of houses built was also unprecedentedly great. In 1861, when the industry of the district was declining, there were actually 127 uninhabited houses, and in 1881 at the end of the period of depression prior to the expansion of the coal-mining industry, there were as many as 305 uninhabited houses in Brynmawr, and this has been a constant factor in the maintenance of family solidarity and self-sufficiency.

The types of property built at different times reflect the economic conditions prevailing in the community. To the original farms and shepherds' cottages further cottages and a few shops and inns, including the important Coaching Inn, the Griffin Hotel, were added prior to 1830. In the period of industrial and trading prosperity between 1830 and 1840 were added not only cottages, but the shops in the present main street, and two important chapels. The next decade brought three more Chapels, the British Foreign School, and some larger houses. Between 1860 and 1880 there was less building of cottage property, but the railway station and all the present elementary school buildings were erected. With renewed industrial prosperity and growth of the town as a trading centre from 1880 onwards a wide new street was added with substantially built cottages on each side; existing shops were re-modelled and others were built, together with a new Market Hall and the Secondary School.

Unlike the industrial settlements of Nantyglo, Beaufort, Blaenavon, and to a lesser degree Clydach, where the iron works were actually situated, the dormitory town of Brynmawr owed little in the way of building enterprise to the great employers. Individual workers built their own cottages here and there along the tramroads in the very early days, and shortly afterwards tradesmen who, like the workers, were attracted by the central position of the town, began to build courts and rows of houses as a commercial speculation. Later still, thrifty workers, who built their own cottages, invested what was left of their savings in the building of an additional cottage which was inhabited by a married member of their family or let to a fellow worker, and speculative builders put up rows of houses. Thus the tied cottage belonging to the employers has never been a feature of Brynmawr life, and in consequence of this labour has been mobile and workers have been able to move from one colliery to another within traveling distance from Brynmawr in the search for work in bad times.

The influence of transport and communications upon trade is apparent throughout the history of Brynmawr. From its early days it was brought into touch with the outside world by the fact that the coach-road from Merthyr to Abergavenny, which was used by Nelson on his way from Pembroke Dockyard to the north, ran through its site and horses were changed at the 'Grand Stand' there. Very soon an important Coaching Inn grew up to cater to travelers along the main road. This road has remained the shortest route from England to the South Wales Coalfield and has thus brought traders and goods through Brynmawr.

The tramroads leading to the iron works and other rough local roads also passed through the town and along them came Breconshire farmers bringing produce for sale to the Company Shops and to the residents of both Brynmawr and Nantyglo. The greatest bulk of trade in farm produce in the early days, however, appears to have come from West Wales. Carriers from Cardiganshire and West Carmarthenshire brought dressed pigs and casks of butter to the "hills" of South Wales, and every week the open-sided red "Cardy" carts drawn by the free-stepping, light brown "Cardy" horses might have been seen in strings of ten or twelve on their way from Teify-side through Brecon and Llangynidr to the Company Shop at Nantyglo.

The early shopkeepers in Brynmawr found their trade somewhat restricted by the competition of the Company Shops at Clydach, Llanelly Hill and Nantyglo, and from about 1840 onwards in Brynmawr itself. Although the Truck Acts of 1817 and 1820 made payment in kind illegal, the fact that wages were drawn in money only once in six or eight weeks and also that debt at the Company Shop was recognized as a kind of security for continued employment, made it difficult for workmen to trade elsewhere.

As early as 1844 a Market Hall was built and after various alterations was replaced by a new and larger hall in 1894. The trade done in the market was largely wholesale, but in addition several local shopkeepers had stalls there, and applications for places in the market were received from as far afield as Sheffield. Christmas poultry fairs were held in the hall, and stock fairs on the adjoining ground. The comfort of the country buyers and sellers was catered for by an enterprising Brynmawr tradesman who provided meals for them on the premises. The importance of the market to the town was so fully recognised that the Board of Health continually pressed for special Saturday market fares from Blaenavon, Blaina, Abertillery and even as far afield as Aberbeeg, and in 1889 the rights of the Market Company were bought out by the town. The new hall was built at the public expense and was opened by a civic ceremony and lunch to which two hundred guests were invited.

XII. The Region to the North of Brynmawr

☞ Follow this link for a map of villages and sites of former industry works in Clydach Valley.

From the start Brynmawr has had close ties with Llanelly Parish and other parts of the Crickhowell Rural District. Hundreds of years before the town of Brynmawr existed, a small farming population lived at the lower or northern end of the Parish, where a church was built, which is now some distance from the main villages and hamlets. The principal aggregation of population are now to be found at Gilwern, the centre of the farming, trading and residential part of the parish; at Clydach, where a forge was erected as early as the seventeenth century and where the opening out of the Iron Works at the end of the eighteenth century and the beginning of the nineteenth century, caused a rapid increase of population together with an admixture of stocks similar to that which took place in Brynmawr; and in the smaller scattered hamlets which make up the district of Llanelly Hill, the home of the iron-ore and coal-mining in the Parish.

Owing probably to the existence of a plentiful water-supply, Clydach was the scene of industry earlier than Brynmawr; Works accounts dated 1711-12 are extant, and in 1800 the Iron Works and forge employed four hundred hands. At the time of the 1811 census, the population of the Parish was already mainly occupied in industry, and by 1822 the proportion of industrial workers has still further increased. Owing to lack of capital many difficulties were experiences at the Iron Works, and the early records reveal fluctuations in trade and sometimes difficulty in affording steady employment to the workmen.

As in Brynmawr, nonconformity was predominant among the workers, and chapels were built early in the nineteenth century. In the Gilwern district, however, there was a tradition of church membership among the wealthy residents as well as some of the families of farmers and tradesmen, and at one time a stream of carriages could be seen every Sunday making their way up the hill to Llanelly Parish Church.

Below: Beautiful Llanelly parish church near Brynmawr dates from the late 12th century and is dedicated to Saint Elli.

From the earliest days of industrial development there has been a social and occupational cleavage between the Gilwern district with its rich beauty and wooded valleys, fertile fields and river and the more rugged mining districts of Clydach and Llanelly Hill. The Gilwern area early became the home of members of landed proprietors and of the great employing families, the Crawshays and Jaynes, and later even a few of the wealthier Brynmawr tradesmen; the social makeup of the population was thus varied and included a local aristocracy of leisured and well-to-do people, which is

conspicuously lacking in mining towns in South Wales. In addition, there were not only farmers and small shop-keepers but rural craftsmen such as farm carpenters, blacksmiths, clog-makers, wood-carvers, and sawyers. Colliers and quarrymen also penetrated the district, but not in sufficient proportions to make the outlook predominantly industrial as in Clydach and Llanelly Hill.

The industrial parts of Llanelly Parish have perhaps suffered even more severely than Brynmawr from successive failures of industry. After the Clydach Iron Works were closed down in 1861, the distress of the population, congregated in the district almost entirely owing to the local demand for labour, was very great and was reflected in the increase of persons receiving Poor Law Relief between 1861 and 1871, and in the sudden decrease in population due to migration. Efforts were made to revive the trade of the Works on other lines, first by the opening out of a gate and hurdle department and later by the development of entirely different industries on the former site, such as a Flannel Factory and Soap Factory. None of these efforts were for long successful, and the district sank back to the status of a dormitory for workers in distant collieries. Since Clydach was even further from the developing mines of the Western Valley than was Brynmawr, the difficulty in obtaining and retaining employment was accentuated. Many of the workers indeed found the expense and difficulty of traveling so great, especially before motor transport was developed, that they returned to their homes and families only at week-ends.

http://thomasgenweb.com/brynmawr_history.html

132

Destination America, by Maldwyn A. Jones, 1976, Thames Television Ltd., p. 31

Departure from Liverpool, 1850; An emigrant sailing packet is about to be towed out into the Mercy.

Joseph and Sarah Hodge left Liverpool, England for the distant shores of America. This scene could well have included the Hodge family. The ships of 1850-1870 carrying the immigrants were built of wood and iron. They had sails as well as steam boilers to provide power for sailing. Crowded conditions made for an uncomfortable and difficult trip. By this time, however, steam power had shortened the crossing time to less than 14 days, if all went well. Here we see some of those departing wave to the crowd on the dock.

Destination America, by Maldwyn A. Jones, 1976, Thames Television Ltd., p. 36

Life below deck, 1872. Even at this date steerage accommodation remained cramped. Emigrants line up for food from the ship's galley. Separate dining rooms for steerage passengers were not generally introduced until later. The Joseph and Sarah Hodge family would fit quite well into this scene as they immigrated in 1870. The steerage class passengers are hungry and wait their turn to be served. Note the dinner plates held high. It appears as though the women and children are being served first. A young girl has fallen and spilled her meal on the wooden deck.

Joseph Hodge Heritage in Helfenstein
Eternal rest in Mt. Carmel, Pennsylvania

Sarah Hodges second marriage to William Riddle

Reed's Cemetery, also called Pioneer Cemetery, between Taylorsville and Lavelle

The earliest road passed through this part of the Mahanoy Creek Valley. A young girl, Mary Hodge, born 20th of May, 1869, is buried here. Mary Hodge's birth record has been located. She was born on King Street, Brynmawr in South Wales. The Joseph Hodge family must have emigrated after her birth date.

The following document names the children of Louisa Kidson. Louisa's first marriage to James Marsh is documented by a marriage certificate from South Wales. Sarah Hodge's name is also documented from Wales records as born name of Mass or Marsh.

Northumberland County Court House, Sunbury, Pa., Deed Book 97, page 13
Deed: George Kidson et.al to Ellis F. Orner, entered May 3, A.D. 1887

This indenture, made the 26th day of February, in the year of our Lord 1887 between **George Kidson**, *of the borough of Shamokin*, County of Northumberland and State of Pennsylvania, widower, **Mary** Skelding, nee Kidson, and Jonathan Skelding, her husband, and **Sarah** Hodges, nee Kidson and Joseph Hodges, her husband of the Township of Eldred, County of Schuylkill, and state aforesaid, children and **heirs at law of Louisa Kidson**, *late of the borough of Shamokin* in said County of Northumberland, deceased of the first part and Ellis F. Orner of the Township of Cameron, County of Northumberland and state aforesaid of the second part: Witness, That the said parties of the first part, for and in consideration of the sum of $20 lawful money of the United States of America well and truly paid by the said party of the second part to the said parties of the first part,............ at and before the sealing and delivering of these presents, the receipt whereof is hereby acknowledged have granted, bargained, sold, alined, enfeoffed, released, conveyed, and confirmed, and by these presents do grant, bargain, sell, aline, enfeoff, release, convey and confirm unto the said party of the second part his heirs and assigns.........all that certain piece, parcel or tract of land situate in the Township of Cameron, County of Northumberland and State of Pa., and bounded and described as follows, to wit.........beginning at a heap of stones in a line of land of John Weikel, thence by the same south 10 ¼ degrees east 14 perches to a heap of stones thence south 84 degrees west 14 7/10 perches to a red oak tree standing on the northern bank of Mahanoy Creek thence by the same north 13 ½ degrees.....20 4/10 perches to a stone, thence by land late of Mrs. Catharine Derr north 79 ¾ degrees east, ...15/ 2/10 perches to the place of beginning. Containing 1 acres and 35 perches, to be the same more or less and having erected thereon a 1 ½ story plank dwelling house. Excepting and reserving however the full privilege of using at any and all times hereafter and forever a private road which passes over and through said land. This being the same piece, parcel, or tract of land conveyed to the said Louisa Kidson by Charles K. Weikel, and Elizabeth Weikel his wife, and Charles B. Boyer Rush Ann Boyer, his wife, by indenture bearing date the 30th day of July, A.D. 1869 and intended to be recorded.

To have and to hold the said premises the said.....**George Kidson**, **Mary Skelding**, and Jonathan Skelding, her husband, and **Sarah Hodges**, and Joseph Hodges, her husband for themselves, their heirs....shall and will by these presents, warrant and forever defend.

In witness whereof the said parties have hereonto set their hand and seal, signed **George Kidson**, **Jonathan Skelding, Mary Skelding, Joseph Hodges Jr**., (his mark), **Sarah Hodges**, (her mark).

Received the day of the date of the herein foregoing indenture of the said party of the second part the sum of $20 being the consideration money above mentioned in full. Witness: Jeremiah Orner, Rosa E. Latsha, ...George Kidson

Mountain Road from Pitman to Helfenstein crosses the Mahanoy Creek at this bridge.
Louisa, grandmother of Jemima Hodge owned a "plank house" near this location.
Louisa Dainty first married James Marsh, second marriage to Kidson. Louisa was one of
the first settlers along the Mahanoy Creek.

Mahanoy Creek, cloudy from a June rainstorm in 2009.

Residence of Mary Young near the Mahanoy Creek. Louisa, grandmother of Jemima (Hodge) Fetterolf, lived in a "plank house" located nearby. See deed in this book naming Louisa Kidson who purchased the "plank house" from Charles K. Weikel. In recent times, a Charles Weikel lived here also, no doubt a descendant of the earlier landowner.

Residence of Agnes Haas, age 98 years old. Agnes is the oldest living resident from Helfenstein. She is presently a resident at Mountain View Manor. Agnes moved to Helfenstein when she married Ole Haas. This house is next door to Mary Young near the Mahanoy Creek.

Chronology of Hodge Deeds Recording Purchase and Sale of Land and Houses
Early Schuylkill and Northumberland County, Pa. Records

Deed Transfers:

1869, Charles B. Boyer and Charles K. Weikel to Louisa Kidson

1879, Charles B. Boyer to Sarah Hodge, lot 13 and 14, Helfenstein

1884, Harriet Brown to Sarah Hodge, lot 16 and 17, Helfenstein

1884, 8 Nov., Deed Book 99, p. 248, Northumberland Co. Court House
Joseph Hodge purchases a lot of ground from the Reading Coal and Iron Company.
Being lot #6 in block #8 on the South side of Third Street, Mt. Carmel, Pa.

1887, Same property as described above, purchased in 1869 by Louisa Kidson. In 1887, Book 97, p. 13, Northumberland Co. Court House Record shows the transfer of this deed from Joseph Hodges Jr. and Sarah and others, selling a plank house and 1 acre plus 3 perches of land in Cameron Twp. to Ellis F. Orner. See this deed in this book. George Kidson, Mary Skelding, and Sarah Hodge, (children of Louisa Kidson) to Ellis J. Orner.

1892, 2 Sept., Sarah (Hodge) Riddle selling to William Riddle the lot purchased by Joseph Hodge in Mt. Carmel. See 1884 deed above. Document description by Hope Conrad in this book.

1899, Charles B. Maurer to John Hodge

1903, Henry Knock to Sarah Hodge, lot 11 and 12, Helfenstein

1914, J.M. Merwins to James Hodge, Helfenstein

A Charles Weikel lived in Helfenstein near the Mahanoy Creek Bridge during the time of the previous generation. Refer to deed transfer in 1869 above naming Charles K. Weikel to Louisa Kidson. Louisa was the grandmother of Jemima Hodge Fetterolf. George M. Troutman operated a meat route from Trevorton through the Cameron Valley into Helfenstein. One of his customers was Charles Weikel who lived either in the house that Mary Young lives in today, or the neighboring house where Agnes Haas lived. Bryant A. Troutman later stopped there also, with his butcher truck. Bryant remembers the peacocks calling as they still do today at Mary Young's home. Charles Weikel and his wife sometimes visited the George Troutman farm near Klingerstown.

Joseph and Sarah Hodge residence. This duplex home is under renovation to a single family dwelling. Most of the coal mining families of this portion of Helfenstein were closely related, being parents, children, aunts, and uncles. (Hodges, Skeldings, and Fetterolfs)

After Joseph died, Sarah married William Riddle and remained living here with her children. This home was lately the residence of Benjamin and Hannah Young and is presently owned by Terry Spalti.

Next door to "Soy" Weikel's hotel was the Helfenstein Post Office, located on Shamokin Street. The post office was located on the street level of this lovely home.

Census Records of 1880 for Eldred Twp., Schuylkill Co., Pa.

Joseph Hodges, age 45, coal miner, born in South Wales. His mother and father listed as both born in South Wales.

Sarah, age 35, born in South Wales. Her father and mother born in England.
Children listed:

Joseph T.,	age 15, laborer, b. S. Wales	
William	age 12, slate picker, b. S. Wales	
Elizabeth	age 9	b. PA
John H.	age 8	b. PA
Anna	age 2	b. PA
George	6 month, b. Nov.	b. PA

The ages given for Joseph and Sarah do not correspond with their known birth dates. Joseph was born in 1840, and Sarah was born in 1843, according to tombstone records. In this census Sarah states her emigration date as 1862. In 1910 Census Records, Sarah's son William states the year of his emigration as 1867. The Joanthan Skelding Family emigrated in 1866. Joanthan Skelding married Mary Ellen, Sarah's sister.

Census Records of 1890 for Eldred Twp., Schuylkill Co., Pa

Joseph Hodges, age 50, no occupation is given for any of this family
Sarah (wife), John, 16, George 12, Jemima, 9, James, 7, Martha, no age, Mary, (Bertha M.), no age.
Joseph Hodge, age 26, is a coal miner living next door, wife Sarah and daughters Elizabeth and Sarah R. This would be old Joseph's son.
George Kitson (Kidson), age 64, laborer. George is a brother of Sarah Hodge and Mary Ellen Skelding.

Census Records of 1900 for Eldred Twp., Schuylkill Co., Pa.

William Riddle, born December 1851, laborer, born in England.
Sarah, listed as born January 1842, married 9 years with 16 children, 6 living
Step children listed: George, born May 1880, James, born June 1884, Bertha, born May 1886. These are the children of Sarah and Joseph Hodge. (Jemima is not listed here.)
Here we see recorded the second marriage of Sarah Hodge to William Riddle
Although these birth dates given do not correspond exactly to the tombstone carving, the family members are named correctly.

August and Jemima Fetterolf. Jemima b. Pa., both parents b. England, 3 Children, 2 living

As per recent Welsh research, 2009, documenting birth records for Joseph and Sarah, notice is made that the person giving census data did so in error. Sarah's age and the date of emigration are incorrect in the census. Emigration date must be after 1869, because child Mary's birth is recorded in Brynmawr, Llanelly Parish, South Wales in 1869.

Census Records of 1900 for Aston Township, Delaware Co., Pa.

Joseph T. Hodge, born 1864, in Wales. Father born in Wales, mother born in England. Sarah born August 1871, in Pa. Father and mother born in England. Children, Sarah, (Jan. 1889), Margaret, (July 1892), Son, (April 1895), Thomas, (Jan. 1897).

Census Records of 1910, Pottsville, 5th Ward, #148-155

John H. Hodges, age 35, engineer in a steel mill. Wife Edith, age 33, (1876-1973) Children, Myrtle L. (12), Floyd J. (age 8), Edith R. (1 month) Mt. Laurel Cemetery near Seltzer, Hodge/Turner, Edith (1876-1973), Annie (1847-1918),George W., (1846-1921)

Census Records of 1910 for Eldred Twp., Schuylkill Co., Pa.

William Hodge, age 45, born in Wales, coal miner, emigrated 1867 Wife, Catherine, age 43, Sarah, age 8, William, age 3 William is the son of Joseph and Sarah Hodge and we can assume Joseph, Sarah, and children Joseph T. and William Hodge all emigrated together in 1867. William states here the year of his emigration is 1867.

August and Jemima J. Fetterolf. Jemima's parents both born in England, 10 children, 7 living, married 13 years. Comment: Here we see that stating England, rather than Wales, as ones birthplace, is the same as stating America, rather than Pennsylvania.

James Hodge, (brother of Jemima), born in Pa., both parents born in Wales, 4 children, 3 living, married 6 years.

Sarah Riddle, (next door to James), (his mother), age 66, born in Wales, both parents born in England.

Census Records of 1920 for Eldred Twp., Schuylkill Co., Pa.

James Hodge, age 35, stationary engineer in coal mine Mary Ellen, (wife), age 35, children: Russell Winfield, 15, Dorothea M., 12, Adah M., 8, Sarah E., 6, John T., 3 year, 4 month, Mary E., 1 year, 9 month.

At St. Paul's Evangelical Lutheran in Franklin Square, Eldred Twp., married 4 April, 1931, James Kahler of Pitman and Sarah E. Hodges of Helfenstein.

August and Jemima Fetterolf's Children listed in 1920

Ellen Fetterolf, 17, Frank E., 18, Althesta, 13, Wesley T., 12, Clayton H., 11, Harvey L., 10, Clyde W., 5, Archiblad G., 3y, 8 mo.

High Street looking west - Kahler's Gunshop, center photo. Joseph Hodge's home was next door on the west side.

This large double home called a "duplex" was the childhood residence of Jemima Hodge, later married to Ausgust Fetterolf.

The last will and testament of Joseph Hodges, dec'd.
Schuylkill County Courthouse, Pottsville, Pa., Will book #8, p. 102
Northumberland County Courthouse, Sunbury, Pa., Will book#18, p. 138

Be it remembered that, I, Joseph Hodges of Eldred Township, County of Schuylkill and State of Pa., miner, being of sound and disposing mind and memory, do make and ordain my last will and testament in manner following.
I direct all my just debts and funeral expenses to be fully paid by my execure here in after named as soon as conveniently may be after my decease. All the rest residue remainder of my estate real and personal and mixed whatsoever and wheresoever I order and direct to be converted into money as soon as the same can conveniently be done after my decease, and for that purpose I hereby authorize and empower my said executors here in after named, and the survivors of them to sell and dispose either by public or private sale or sales for the best price or prices that can be gotten for the same and by proper deed or deeds conveyances or assurances in the law to be duly executed, acknowledged and perfected to grant convey and assure the same to the purchaser or purchasers thereof in fee simple, and when the whole of my said residuary estate shall be converted into money as aforesaid then I will order and direct all just debts shall be paid . . . . . and after all my just debts are paid I devise and bequeath the balance to my beloved wife **Sarah Hodges** in trust that she shall use the said balance or so much therefore as shall provide for the wants of the surviving children yet in helpless circumstances, and the remainder if any shall be left at the death of my said wife **Sarah Hodges shall be divided in equal share among my surviving children**, and I appoint my said wife sale executrix of my last will and testament.
In witness where of I Joseph Hodges the testator have my last my last will and testament written on one sheet of paper, my hand and seal this 9th day of January, A.D., 1890.
Signed, sealed, published and declared by above named Joseph Hodges as and for his last will and testament which have here unto subscribed our names at his request as witness the presence of each.
Bodo Otto, John Skelding, James Romberger
Joseph "X" Hodges, his mark and "seal"

GAP COLLIERY & BREAKER,
ZIMMERMAN & PURSEL

Gap Colliery and Breaker. After the Helfenstein Colliery closed many of the miners walked north across the mountain to Locust Gap where this deep mine was located.

The last will and testament of Joseph Hodges, dec'd., continued
State of Pa., County of Schuylkill

Before me Samuel Beard, Register for the probate of wills and grant letters of administrations in and for Schuylkill Co., personally appeared Bodo Otto, and James Romberger subscribing witness to the above and forgoing instrument of writing purporting to be the last will and testament of Joseph Hodges late in the township of Eldred, in said county deceased who being by me duly sworn according to law, did depose and say that they were present and did see the testator, Joseph Hodges, now deceased, sign, seal, and heard him publish pronounce and declare the above and forgoing instrument of writing as and for his last will and testament, and at the time of the doing thereof, the said Joseph Hodge was of sound mind, memory and understanding to the best of their knowledge and belief.
Sworn and subscribed before me this 20th day of May, A.D., 1891, Samuel Beard, Register of Wills, witness Bodo Otto and James Romberger

Estate of Joseph Hodges desceased, Schuylkill Co., Pa.
You do swear that as executrix of Joseph Hodges deceased you will and truly administer the goods and chattels, rights and credits of the decedent according to law and diligently and faithfully regard and will truly comply with the provisions of the law relating to inheritances.
Sarah Hodges, her mark and seal, filed 20th May, 1891
Sworn and subscribed before me 20th May, A.D., 1891, Samuel Beard, Register of Wills

Sarah's Second Marriage to William Riddle

Joseph Hodges died January 14, 1891, at the age of 50y, 9m, 24d. He left behind his wife Sarah, age 48 and 10 children. His son Joseph T., born in Wales in 1864 was age 27. William, born in Wales was age 23. Elizabeth was 20, John "Jack" was 19. Sarah Ann had passed away in 1888, three years before at age 11. George W. was 12, Jemima Jane was 10, James was 8, Martha was 6, Bertha Mary was 5.

By this time some of Joseph and Sarah's older children were married, but Sarah had 5 young children remaining at home as minors. In this period of history, widowed mothers soon remarried, if at all possible. Sarah married William Riddle as her second husband. The census of 1900 states William Riddle and Sarah were married 9 years at that time. This suggests 1891 as the marriage date. So it would seem that Sarah was remarried less than a year after Joseph died.

William and Sarah had no known children together. One year after their marriage Sarah transferred real estate purchased by Joseph Hodge (in 1884), a house lot in Mt. Carmel, to William Riddle (1892). This lot was then sold by William and Sarah to David J. Lewis. This was probably a family member. See deed records in this book.

We do not know when William Riddle died, or where he is buried. Joseph and Sarah Hodges are buried together in Mt. Carmel Cemetery, west of Mt. Carmel.

Hope Conrad of 335 Derr Road, Sunbury, Pa., 17801, researched Northumberland Co.
Kidson, Hodge, Rittle, and Skelding deeds recorded in Sunbury Court House.

SARAH RITLE (EXECUTRIX_)
sells to
WILLIAM RITLE.........
IT READS LIKE THIS...
TO ALL TO WHOM THESE PRESENTS SHALL COME, SARAH RITLE (FORMERLY SARAH
HODGES) OF SCHUYLKILL CO. PA. (EXECUTRIX) OF T HE LAST WILL AND TEST. OF
JOSEPH HODGES LATE OF
SCHUYLKILL CO. PA. SEND GREETINGS.....
WHEREAS THE SAID JOSEPH HODGES BY HIS LAST WILL AND TESTAMENT DULY
PROVED AND RECORDED IN THE REGISTERS OFFICE AT SCHUYLKILL CO PA. HE
ORDERED AMONGST OTHER THINGS THAT THE WHOLE OF HIS ESTATE SHOULD BE
SOLD BY HIS EXECUTRIX THEREIN
MENTIONED , OF WHICH SAID WILL HE APPOINTED SARAH HODGES (NOW SARAH
RITLE) EXECUTRIX
AS IN AND BY SAID RECITED WILL SINCE HIS DECEASE DULY PROVED AND REMAINING
IN THE REGISTRARS OFFICE AT POTTSVILLE RECORDED BEING THERE UNTO
APPEARS. WHEREAS THE SAID
JOSEPH HODGES BY VIRTUE OF DIVERS GOODS AND CONVEYANCES AND
ASSURANCES IN LAW , DULY HAD AND EXECUTED BECAME IN HIS LIFETIME SEIZED IN
HIS DEMISE AS A FEE OF AND IN ALL THAT CERTAIN LOT OR PIECE OF GROUND
SITUATE ON THE SOUTH SIDE OF THIRD STREET IN THE HOUGHES ADDITION TO THE
TOWN OF MR. CARMEL.

(SEE THE PROPERTY LOTS OF DEED BOOK 99 PAGE 248.....) this is the property that Sarah
is conveying
to WILLIAM RITLE her husband ....for $1,500. William of Eldred Twp. Schuylkill co. Pa. Sept 2nd
1892
(deed book 99 page 248 stated that Joseph Hodge bought it from the Phila. and Reading Coal
and Iron Co on
Nov. 8th 1884)....)

at the bottom of this deed book 108 page 231...(Sarah Ritle selling to Wm. Ritle) there is an
addendum....saying
" RELEASE.....AND AGREEMENT.".'......Sarah 'Ritle (Extrix) to the Citizens Building and Loan
of MT.Carmel
(Sept. 3rd) 1892...states that she has this day sold the estate Property in Mt. Carmel to WILLIAM
RITLE
for $1,500. and having taken a mortgage from the said William Ritle for the payment of $11,000.
of t he purchase money, covering said lot. The said William Ritle having borrowed the sum of
$400. from the Citizens Building
and Loan Assoc. of Mt. Carmel, executed a mortgage to the said Citizens Building and Loan
Assoc. and the said sum of $400. i do hereby wave the right of the priority of the lien of the
mortgage given by the said William
Ritle in favor of one given to the citizens Building and Loan Assoc. and do hereby agree that the
said mortgage in favor of the said Building and loan Assoc. shall rank ahead and take
precedence of the one given to me and that in case the said lot should be sold so as to discharge
the lien of the said mortgage ..then the one in favor
of the C.B.& Loan Co shall be 1st paid out of the proceeds of such sale....(signed Sep. 2 1892
...)^^^
^^^^^^^^^^^^^^^^^^^^^^^^^^

I told you how in book 99 page 248 the Phila. and Reading Coal and Iron co...sold to Joseph
Hodges...of Mt.Carmel for $175.00......but this deed can be traced back further..........IN DEED
BOOK 62 PAGE 46...the

Mt. Carmel Coal and Iron Co. by deed dated 27th day of Jan 1872 granted and conveyed to the
Phila. and Reading Coal and Iron Co. ......I did not go to Book 62 and page 46 to see how the Mt.
Carmel Coal and Iron
had obtained it in 1872
but it is the same property which got passed from the Coal and Iron co to Joseph Hodge and
then to
Sarah Hodge and then to Wm. Ritle and then to David J. Lewis in 1892 for $100. and I suspect
that if you
trace David J. Lewis deed forward you will find that he was KIN to the Hodge family or the Ritle
family
or even to the maiden name family of Sarah...(the Kidson...or Kedson family name) ....
to have gotten this home which Sarah Hodge Ritle had sold for $1,500 at one time....but David J.
Lewis only
pays $100. for it now....seems to mean that he is "family" in some way.....

^^^

^another DEED I copied in the court house today...\
DEED BOOK 107 PAGE 375
WILLIAM RITLE AND OTHERS...SEPT 3rd 1892....
                sells to
DAVID J. LEWIS

it reads.......William Ritle and Sarah his wife of ELDRED Township, Schuylkill Co. Pa. sell to
DAVID J. LEWIS
OF THE borough of MT. CARMEL IN NORTHUMBERLAND COUNTY, PA. FOR $100. (ONE
HUNDRED)

A LOT OF GROUND SITUATE IN THE SOUTH SIDE OF 3RD STREET IN HOUGH'S ADDITION
TO THE TOWN OF MT. CARMEL ...BEING LOT #6 IN BLOCK #8

36 &1/2 FRONTAGE ON THE SOUTH SIDE OF 3RD STREET....IN HOUGH'S ADDITION OF
THE TOWN OF MT.
CARMEL BEING LOT #6 IN BLOCK #8 ...
36 1/2 BY 150 DEEP BOUNDED BY LOT #7

IT BEING THE SAME PIECE OF GROUND WHICH SARAH RITLE...FORMERLY SARAH
HODGES (executrix)
THE LAST WILL AND TESTAMENT OF Joseph Hodges (DECEASED) BY HER DEED DATED
Sept.2nd 1892 RECORDED IN THE OFFICE OF RECORDING OF DEEDS IN THE COUNTY
OF NORTHUMBERLAND
DEED BOOK (?) PAGE (?) GRANTED AND CONVEYED TO THE SAID WILLIAM RITLE
..PARTY OF THE 1ST PART SUBJECT TO THE LIEN OF THE MORTGAGE IN FAVOR OF THE
CITIZENS BUILDING AND LOAN ASSOCIATION AND THE MORTGAGE IN FAVOR OF THE
SAID RITLE (FORMERLY , SARAH HODGE)
EXECUTRIX AFORESAID..
WILLIAM RITLE AND SARAH RITLE (HUSBAND AND WIFE_) SIGNED THE DEED TO DAVID
J. LEWIS
                BOOK 108 PAGE 231...THE YEAR S 1892

The last will and testament of Sarah Hodge, dec'd., Will Book 23, p.70
Register of Wills – Clerk of the Orphans' Court, P.O. Box 1271,
Schuylkill County Court House, Pottsville, Pa.17901-2520

In the name of God, I **Sarah Hodge**, single of the Town of Helfenstein, County of
Schuylkill, State of Pennsylvania, being of sound mind, memory, and understanding, do
hereby make, publish, and declare, my last will and testament, thereby revoking and
making void any and all former wills by me at any time heretofore made, I direct that all
my just debts, funeral expenses and charges of settling up my estate be in the first place
fully paid and satisfied.

I give, devise, and bequeath unto my son **John Hodge**, ($100), One Hundred Dollars, to
my son **William Hodge**, I give, devise, and bequeath ($100), one hundred dollars, and
the residue of all my estate real, personal, and mixed of whatsoever in nature and kind the
same may be and wherever the same may be, I give, devise, and bequeath to my sons
Joseph Hodge, **James Hodge**, and my daughter **Bertha** intermarried with Curtis Willier,
and **Jamima**, deceased, (her legal heirs) share and share alike.

I do hereby constitute and appoint my son **James Hodge** as executor of this my last will
with full and complete to execute and deliver any and all deeds or other instruments of
writing that may be necessary to carry into effect any and all parts of this my will and
testament.

In witness thereof, I Sarah Hodge testatrix, have to this my last will and testament set my
hand and seal the 5th Day of September, A.D. 1919.
Signed, sealed and published and declared by the above Sarah Hodge, as and for her last
will and testament in the presence of us who have here unto subscribed our names at her
request, as witnesses here to in the presence of the said testatrix and each other.

Signed   P. B. Maurer, William J. Weikel, Sarah Hodge, (mark and seal)

In the matter of probate of the last will and testament of **Sarah Hodge**, late of Eldred
Township, Schuylkill County, Pa., deceased, Schuylkill County.
Personally appeared before me Frank C. Ball, Register of Wills for the County of
Schuylkill, P.B. Maurer, who being duly sworn, doth depose and say that he is a resident
of Barry Township, this County, that Sarah Hodge, the decedent above named requested
the deponent to write her last will and testament, that on the 5th day of September, 1919,
the deponent wrote the said last will and testament hereto attached, which was duly
signed, sealed, published, and declared by the said Sarah Hodge as and for her last will
and testament, by placing at the end thereof her mark, that your deponent signed the
name Sarah Hodge with said mark at the end of said last will and testament instead of the
proper name **Sarah Hodge Riddle**, that the name of the testatrix by her first marriage
was **Sarah Hodge** and by her second marriage, **Sarah Riddle**, and that the true name of
the said Sarah Hodge and Sarah Riddle was one and the same person this 17th day of
September, 1919. Probated September 17th, 1919   Examined September 20, 1919
Signed Frank C. Ball, Register, P.B. Maurer and seal, Decedent died September 11, 1919

Two 17th day of September 199.

Frank O'Ball
Register

State of Pennsylvania,
County of Schuylkill } ss.

BEFORE ME, Frank O'Ball, Register for the Probate of Wills and granting Letters of Administration, in and for Schuylkill County, personally appeared P. B. Mauer, and William Merkel subscribing witnesses to the above and foregoing instrument of writing purporting to be the last will and testament of ____ in said county, deceased, who being by me duly sworn according to law, did depose and say that they were present, and that they saw the testator Sarah Hudge, late of Township of Blank, not deceased, sign, seal, and heard the said Sarah Hudge publish, pronounce and declare the above and foregoing instrument of writing as and for her last will and testament and at the time of the doing thereof, the said Sarah Hur was of sound mind, memory and understanding, to the best of their knowledge and belief.

Sworn and subscribed before me this
17, day of September A. D. 1919

P. B. Mauer
William Merkel

____
Register of Wills

ESTATE OF ____ Sarah Hudge, DECEASED.

State of Pennsylvania,
County of Schuylkill } ss.

You and each of you ____ Executors of Sarah Hudge Deceased, you will well and truly promise the goods and chattels, rights and credits of the Decedent according to law, and diligently and faithfully regard and well and truly comply with the provisions of the law relating to collateral inheritance.

Sworn and subscribed before me this
17 day of Sept. A. D. 1919

Register of Wills

Registered Sept 17—1919
Granted Sept 20, 191
Decedent died Sept 11 1919

(Seal)
(Seal)
(Seal)

March 28, 2009 – Upon receipt of Elaine Schwar's correspondence from 3384 Harwood Lane, Sinking Spring, Pa. 19608-8811, and correspondence via e-mail from Hope Conrad @ soberconrad@evenlink.com , Steve E. Troutman traveled to Mt. Carmel, Pa.

Steve crossed over the Helfenstein Mountain and Mahanoy Mountain to Locust Gap, and a mile further east to the Mt. Carmel Cemetery. Elaine's directions enabled him to find the Hodge monument. The cemetery is divided into sections by paved avenues. The Hodge monument is located in Section 8 where the chapel is located. The Hodge monument is in Row 23, west of the chapel, near the east/west avenue. The monument is approximately 6 feet tall, with a broad base tapering to a steeple like top. Three sides of the monument are carved with family vital data as follows:

East Side: SARAH HODGE-WIFE OF – JOSEPH HODGE- BORN – MAY 12, 1843-DIED – SEPT. 11, 1919

South Side: OUR BELOVED SON – GEORGE HODGES – 1879-1905

West Side Top: SARAH ANN – DAU. OF – JOSEPH AND SARAH – HODGES – BORN NOV. 17, 1877- DIED – FEB. 15, 1888- poem unreadable.

West Side Bottom: JOSEPH HODGES – BORN – MAR. 20, 1840- DIED – JAN. 14, 1891- AGED 50Y. 9MS. 24D.
Poem inscription: Call not back the days departed – Anchor safe where storms rare are – On the borderland we left them – Soon to meet to part no more.

Mt. Carmel Cemetery: Section 4, Row 3
Two stones, side by side, possibly related
HODGES – J.S. HODGES – 1880-1935- HIS WIFE - VIOLET A. – 1883-1920
KREISCHER – VIOLET E. – 1908- 1999 – DAVID K. – 1902-1955

Dear Elaine and Hope,
    Enclosed find the tombstone inscriptions for Mt. Carmel Cemetery. My wife Joan is typing for me. With the aid of Elaine's map I found the Hodge stone in about 30 minutes. Mt. Carmel Cemetery is a very large burial ground with many avenues. I first saw a tall thin monument about 6 feet high with a broad base with carving " born in Wales " of the mid 1800's. But the name was not Hodge. I continued searching in this area. I soon found another similar monument with the name Hodge and couldn't believe my eyes! Here it said Sarah Hodge, wife of Joseph Hodge, plain as day. Imagine my surprise as I walked around this singular monument and saw all the family data. This was about 6 pm Saturday. Thank you both! Elaine's phone number is: 610-678-0313.

                                        Sincerely,   Steve

March 28, 2009 – Upon receipt of Elaine Schwar's correspondence from 3384 Harwood Lane, Sinking Spring, Pa. 19608-8811, and correspondence via e-mail from Hope Conrad @ soberconrad@evenlink.com , Steve E. Troutman traveled to Mt. Carmel, Pa.

Joan Troutman standing next to Joseph and Sarah Hodges' obelisk. An obelisk is a " tall four-sided tapering stone rising to a pyramid point."

West Side Bottom: JOSEPH HODGES – BORN – MAR. 20, 1840- DIED – JAN. 14, 1891- AGED 50Y. 9MS. 24D.

Poem inscription: Call not back the days departed – Anchor safe where storms rare are – On the borderland we left them – Soon to meet to part no more.

East Side: SARAH HODGE-WIFE OF – JOSEPH HODGE- BORN – MAY 12, 1843-
DIED – SEPT. 11, 1919

South Side: OUR BELOVED SON – GEORGE HODGES – 1879-1905

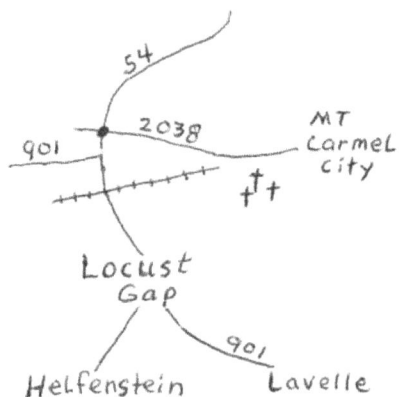

West Side Top: SARAH ANN – DAU. OF – JOSEPH AND SARAH – HODGES – BORN NOV. 17, 1877- DIED – FEB. 15, 1888- poem unreadable.

Steve crossed over the Helfenstein Mountain and Mahanoy Mountain to Locust Gap, and a mile further east to the Mt. Carmel Cemetery. Elaine's directions enabled him to find the Hodge monument. The cemetery is divided into sections by paved avenues. The Hodge monument is located in Section 8 where the chapel is located. The Hodge monument is in Row 23, west of the chapel, near the east/west avenue. The monument is approximately 6 feet tall, with a broad base tapering to a steeple like top. Three sides of the monument are carved with family vital data,

Dear Elaine and Hope,
    Enclosed find the tombstone inscriptions for Mt. Carmel Cemetery. My wife Joan is typing for me. With the aid of Elaine's map I found the Hodge stone in about 30 minutes. Mt. Carmel Cemetery is a very large burial ground with many avenues. I first saw a tall thin monument about 6 feet high with a broad base with carving " born in Wales " of the mid 1800's. But the name was not Hodge. I continued searching in this area. I soon found another similar monument with the name Hodge and couldn't believe my eyes! Here it said Sarah Hodge, wife of Joseph Hodge, plain as day. Imagine my surprise as I walked around this singular monument and saw all the family data. This was about 6 pm Saturday. Thank you both! Elaine's phone number is: 610-678-0313.

Sincerely, Steve

155

1875 Map of Schuylkill County, Pa.

Note:

Residence and office of Honorable Judge Wm. L. Helfenstein.

The coal colliery where August Fetterolf was killed in 1918, and the co. houses nearby.

HELFENSTEIN

ELDRED TSP

Scale, 25 Rods to the inch

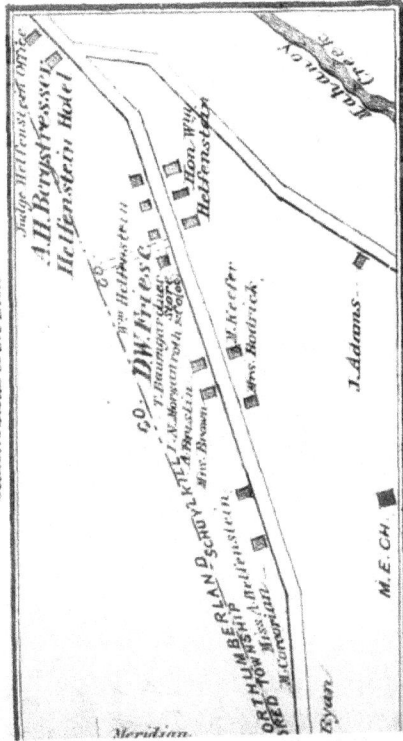

Residents of Helfenstein in 2009 can identify the house occupied by James and Mary Hodge. James was the brother of Jemima. August and Jemima lived here in the village also, as well as Joseph and Sarah Hodge, Jemima's parents.

Jemima and August Fetterolf lived next to James Hodge, (her bro.) James Hodge residence earlier identified here as the company store. The Skeldings lived across the street from Jemima and August Fetterolf, (Jemima's aunt).

Jonathan and Mary Skelding (Jemima's aunt), and other relatives, (neighbors) aided in the care of the orphaned family of August and Jemima Fetterolf.

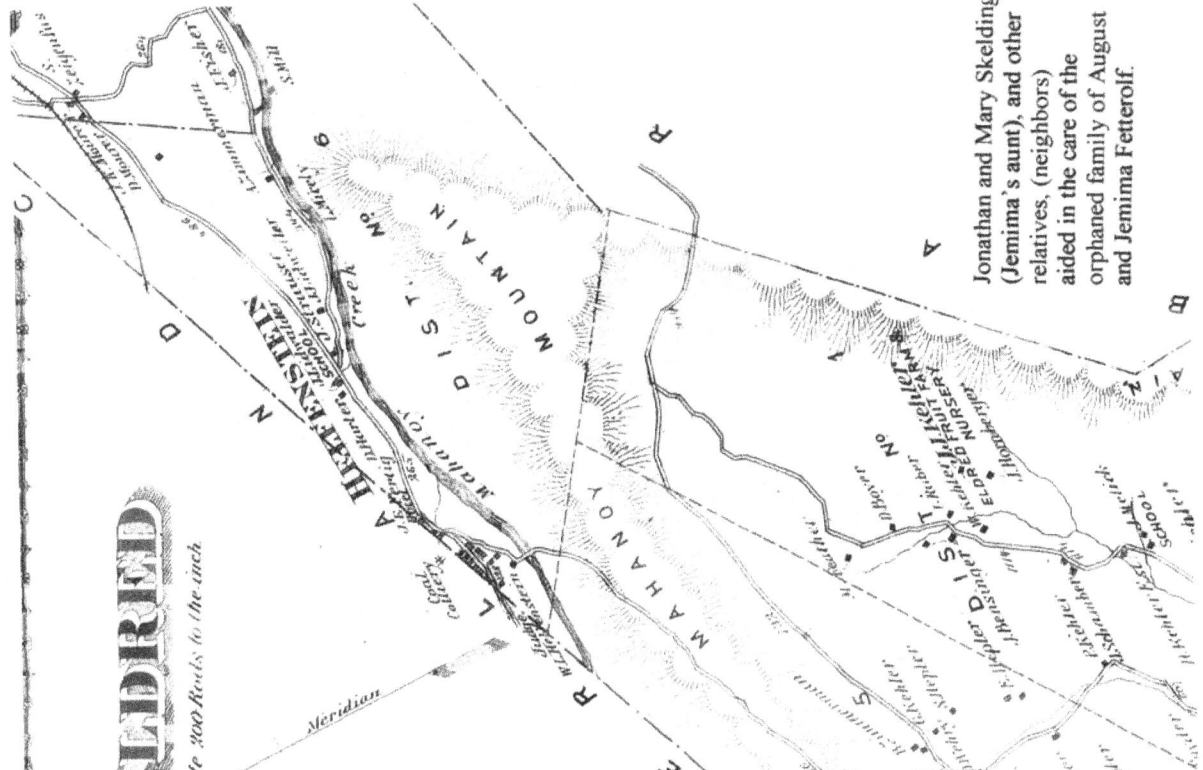

ELDRED

Scale 200 Rods to the inch

Mary Young and Joan Masser Troutman. Mary lives on Pitman Mountain Road in Helfenstein, near the bridge over Mahanoy Creek. Mary recalled the story of Jemima Fetterolf, ("Mime", as she called her), and her untimely death as told to her by her mother Hannah. Hannah was married to Benjamin Young. Mary also identified the dwelling of August and "Mime" Fetterolf.

Mr. and Mrs. Paul Fenstermaker at their home, 859 High Road, Helfenstein. Paul and Lucine live in a remodeled duplex formerly occupied by John and Mary Ellen Skelding. Lucine has lived in Helfenstein her entire lifetime and recalls the duplex home of James and Mary Hodge across High Road on the north side. James and Mary Hodge's residence is now removed, and only the east side remains. This is the residence of Mrs. Lute. James Hodge was the brother of Jemima (Hodge) Fetterolf.

Paul and Lucine Fenstermaker live here today as Paul remodeled the Skelding duplex at 859 High Road, Helfenstein. This dwelling is across the highway, south of the home of August and Jemima Fetterolf. Mary Ellen Skelding was an aunt to Jemima Fetterolf, Jemima's mother Sarah and Mary Ellen were sisters.

Duplex home of John and Mary Ellen Skelding after 1905 when this house was built as their second residence. James (son of John and Mary) and wife Emma Skelding lived here also. The Mahantongo Mountain is in the background and a water pump stands at the corner of the porch. In the census of 1920, John S. Skelding, age 75, lived here with the James H. Skelding Family. Currently this is the home of Paul and Lucine Fenstermaker.

The Helfenstein Methodist Church stood at the end of this street. This gravel roadway is south of High Street. Many residents were sad to see this well known land mark demolished.

Christ Reformed Church, High Street, Helfenstein. Photo taken on a sunny day in June prior to worship service. Many local residents walk to attend Sunday services here.

Christ Reformed Church built in 1916. In the background is the former residence of Robert Kahler. In earlier times this was the residence of George "Hootie" Skelding. The Skeldings provided the land for the church building, according to Lamar Kahler. George Skelding is the son of John and Mary Ellen Skelding

The duplex home being remodeled by Terry Spalti, (2009) was lately the home of Benjamin and Hannah Young. According to the census of 1900, William Riddle and Sarah Riddle lived next door to John and Mary Skelding. This was the first Skelding residence and also the home of Joseph and Sarah Hodge. After Joseph's death, Sarah remarried William Riddle. Sarah and Mary Ellen were sisters.

Mr. Zimmerman resides near the center of Helfenstein, Pa. at the intersection of the Cameron Valley Road, 49012, and the Gap Road to Locust Gap, 49016, and the Hefenstein Mountain Road from Pitman. His large home was also used as a church of the Pilgrim Holiness for some years. The dwelling was also a store for some years. Robert was very familiar with the coal mine drift where August Fetterolf was killed in 1918. A drift is a coal miner's name for a tunnel. This drift is adjacent to the abandoned railroad bed, located half way up the mountain north of the village. Robert said the railroad track went as far west as the neighboring Village of Doutyville, where another drift was established. The tracks were removed in the 1930's when large scale mining was abandoned in these Mahanoy Mountain tunnels. Steve Troutman visited the Helfenstein drift location and saw huge native stone foundations and walls remaining. At a later date other local men reopened the Helfenstein tunnel and used Mack trucks with chain drive to bring coal down the mountainside via a haul road into Helfenstein. This haul road exited near Robert Zimmerman's home. The Weikel's Beergarden and community park is also nearby. Robert remembers seeing the steam engines on the track and how the white smoke could be seen above the village high on the mountainside rising above the green tree tops as coal cars were pulled between the Mahanoy Mountain Mines and Lavelle.

Coal mining was eventually abandoned at the Helfenstein drift because the top rock was dangerously loose and susceptible to falling. Perhaps August was killed by falling top rock, inside the mine. Miners that last worked the tunnel said there were mine buggies still on the tracks, some loaded with coal when the tunnel was abandoned.

Robert Zimmerman also knew Kenny Minnick, (married to Elnora, granddaughter of Joseph Hodge), who told Joan Troutman the location of August Fetterolf's mining accident. Kenny often walked with his father Rathmus M. Minnick and the other Helfenstein miners to work across the Mahanoy Mountain to Village of Locust Gap where the Gap Colliery was established. Here the men worked in the underground mine which was several thousand feet deep. Rathmus operated the winches which hoisted the twin cages in the mine shaft up and down, lifting and lowering coal, men, and supplies. Mr. Zimmerman also identified the residence of James (brother of Jemima) and Mary Hodge, located on the north side of the road, a quarter mile west of the Zimmerman home. [End of interview].

Joseph Hodge is named in the 1880 census of Eldred Township, Schuylkill Co., Pa., as a coal miner born in South Wales. Joseph's mother and father are listed as born in South Wales. Joseph's wife Sarah (Marsh) is listed as being born in England. Sarah's mother and father are listed as born in England.

Rathmus M. Minnick operated the cable hoisting windless at the deep mine in Locust Gap. (See Robert Zimmerman interview above.)

The 1920 census of Eldred Township lists James Hodge (son of Joseph) age 35, occupation as "stationary engineer". Perhaps this entailed operating the cable hoist in the mine shaft also. In many cases, the Welshmen were engineers and middle level management holding positions high in responsibility.

One of the largest dwellings in Helfenstein was originally Jesse Lambach's General Store. It was also occupied by a Holiness church congregation after the store closed. Presently it is the home of Robert Zimmerman, age 84, in 2009. Robert remembers seeing the steam engines pulling coal car trains from the Helfenstein colliery on Mahanoy Mountain above this residence.

This residence on High Street in Helfenstein has an interesting history. It was originally built as Liberty Barn, as a stopping place for market hucksters with horse drawn wagons. It was remodeled later by the Weikel Family and named Weikel's Dance Hall. Remodeled again some years ago, it is now a residence.

August Fetterolf and Jemima Hodge

Family Homestead in Helfenstein

The house with the red banister and porch railing is identified by Mary Young as the home of August and Jemima Fetterolf. This is a single family dwelling. The adjacent brown colored house seems to be identical in style. The August Fetterolf home is now occupied by the Boyer Family and is nicely restored. The house is located on High Street, Helfenstein, Pa. August had a short walk to the coal mine, located directly above, on the mountainside.

Family picture of August Fetterolf and Jemima (Hodge) Fetterolf.

Photo Caption: Left to Right: Grandparents, Aunts, and Uncles. Courtesy of Evelyn Minnich of Hatboro, Pa.

Frank Fetterolf, Charles Fetterolf, father August Fetterolf, holding Clyde Fetterolf, Mother, Jemima (Hodge) Fetterolf, holding Althesta (Fetterolf) Adams, Standing, Martha (Fetterolf) Hepler, married to John Hepler Kneeling, Eleanor (Fetterolf) Minnich

Family not on the picture: Wesley Fetterolf, Harvey Fetterolf, Clayton Fetterolf, Archibald Fetterolf.

August and Jemima Fetterolf's homestead. View looking west. The family photo of
August, Jemima, and children was taken on the back porch. This porch is now removed
for the additional living quarters added later. The old family photo seen is of a rough
plank porch floor with a dish towel drying on a wash line. This is typical of a back
porch. The family posed for the photographer at the northeast corner of the original
house. (S.E.T.) The steps and the back porch are now removed.

After the August Fetterolf Family lived here, others included the families of Hoover,
Hummel, (restored and remodeled the house) and Boyer, 2009.

Location of the James and Mary Hodge residence. This duplex home was lately
remodeled into a single family dwelling. The James Hodge family lived in the portion of
the house that is now removed, where Joan Troutman is standing. The next house to the
east was the home of August and Jemima Fetterolf. James Hodge and Jemima Fetterolf
were the children of Joseph and Sarah Hodge.

Kahler's Gun Shop, located in the village of Helfenstein, is close by a Hodge dwelling place.

Mazie Kahler lived a few doors east of this shop along the main road. This Kahler residence was formally occupied by Mary Hodge. This dwelling is now removed and a newer home occupies the location. Mary Hodge is well remembered by neighbors.

I remember my mother, Pauline (Fetterolf) Masser telling me that she worked as a maid for a cousin Hodge in Pottsville, when she was a young teenage girl. This probably was Floyd Hodge.

By Joan (Masser) Troutman, September 16, 2007

Communication with Edward Jones of Lavelle: He remembers growing up near Helfenstein. A Hodge family lived south of the flagpole which still stands in Helfenstein in 2009. Edward is a retired electric line worker and lives east of Lavelle Fire Company. As a boy, Edward played with Hodge children. Edward Jones is of Welsh descent.

The British Isles

The people of Wales kept their own ancient traditional language. It is one of the oldest languages in Europe and is of Celtic origin.

Scotland

Northern Ireland

Ireland

Wales

England

South Wales, Clydach Gorge →
Iron and Coal Industry

©EnchantedLearning.com

167

Interviews with Mary Young, age 86, born 1922. May 2, 9, 2009

Mary has lived her entire life in or near Helfenstein, Pa. Her current residence is near the Mahanoy Creek Bridge on Pitman Mountain Road. Her home is the first house on the left. Mary is the daughter of Benjamin and Hannah Young. In 1909 Benjamin and Hannah lived in a house near the Helfenstein Reformed Church on High Street. This was a duplex home and the Youngs lived on the west side. This dwelling is the third home east of the Reformed Church and west of Kahler's Gun Shop. The house is now owned by Terry Spalti. He is remodeling the duplex into a single dwelling.

Mary recalls her mother telling her about her friend "Mime" Fetterolf. Jemima was married to August Fetterolf. This family lived on High Street not far west of the intersection of Pitman Mountain Road. At this intersection several important buildings were located. Jesse Lambach's General Store was on the east side and the Liberty Barn was on the west side. In later years the store became a Holiness Church and the barn became Weikel's dance hall. Presently, the store is the residence of Robert Zimmerman, and the dance hall has been remodeled into a single family home. Mary related that the Liberty Barn was a stopping place for farmers' going to market with horse and wagon. Here the horses were fed, watered and rested, before crossing Mahanoy Mountain on the road to Mt. Carmel.

West of this barn dance hall residence is a newer ranch style home. The next residence to the west was the home of Mazie Kahler. West of Mazie's was the home of August Fetterolf. Mary Young, who has never been married, took a great interest in her local community. Usually on a Sunday her mother would sit and read the Bible, and Mary would ask her mother Hannah about the older town residents, in the days of her mother's youth. "What about Mime Fetterolf?" Her mother was a close friend of Jemima Fetterolf, having lived on High Street as neighbors, separated by a few houses. Hannah told the story that Jemima was in her kitchen. She was a stout woman and stood on a high back chair. She wanted to reach something on the higher cupboard shelves. She attempted to get down from the chair and bared her weight on the back of the chair. The back broke away, and Jemima fell onto the broken high back rails, puncturing her intestines. As there was little medical assistance in those days, Jemima's death was not long after the accident. It was remembered as a horrible event.

Two years later, August was killed in a coal mining accident at the Helfenstein Colliery. After the death of both parents, two of the children went to Pitman to stay with relatives. Martha Fetterolf was one of these children. She married John H. Hepler and later died at a young age of a hunting accident. Martha was husking corn when a stray bullet from a hunter's gun struck and killed her. She had only one child, John, who later was on a butcher truck that came to Helfenstein. Mary recalled others from the family including, Charles, who moved to the Mahantongo, Frank, from Mowery, Harvey, who married a Reinoehl girl, Wesley, from Ashland. Ellie, "Sis" was an older sibling who cared for the youngsters. (Elnora would have been 14 years old when her mother died, and later married Rathmus Minnick, a well known coal miner from the Cameron.)

The old August Fetterolf home is now occupied by the Boyer family. Next door, to the west, was a duplex home. The James Hodge family lived on the west side of the duplex residence. Today only the east side of this residence remains as the home of Nelma Lute. The west side was removed during renovation. James Hodge and Jemima Hodge Fetterolf were siblings, the children of Joseph and Sarah Hodge. Mary Hodge, James' wife, worked as a maid at Fertig's Hotel and boarding house. This building still stands in Helfenstein on Shamokin Street, but has been under construction for 20 years.

Mary Young remembered the grade school and secondary school located at the "Y" intersection of Gap Street and Shamokin Street above Fertig's hotel. Both of these school buildings burned down.

Interview with Lamar Kahler, May 2, and Paul and Lucine Fenstermaker, May 9, 2009

Lamar Kahler of High Road, Helfenstein lives adjacent to the Reformed Church. Lamar's father was Robert Kahler who lived two doors east of the church. This was previously the home of Lamar's grandfather father George, "Hootie" Skelding. Today this is the residence of Terry Spalti. Lamar recalls that John Skelding gave land for the Reformed Church. Lamar Kahler recalls hearing the name Kidson spoken by his Skelding grandparents in conversation. John Skelding married Mary Kidson.

In the census of 1900, John Skelding lived next door to William and Sarah Riddle. John Skelding was married to Mary, and William Riddle was married to Sarah. Sarah was first married to Joseph Hodge and married second to William Riddle. Sarah and Mary were sisters. These dwellings must be the houses near the Reformed Church. Joseph and Sarah (Marsh) Hodge are the parents of Jemima Hodge, who married August Fetterolf. Prior to 1909. the Skeldings seem to have lived in the Robert Kahler homestead and Joseph Hodge lived in the duplex next door. After 1909, John Skelding and son James Skelding lived in a newly constructed duplex home built 1909 presently the home of Paul and Lucine Fenstermaker. Lucine has lived her life in Helfenstein and identified the home of James and Mary Hodge. The Fenstermaker address is 859 High Road, Helfenstein. The Skelding duplex is on the south side of High Road, and the August Fetterolf family home and the James Hodge family home are on the north side of the road.

Interview with Mrs. Agnes (Wolfgang) Haas, May 3, 2009

Agnes is presently a resident of Mountain View Manor. She was born October 8, 1910 in Mowry. She is the oldest living person having lived in Helfenstein. Agnes was married to Ole Haas from Pitman. Ole was raised by Jim and Francis Wetzel. Agnes Wolfgang's roots are from the Mahantongo Valley. Agnes is now 98 years old and blind.

Agnes moved to Helfenstein from Mowry when she got married. She lived most of her married life along the Mahanoy Creek near the bridge on Mountain Road to Pitman. She lived in the second house above the bridge. Agnes recalls James and Mary Hodge, (Jemima's brother and wife), and she lived for a time as a neighbor, separated by an orchard field on High Street. James and Mary lived across the street from the flagpole. The flagpole is a local landmark. (James Hodge residence confirmed by Lucine Fenstermaker). Agnes remembers James Hodge as a "nice man, a quiet man, and honest." She recalled Fertig's Hotel which took in boarders and Mary Hodge worked there as a maid. Agnes also remembered the Weikel's dance hall and the general store that was converted into the Holiness church.

Soy Weikel's residence, hotel, gas station, and coffee shop was earlier called Fertig's Hotel on Shamokin Street. Agnes did not recall the August Fetterolf Family as these people were gone by the time she moved into town. She did not recall hearing the names of Joseph Hodge or John Skelding. She said she has a different view of Helfenstein from a later period. Agnes recalled the Methodist Church which stood west of her home along Mahanoy Creek. This church building was a well known landmark, although abandoned. The church was recently burned down and Agnes predicted that bad luck would come to those that burn churches. Agnes also reflected on schools in the area, and the education of the people of her generation. She replied, there was a well known saying, "the farther down you went, (along the Mahanoy Creek) the dumber they got!"

This large building under renovation, with the upper stories removed, was first established as the Union Pacific Hotel. This was a 24 room hotel with a dining room and a bar room on the street level. A ballroom was located upstairs. Later this establishment became known as Fertig's Hotel. The most recent and last hotel owner operator was Clayton "Soy" Weikel.

There was also another hotel in town operated by the Weikel Family. This building stood near the Liberty Barn. It was torn down in the early 1950's. This hotel was connected to the barn by an additional structure. Information courtesy of Dave Miller of Helfenstein.

August Fetterolf,(1871-1918), md. Jemima Hodge (1881-1916)

November 29, 2003, personal telephone conversation with Evelyn Minnich, (age 80), married to Kenneth Minnich, age 83, of Hatboro. Evelyn grew up in Pitman, maiden name, Brosius. At the time of this interview, Kenneth is the oldest living cousin on Pappy Fetterolf's (Charles) side. Kenneth Minnich is a retired coal miner with a serious lung condition from black lung, a coal miner's disease. He is on oxygen every day.

Kenneth reports his grandfather, August, was killed in 1918, age 47, in a coal mining accident, on top of the mountain above Helfenstein. A well known tavern named Weikel's Beer Garden is located at the base of this mountain in Helfenstein. This hotel is located on the intersection of the road which leads to Locust Gap. Directions to the mine accident site given by Kenneth is to cross over the Line Mountain from Pitman into Helfenstein. Go straight across the intersection, past Weikel's bar room in Helfenstein, to the top of the mountain.

Jemima (Hodge) Fetterolf,, died 2 years before her husband. She died 6 months after the birth of her youngest child Arch Fetterolf. Arch became well known in the Lavelle area and the Mahantongo Valley as a plumbing, heating and electrical contractor. After mother Jemima died, Ken Minnich's mother Eleanor Fetterolf, age 14, took care of and raised her younger brothers and sisters. Sometimes Lizzie Chubb,a neighbor, helped out.

Kenneth's sister, " Sis", now deceased, recalled that Sarah Marsh married Joseph Hodge. Their daughter Jemima Hodge, (1881-1916) married Augustus Fetterolf, (1871-1918). She also recalled Augustus's mother Lucinda Brosius, (1842-1899), married Harrison Fetterolf, (1829-1899). August, Jemima, Lucinda and Harrison are buried at Sunnyside Cemetery near Lavelle. Harrison and Lucinda have a tall monument west of the church. August and Jemima have a lower monument near the steps on the east side of the church. This church is locally known as Huntersville Church.

Anna Specht , daughter of Charles Fetterolf, interviewed at Christ Church, November 16, 2003, described Jemima as a "strict woman, and that's where Charles Fetterolf got his ways". As Charles's granddaughter I Joan recall him being stubborn and authoritative. "Pop" Fetterolf and Grammy Fetterolf (Lottie Reiner) often had picnics on the farm in the Mahantongo, and Hodge people from Pottsville would come to these gatherings.

Lorraine, married to Mark Fetterolf, recalled the Hodge family from Pottsville. Floyd Hodge was married to Pearl Heffner. Pearl had many sisters. Floyd, Pearl and her sisters often attended "Pop" Fetterolf's picnics. Lorraine believes Floyd Hodge is the son of Jack Hodge, a brother of Jemima. Jemima and Jack, are the children of Joseph Hodge and Sara Marsh.

Conversation with Eleanor (Fetterolf) Williard, married to Ray Williard: Charles Fetterolf in his old age, when going to visit May Fetterolf in the hospital, (Eleanor's mother) said to his granddaughter, Eleanor, that it was his grandmother that "came over on a boat from Wales".

August Fetterolf and Jemima Hodge married in 1901 per Northumberland Co. Records.

Mary Young, an old Helfenstein resident, remembers the Hodge and Fetterolf residences in the village. August Fetterolf was killed at the Helfenstein coal colliery. This mine was located on Mahanoy Mountain, above the Village of Helfenstein in Northumberland County. In the Village of Mowery, a coalmine colliery named Laurel Hill was established and at Doutyville a mine tunnel was located also. These 3 coal collieries were connected by a railroad from Lavelle which ended in Doutyville.

Location marked where the August Fetterolf coal mine death occurred in 1918. The mine was located on the south flank of Mahanoy Mountain, near the top.

Schuylkill County, formed in 1811 out of Berks and Northampton, was named for the Schuylkill River, which flows through its territory. This name, which means "hidden stream," was given to the river by the early Dutch explorers because they passed by its mouth at first without seeing it.

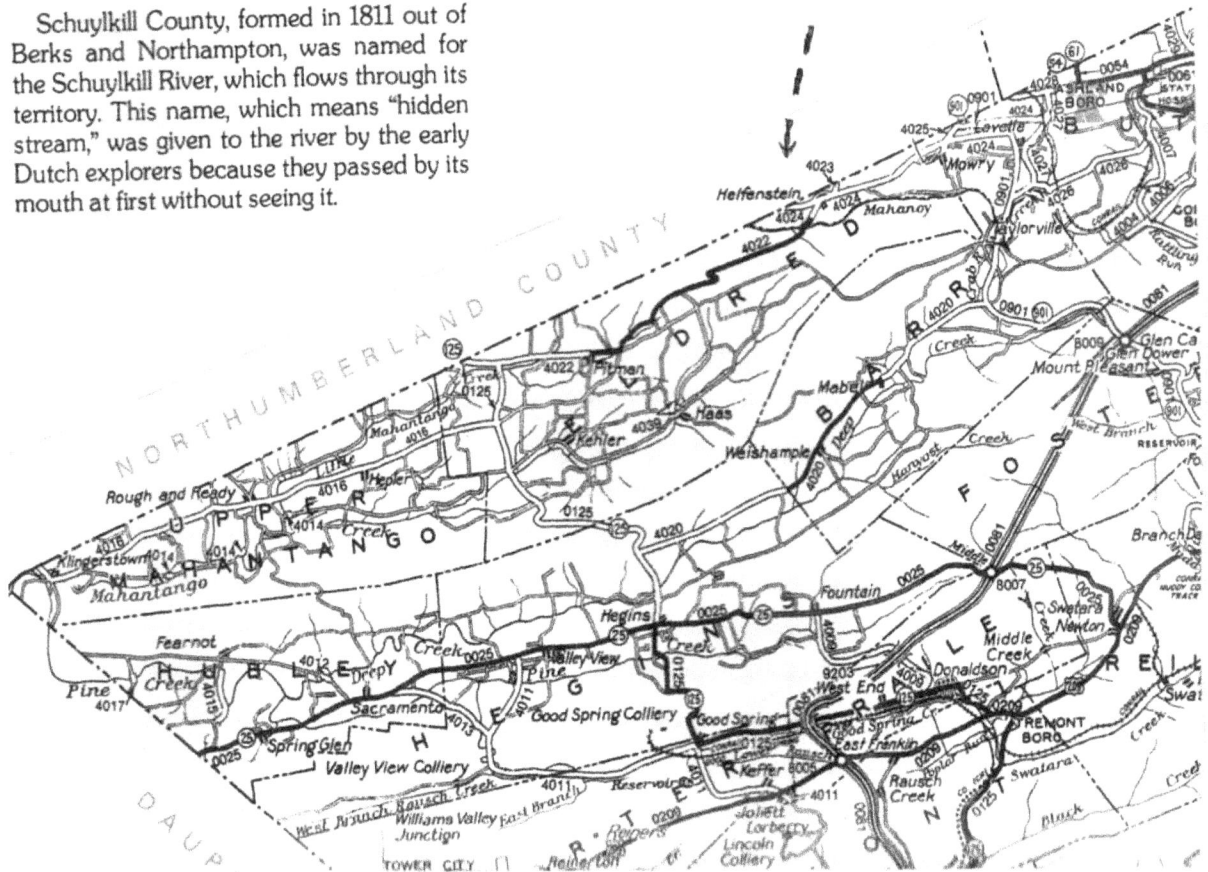

Railroad grade on Mahanoy Mountain above Helfenstein. View is looking west from the railroad intersection with Gap Road. Steam engines pulled coal cars along this track which connected the collieries at Doutyville, Helfenstein, and Mowery to Lavelle and the main line from Ashland to Gordon.

Helfenstein coal colliery foundations. These stone walls were erected without concrete or mortar. This was a very early coal mine, possibly established in the mid 1800's. August Fetterolf was killed here as told by Mr. Kenneth Minnich, a coal miner himself, now deceased.

Reunion Address, 2009
August and Jemima Fetterolf

According to House of Names .Com, the ancestors of the bearers of the names Hodge were of the Anglo-Saxon tribes of Britain. The name Hodge is derived from the baptismal name Roger through its nickname form of Hodge. First found in Northumberland, England where they were seated from very ancient times, some say well before the Norman Conquest and the arrival of Duke William at Hastings in 1066 A.D.

For political, religious, and economic reasons, thousands of English families boarded ships for the American colonies in the hope of finding better lives abroad. The families that survived the trip often went on to make valuable contributions to those new societies to which they arrived. Early immigrants bearing the Hodge surname include a John Hodge, settled in New Jersey in 1685 and Benjamin Hodges settled in Maryland in 1633.

According to The World Book Encyclopedia, Wales is a small mountainous country on the western coast of the island of Great Britain. It is part of the United Kingdom of Great Britain. Cardiff is the capital and largest city. Wales lies to the west of England. It has been united with England more than 400 years and English is the official language of Wales. But the great national pride of the Welsh people, has helped them keep alive their own language and traditions. The people call their country Cymru, which comes from their word for fellow countrymen. They call themselves Cymry. The name Wales comes from the Saxon language and means land of strangers. In literature Wales is sometimes called by its Latin name Cambria.

William the Conqueror subdued England between 1066 and 1071. He declared himself Lord of Wales. He gave lands along the boarder between England and Wales to Norman Barons to keep the Welsh in check. These men, called "Lords of the Marshes", built castles along the boarder and gradually expanded their lands. Soon they held most of the central and southern parts of Wales. In the 1200's the Welsh prince Llewelyn ap Griffith won control of much of the country. King Henry III of England, recognized him as Prince of Wales in 1267. In return for the title, Llewelyn had to recognize Henry as his overlord. The people slowly accepted the idea of union with England and 1536 the two countries were joined under the same system of laws and government.

Coal mining was once the most important industry in Wales. Most of the coal mines are in the south. Cardiff exported more coal than most other ports in the world. Many Welshmen were attracted to settle in the central Pa. coalfields. Pa. received the largest group of Welsh immigrants. By 1900, over 35,000 had emigrated to Pennsylvania, mostly to the coal regions. Coal mining attracted Joseph Hodge to Helfenstein, Schuylkill County. His daughter, Jemima, born in 1881, in Helfenstein, married August Fetterolf. Jemima and August are the parents of Charles whose descendants have established our Fetterolf Family Reunion. The following presentation was given:

June 14, 2009, Charles and Lottie Fetterolf Reunion
Klingerstown Park, Sunday afternoon

This gathering here today is a reunion of the descendants of Charles and Lottie (Reiner) Fetterolf. Today I want to talk mostly about Charles Fetterolf. Although he is no relation to me, he is to my wife and children. I know there are quite a few here today that do not remember Charles Fetterolf. He died in 1972. To Joan, my wife, he was known as "Pop"

Fetterolf. I understand that many of his grandchildren called him "Pappy". Lottie was known either as "Grammy" to some, "Mammy" to many others.

Pappy and Mammy Fetterolf lived where Dennis Fetterolf lives today, on the farm along the Mahantongo Creek, near the Village of Hepler. Charles was born in Helfenstein. He was the oldest child of August and Jemima Fetterolf's 10 children. The youngest of the family, Arch, was born 19 years after Charles.

Charles's father, August Fetterolf, was a coal miner. He lived in Helfenstein along the main road, called High Street. Helfenstein is located across the Line Mountain from Pitman. Many of us are familiar with the "stair steps" mountain road which connects the Mahantongo Valley and the Cameron Valley. Old timers recall the road was built in a step like fashion to accommodate farmer huckster horse drawn wagons. As the heavy market wagons ascended the mountain, the horses could rest on the flat steps. As the wagons descended the mountain, the steps allowed the horses to hold back the wagons. On top of the Line Mountain are two sharp curves between the bedrock. The narrow macadam road descends into the lovely green deep valley of the Mahanoy Creek to the Village of Helfenstein.

When August and Jemima Fetterolf lived here, coal mining was the main industry. Helfenstein had its own colliery near the center of the village. August could easily walk to work. The mine was called a "drift" or tunnel into Mahanoy Mountain located just above his house. Other nearby tunnels were located at Mowry, called Laurel Hill Colliery, and at Doutyville. These three mines were connected by a railroad from Lavelle and steam engines pulled the coal cars east toward Ashland. In the late 1800's and early 1900's, Helfenstein was a busy place. In addition to all the residents, several stores were located here as well as a Methodist Church, several boarding houses and several hotels. The village is divided by the county line, therefore public schools were located in Northumberland County at the west end of town, and public schools were located at the east end of town, in Schuylkill County. Some businesses that August would have known are the Union Pacific Hotel, Weikel's Beer Garden, Weikel's Dance Hall, Jesse Lambach's General Store. The old Methodist Church is now gone, as well as many of these buildings.

When Judge Helfenstein established the community, he had the town surveyed with many streets and avenues. He envisioned a city the size of Ashland. It was not to be. Only half a dozen streets were built with houses located on them. There were many more houses years ago. The coal mines on the Mahanoy Mountain employed hundreds of men but the work was dangerous. One problem was loose top rock which could fall and injure the miners. The coal was mined with dynamite, picks, and shovels. These men used mules to pull the coal cars through the tunnels.

August and Jemima lived and breathed the coal industry every day. Jemima was your Pappy Charles' mother. Jemima's parents, Joseph and Sarah Hodge, lived a few doors away, in a duplex home. On the other side of this duplex home, Sarah's sister Mary Ellen, (Jemima's aunt), lived with her husband, Joanthan Skelding. Many of the houses on High Street were occupied by the Hodges and the Skeldings, related through the sisters Sarah and Mary Ellen who were born in Wales.

According to the 1880 census records, Sarah Hodge and her sister Mary Ellen Skelding migrated from South Wales in 1867. Jemima Jane, daughter of Sarah Hodge, is not listed, as she was born in 1881. *County deed records indicate Sarah and Mary Ellen were born Kidson.* Sarah, Mary Ellen, and George are named as the children of Louisa Kidson in a deed from 1887. This deed is for land along the Mahanoy Creek in Cameron Township, Northumberland County. The deed transfer also names Sarah's husband Joseph Hodge.

Is Sarah Hodge's Maiden Name Kidson or Marsh?

A death record for Sarah names her father as James Marsh. Family tradition recalls Sarah's maiden name as Marsh. We cannot explain why the county deed record gave Sarah's maiden name as Kidson, unless Louisa Marsh, Sarah's mother, remarried Kidson as her second husband. (September 2009, we now know Sarah was born name of Marsh, see birth record in this book). Both records certainly pertain to the same Sarah. Joseph and Sarah Hodge, according to the census records had 16 children, 7 of which survived. Two were born in South Wales and came to America as young children. Joseph and Sarah Hodge are buried at Mt. Carmel Cemetery. Their daughter Jemima, one of the younger children, was born in the Village of Helfenstein. She grew up there and August Fetterolf married her and they lived there. We can assume that August Fetterolf was also born in the Cameron Valley. He was the son of Harrison and Lucinda (Brosius) Fetterolf. Both are buried at Christ Independent Church of Lavelle.

This marriage of August and Jemima Fetterolf survived for 19 years. Jemima Fetterolf's untimely death was explained by Mary Young. Mary Young, age 86, of Helfenstein, has never been married. She took a great interest in her local community. Usually on a Sunday her mother would sit and read the Bible, and Mary would ask her mother Hannah about the older town residents, in the days of her mother's youth. "What about Mime Fetterolf?" Her mother was a close friend of Jemima Fetterolf, having lived on High Street as neighbors, separated by a few houses. Hannah told the story that Jemima was in her kitchen. She was a stout woman and stood on a high back chair. She wanted to reach something on the higher cupboard shelves. She attempted to get down from the chair and bared her weight on the back of the chair. The back broke away, and Jemima fell onto the broken high back rails, puncturing her intestines. As there was little medical assistance in those days, Jemima's death was not long after the accident. It was remembered as a horrible event. She died in 1916, age 35.

Two years later, in 1918, August was killed in a coal mining accident at the Helfenstein Colliery. He was 47 years old. Kenneth Minnick, grandson of August Fetterolf, described the location of the Helfenstein Colliery where August was killed. After the death of both parents, some of August's children remained in their home cared for by relatives. Two of the children went to Pitman to stay with relatives. Martha Fetterolf was one of these children. She married John H. Hepler and later died at a young age of a hunting accident. Martha was husking corn when a stray bullet from a hunter's gun struck and killed her. She had only one child, John, who later was on a butcher truck that came to Helfenstein. Mary Young recalled others from the family including, Charles, who moved to the Mahantongo, Frank, from Mowry, Harvey, who married a Reinoehl girl, Wesley, from Ashland. Ellie, "Sis" was an older sibling who cared for the youngsters. (Elnora would have been 14 years old when her mother died, and later married Rathmus Minnick, a well known coal miner from the Cameron.)

1848, Coal Township, Northumberland Co., Civil Record lists David Hodge. This David is probably the son of Archibald Hodge.

Of special interest to Hodge research: Here we have the names Archibald, James, and Jemima recorded. These are people of a generation previous to Jemima Hodge, (married to August Fetterolf). The repetition of names in these Schuylkill Co. families suggest they are related to James Hodge, brother of Jemima Hodge, (married to August Fetterolf), and her youngest son named Archibald.
Schuylkill Co. Deed Book 36, P. 780, 2nd of May, 1850.
Archibald Ronaldson for James Ronaldson and wife Ellen Jemima of Pottsville, Pa., to Archibald Hodge of Pottsville, Pa.
$125 for land on the northwest side of Mt. Carbon Railroad in Norwegian Twp. (112 P.) on the new road to Pottsville with reference to coal and mineral rights
1854, Coal Township, Northumberland Co. Court House Deed.
Archibald and Jannet Hodge sell land to William W. McWilliams. Our ancestor, Joseph Hodge, born in Wales in 1840 would have been 14 years old, living in South Wales at the time of this land transaction.

Archibald Hodge is an early name recorded in Schuylkill County Deed Records, Book 60, p. 80. On 9th of December, 1858, Archibald purchased 72 A., 18P. in North Manheim Twp., Schuylkill Co., Pa. from Daniel Britton. This is land south of Pottsville with reference to mineral rights.

Hodges, Marshes and Brittains

Some feel Hodge is an English name and Marsh is a Welsh name. Hodge is found in England as well as Wales. One older Fetterolf relative recalled the family name Britton associated with Joseph and Sarah Hodge. (See early Schuylkill County Deed Record, 1858) naming Archibald Hodge and Daniel Britton. This same relative states that Joseph's full name was Joseph William Hodge.
James Hodge (1883-1943) married to Mary E. Hodge (1883-1964) is buried in the Sunnyside Cemetery churchyard of Huntersville Christ Independent Church of Lavelle, Pa. This is the same cemetery where August Fetterolf (1871-1918) and Jemima (Hodge) Fetterolf (1881-1916) are buried. James and Jemima are siblings, children of Joseph and Sarah Hodge.

Henry Lippiatt was a miner in England where his entire life was passed. He married Ann Hodges who after her husband's death brought her three children to America, landing at New York City in May of 1864. They first located at Locust Gap, Pa., but in 1865 came to Shamokin. Her children were Thomas H. and Elizabeth of Shamokin. Thomas continued to work in the mines for 17 years and later became owner, operator of a photography and furniture sales business on Independence Street. Above information from Gen. and Bio. Annals of North'd. Co. by Floyd, p. 656.

Early Hodge Cemetery Records by Joseph Meiser for Northumberland Co. include:
Ann E. Hodge, 1825-1914, married John Lovell, 1833-1889.
David, 1830-1901, son of Archibald and Effy, md. Henrietta Lamont, 1833-1910.
James, md. Sarah Price, 1835-1891.
William, 1842-1923, son of Archibald and Effy, md. Katherine Walter.

Kidson's and Skelding's in Helfenstein

Hodge Family Relatives

Skeldings and Kidsons

Skelding Family History by descendants: Carollee Kimble, 429 Lamplighter Vlg., Clarkdale, Az., 86324 and her uncle Noel (date of birth 9-5-1925) of Allentown, Pa.

1870 Census lists Jonathan Esquire Skelding as a coal miner, age 22, born in England, married in December 1870. Jonathan emigrated in 1866 and married Mary Ellen Kidson who also emigrated in 1866. Perhaps this marriage took place at the old Methodist Church in Helfenstein.

1880 Census lists Jonathan Skelding, born in England, children, Louisa, Sarah, and Mary. Their firstborn was named Louisa after Mary Ellen's mother Louisa Kidson.

1890 Census Records of Helfenstein from Eldred Township, Schuylkill Co., Pa, list: John Shelding, 46, miner, Mary E. (wife), Sarah J., Mary, Adam (8), James H. (3), George J.

1900 Census lists Helfenstein Village home #198: Jonathan Skelding born 9-1844 in England, emigrated in 1866, wife Mary, born 2-1850, children, Adam, James, (Carollee Kimbel descendant), George, (Lamar Kahler descendant), and Eva. House next door is William Riddle and family (Sarah Hodge and children).

Jonathan worked at the Helfenstein Colliery as did his sons named James (born 1884), and George (born 1889). This George nicknamed "Hootie" is the grandfather of Lamar Kahler of Helfenstein today where the family owns and operates Kahler's Gun Shop. George gave the land to establish the Reformed Church on High Street in Helfenstein and is buried at St. Paul's Reformed Cemetery in Gowen City.

Kidson is a Scottish name. Noel Skelding recalls an oral tradition that his grandmother Mary Ellen came from the Highlands of northern Scotland. She was middle class. Her father was the mayor of Edinberg, a village located in the Highlands north of the large city of Edinburgh which is the capital of Scotland. The capital city is located in the Central Lowland region.

Carollee Kimble has traced the Skelding family to its English origins in a rural parish in England where the Skell River is located. One original family spelling is "Skeleden". Civil records found in Pennsylvania are written Skeldon, Shelding, and Skelding. Residents from the Skell River Parish confirmed the emigration of Jonathan Skelding. The name Jonathan is often known by the nickname "Jack". Jonathan married Mary Ellen Kidson. They lived their married life in Helfenstein. Mary Ellen was knitting and pierced her breast with the knitting needle resulting in an infection which caused her death

Photo of Mary Ellen Skelding, Helfenstein, Pa.
Sister of Sarah Hodge, Helfenstein, Pa.
Contributed by Carollee Kimble

Mary Ellen Kidson
in Helfenstein

Skelding Family Census Records, Eldred Twp., Schuylkill Co., Pa

1870, Cameron Twp. Joanthan Skelding, age 22, Miner, b. in England, md. in Dec., wife Mary, age 19, Louisa, age 5 mo., b. Jan. (Mary is Sarah Hodge's sister).

1900, Eldred Twp., John Skelding, b. Sept., 1844, England, laborer, md. 33 years, emigrated 1866.
Mary, b. Feb. 1850, b. in England, 18 children, 7 living, Adam, b. 1881, James, b. 1884, George, b. 1889, Eva, b. 1891. (They live next door to Wm. and Sarah Riddle.)

1920, Eldred Twp., George J. Skelding, age 30, wf. Carrie F., age 31. Carrie A., 3y, 11 m., Walter F., 2y, 10m.

James H. Skelding, age 35, wf. Emma J., age 35, John S. Skelding, age 75, father,
Mary E., 14, Charles M., 13, Woodrow T., 6, Erma E., 3y, 6m.
The James Skelding family lives two doors away from the August and Jemima Fetterolf family children.
Cemetery Record, Simpson United Methodist of Gordan
James Henry Skelding and Emma J. Skelding, children Mary Ellen, 1905, Charles Monroe, 1906. James Henry is the son of Mary Kidosn
Citizen's Cemetery, Lavelle. Charles Skelding, 1906-1934, child, Nettie and John

Home of John and Mary Ellen Skelding and James and Emma Skelding.
Duplex home in Helfenstein. Presently the Fenstermaker residence.

James & Emma —
my grandparents —
in Allentown

James and Emma Skelding, (grandparents of Carollee Kimble),
as retired in Allentown, Pa.

Family Group Charts

James Marsh md. Louisa Dainty
Joseph Hodges md. Sarah Marsh
Joseph T. Hodges md. Sarah
William Hodges md. Catharine
John H. Hodges md. Edith Turner
James Hodges md. Mary E.
Curtis H. Willier md. Bertha Mary Hodges

United Kingdom, Wales researcher, Christian Phillips-Gunter
(find my ancestors@btinternet.com)
13 Hampton Street, Twynyrodyn, Merthyr Tydfill, CF47 ORR

James Marsh

I have a found a possibility for the family in 1851 (as attached), living in Bridgnorth St Mary, Shropshire. They do have a daughter Sarah (age 3 or so it seems - arrgghh!!) as well as a son James (age 1) and another daughter called Jane (who be 3 or 9!). Father is James, age 32 (approx 1819), a Miner & his wife is Louisa, also 32 - all born in Sedgley, Staffordshire (which is about 4 miles from Tipton, Staffordshire).

Louisa Dainty

Could Louisa have been known as Susan? Could the marriage I found - James Marsh married a Louisa Dainty on the 4th July 1837 at ***Tipton, Staffordshire*** - be the right one??

Researched by Elaine Schwar
3384 Harwood Ln., Reading, Pa. 19608-8811

	HUSBAND	James Marsh
Born		
Chr		
Mar		
Died		
Bur		
HUSBAND'S FATHER		
HUSBAND'S OTHER WIVES		

	WIFE	Louisa Dainty
Born		
Chr		
Died		
Bur		
WIFE'S FATHER		
WIFE'S OTHER HUSBANDS		

SEX M&F	CHILDREN GIVEN NAME	SURNAME	WHEN BORN DAY	MONTH	YEAR	WHERE BORN TOWN	COUNTY	STATE COUNTRY	DATE OF FIRST MARRIAGE TO WHOM	WHEN DIED DAY	MONTH	YEAR
1	George Kidson age 64 in		1890 census		1826							
2	Sarah Marsh		12	May	1843		South Wales		Joseph Hodges Jr.		11 sept	1919
3	Mary			a -1850			md. 1866	England	Nonathan Skelding b. 9-1844			
4									Jonathan & Mary both emigrated 1866			
5	Skelding family								still living in 1890 when he signed Joseph Hodges Will			
6	From: Carollee Kimble (carolleek@gmail.com)											
	Sent: Sun 5/03/09 9:49 PM											
7	To: troutman425@hotmail.com					Sheet 13 Line 97			Pregnancies 18 still living 7			
	1880 Federal Census for Schuylkill County.					John Skelding dob 9/1844 55yrs old England Wife Mary (this would be Kidson) dob 2/1850 49 yrs old place of birth-?			Rented home-both can read & write Children Adam, James(my grandfather) George, Eva E. Eldred Township, Helfenstein Village, House #198			
8						1900 Census-Eldred Township, Schuylkill County Vol. 200 ed 143						
9	Jonathan Skelden, birth- England					Immigrated to U.S. 1866-both Years in U.S. 33			Next door neighbors were William Riddle & family I have this copied-original was not easily legible.			
10	wife & kids–Louisa, Sarah,	Vol 59 ed. 142				years married 33						
11	Mary	Sheet 15 Line 33							1920 Census Helfenstein Village vol 286 ed26 sheet 1 line 87 & 89			

SOURCES OF INFORMATION

This census had John S. (S. is for Squire, we are told) Skelding age 75 living with James H. Skelding (my grandfather) & family-same house.

Conclusion: Louisa's first husband, James Marsh, second husband, named Kidson. Court record naming Sarah Kidson is in error. Should be Sarah Marsh. Perhaps George Kidson is an older step brother to Sarah and Mary Ellen.

ENGLAND

FAMILY GROUP RECORD

United Kingdom, Wales researcher, Christian Phillips-Gunter
(find my ancestors@btinternet.com)
13 Hampton Street, Twynyrodyn, Merthyr Tydfill, CF47 ORR

Researched by Elaine Schwar
3384 Harwood Ln, Reading, Pa. 19608-8811

c. Mary Ann Hodges - June quarter 1869 Volume 11b Page 127

Mary Ann was born 20th May 1869 at King Street, Brynmawr. This must be the daughter you mentioned that is buried in the US which means the family must have emigrated *after* the date of her birth.

HUSBAND	Joseph HODGES	of Eldred twp. South Wales
Born	20 Mar 1840 Place	Husband Wills
Chr	Place	1880 census - coal miner
Mar	14 Jan 1891 Place Mt. Carmel Cem. Northumberland Co.	1890 directory - none listed
Died	Place	
Bur	Place	

HUSBAND'S FATHER:
HUSBAND'S MOTHER:
HUSBAND'S OTHER WIVES:

WIFE	Sarah Marsh
Born	12 May 1843 Place South Wales
Chr	Place
Died	11 Sept 1919 Place Mt. Carmel Cem.
Bur	Place

in 1900 census she said she'd had 16 children, 8 which 8 were living. Actually 7 were alive!

Her place of birth is given as ****Tipton*** in Staffordshire.

WIFE'S FATHER: 2nd William RIDDLE   Louisa
WIFE'S MOTHER: Census of 1900 states Wm. Riddle and Sarah are married 9 years

SEX M/F	GIVEN NAME	SURNAME	DAY	MONTH	YEAR	TOWN	COUNTY	STATE/COUNTRY	TO WHOM	DAY	MONTH	YEAR
1 W	Joseph T.	Age in 1880 census 15		Feb	1864			South Wales	Sarah			
2 W	William	12						South Wales	Catharine			
3	Mary H.	9	20	May	1869				None bur. Taylorsville	15	July	1870
4	Elizabeth	9					PA		None			
5 M	John H. "Jack"	8							Edith TURNER	15	Feb	1889
6	Sarah Anna	3	17	Nov	1877				None bur. Mt. Carmel			
7	George W.	6 mos		Nov	1879				None bur. Mt. Carmel			1905
8	Jemima Jane				1881		m.d. 1901		Augustus FETTEROLF			1916
9	James				1883	a Grace Evang. Luth.			Mary E.			1943
10 W	Martha Alberta		28	Jan	1885				None			
11 W	Bertha Mary				1886				Curtis H. WILLIER			1929

Named in Sarah's will
ted. - in her heirs

SOURCES OF INFORMATION

as attached - a Sarah Marsh.

Father James Marsh, a Miner, age 39 (B c1822) POB, Tipton, Staffs

Mother Susan Marsh, a Miner's wife, age 39 (B c1822) POB, Tipton, Staffs

If you look at the census image - she is living at Clydach Bridge - ring any bells?? Yup - a few houses away from where Joseph Hodges was recorded living at on the 1851 census. Only fly in the ointment is the fact that Sarah is recorded as being 14. I think this could be a mis-transcription as if you look at the image, her age could be 19 which would tie in with her approx age on the marriage certificate.

NECESSARY EXPLANATIONS

FAMILY GROUP RECORD

185

Researched by Elaine Schwar
3384 Harwood Ln., Reading, Pa. 19608-8811

United Kingdom, Wales researcher, Christian Phillips-Gunter
(find my ancestors@btinternet.com)
13 Hampton Street, Twynyrodyn, Merthyr Tydfil, CF47 ORR

HUSBAND	Joseph T. HODGES / HODGE		
Born	Feb 1864	Place	South Wales
Chr		Place	
Mar		Place	
Died		Place	
Bur		Place	
HUSBAND'S FATHER	Joseph		
HUSBAND'S OTHER WIVES		HUSBAND'S MOTHER	Sarah Marsh

WIFE	Sarah		
Born	Aug 1871	Place	PA
Chr		Place	
Died		Place	
Bur		Place	
WIFE'S FATHER		WIFE'S MOTHER	

WIFE'S OTHER HUSBANDS

SEX M/F	CHILDREN GIVEN NAME	SURNAME	WHEN BORN DAY	MONTH	YEAR	WHERE BORN TOWN	COUNTY	STATE	DATE OF FIRST MARRIAGE COUNTRY	TO WHOM	WHEN DIED DAY	MONTH	YEAR
1	Elizabeth					(was not in 1900 census)							
2	Sarah B.			Jan	1889								
3	Margaret			July	1892								
4	? (a son)			Apr	1895								
5	Thomas			Jan	1897								
6													
7													
8													
9													
10													
11													

NECESSARY EXPLANATIONS

lived next to parents in Ektrd twp. in 1890 - was a miner in 1900 census - Aston twp.

Delaware to worked in a Dyehouse. He said he emigrated in 1870.

Can't find in 1910.

SOURCES OF INFORMATION

a. Joseph Thomas Hodges - March quarter 1864 - Volume 11b
Page 133

Joseph Thomas born 7th February 1864 at Bailey Street, Brynmawr.
Bailey Street is in the centre of Brynmawr and still exists today.
Thought this may be of help.

http://www.thomasgenweb.com/brynmawr_photos.html

OTHER MARRIAGES

Kidson or Marsh? Northumberland County, Pa., Court House Record, Deed Book 97, P. 13 in 1887 states George, Mary, and Sarah are the children of Louisa Kidson. Mary Skelding family tradition recalls Mary's maiden name as Kidson.

Sarah Hodge Riddle Death Certificate as completed by William, her son, in 1919, states Sarah's father is James Marsh. Sarah Hodge family tradition recalls Sarah's maiden name as Marsh.

Conclusion: Louisa's first husband, James Marsh, second husband, named Kidson. Court record naming Sarah Kidson is in error. Should be Sarah Marsh. Perhaps George Kidson is an older step brother to Sarah and Mary Ellen.

Researched by Elaine Schwar
3384 Harwood Ln., Reading, Pa. 19608-8811

United Kingdom, Wales researcher, Christian Phillips-Gunter
(find my ancestors@btinternet.com)
13 Hampton Street, Twynyrodyn, Merthyr Tydfil, CF47 ORR

HUSBAND William HODGE

Born	1865	S. Wales	Place	South Wales
Chr		Place	1910 census named coal miner
Mar		Place	emigrated in 1867
Died		Place	
Bur		Place	

HUSBAND'S FATHER Joseph

HUSBAND'S MOTHER

HUSBAND'S OTHER WIVES

WIFE Catherine

Sarah Marsh

Born	43	Place
Chr		Place
Died		Place
Bur		Place

WIFE'S FATHER

WIFE'S MOTHER

WIFE'S OTHER HUSBANDS

husband
wife 1910 – Eldred twp. -miner

SEX M/F	CHILDREN GIVEN NAME	SURNAME	WHEN BORN DAY	MONTH	YEAR	WHERE BORN TOWN	COUNTY	STATE	COUNTRY	DATE OF FIRST MARRIAGE TO WHOM	WHEN DIED DAY	MONTH	YEAR
1	Sarah	age in 1910 census 8											
2	William	3											
3													
4													
5													
6													
7													
8													
9													
10													
11													

b. **James Hodges** - December quarter 1865 Volume 11b Page 123

James was born 15th November 1865 at King Street, Brynmawr (see above link). Could this be the William Hodges that you mentioned in earlier emails?

SOURCES OF INFORMATIC

Kidson or Marsh? Northumberland County, Pa., Court House Record, Deed Book 97, P. 13 in 1887 states George, Mary, and Sarah are the children of Louisa Kidson. Mary Skelding family tradition recalls Mary's maiden name as Kidson.

Sarah Hodge Riddle Death Certificate as completed by William, her son, in 1919, states Sarah's father is James Marsh. Sarah Hodge family tradition recalls Sarah's maiden name as Marsh.

Conclusion: Louisa's first husband, James Marsh, second husband, named Kidson. Court record naming Sarah Kidson is in error. Should be Sarah Marsh. Perhaps George Kidson is an older step brother to Sarah and Mary Ellen.

FAMILY GROUP RECORD

187

NECESSARY EXPLANATIONS

Researched by Elaine Schwar
3384 Harwood Ln., Reading, Pa. 19608-8811

HUSBAND John H. HODGES "Jack" HODGE

Born	age 35 in 1910 Eldred twp. Schuylkill Co.	Place
Chr		Place
Mar		Place
Died	not in State in 1920	Place
Bur		Place

in Pottsville, 5th Ward in 1910 census. Engineer in Steel Mill

HUSBAND'S FATHER Joseph

HUSBAND'S MOTHER

HUSBAND'S OTHER WIVES

WIFE Edith TURNER   Sarah Marsh

Born	1896	Place England
Chr		Place
Died	1973	Place
Bur		Place

Edith found in 1920 census in Pottsville her father lives with her & the 3 children

WIFE'S FATHER 1846 George W. Turner 1921

WIFE'S MOTHER

Mt. Laurel Cem. near Seltzer with parents. Geo. W. Turner cem on Bulls head road Arline 1847-1918

WIFE'S OTHER HUSBANDS

SEX M/F	CHILDREN GIVEN NAME	SURNAME	WHEN BORN DAY	MONTH	YEAR	WHERE BORN TOWN	COUNTY	STATE COUNTRY	DATE OF FIRST MARRIAGE TO WHOM	WHEN DIED DAY	MONTH	YEAR
1	Myrtle L.	Age in 1910 census 12				Age in 1920 21						
2	Floyd J.	8				17						
3	Edith R.	1 mo.		1910					Pearl "HEFFNER"			
4	Arline					19						
5												
6												
7												
8												
9												
10												
11												

SOURCES OF INFORMATION

Kidson or Marsh? Northumberland County, Pa., Court House Record, Deed Book 97, P. 13 in 1887 states George, Mary, and Sarah are the children of Louisa Kidson. Mary Skelding family tradition recalls Mary's maiden name as Kidson.

Sarah Hodge Riddle Death Certificate as completed by William, her son, in 1919, states Sarah's father is James Marsh. Sarah Hodge family tradition recalls Sarah's maiden name as Marsh.

Conclusion: Louisa's first husband, James Marsh, second husband, named Kidson. Court record naming Sarah Kidson is in error. Should be Sarah Marsh. Perhaps George Kidson is an older step brother to Sarah and Mary Ellen.

FAMILY GROUP RECORD

188

NECESSARY EXPLANATIONS

Researched by Elaine Schwar
3384 Harwood Ln., Reading, Pa. 19608-8811

HUSBAND James HODGE "Jim" of Eldred twp.
Born	1883 Place Eldred twp. Schuylkill Co.
Chr	Place
Mar	Place
Died	1943 Place
Bur	Place

HUSBAND'S FATHER: Joseph
HUSBAND'S MOTHER: Sarah marsh
HUSBAND'S OTHER WIVES:

coal miner in 1910
stationary engineer in coal
mine in 1920

WIFE Mary E.
Born	1883 Place Sunnyside (Huntersville) Lavelle
Chr	Place
Died	1964 Place Sunnyside
Bur	Place

WIFE'S FATHER:
WIFE'S MOTHER:
WIFE'S OTHER HUSBANDS:

SEX M/F	CHILDREN GIVEN NAME SURNAME	WHEN BORN DAY MONTH YEAR	WHERE BORN TOWN COUNTY STATE COUNTRY	DATE OF FIRST MARRIAGE TO WHOM	WHEN DIED DAY MONTH YEAR	NECESSARY EXPLANATIONS
1	Winfield Russel	Age in 1920 census 15	1905	Eldred twp	Evelyn C.	1927	bur. Litzsted cem. Lavelle
2	Dorothy M.	12		"		1910-	St. Pauls Reformed cem. Gowen City
3	Winifred			"			
4	Adah M.	8		"	1928 Edward Knarr	1900-1964	
5	Sarah E.	6		"			
6	John T. "Jackie"	3yrs 4mo		"			
7	Mary E.	1yr 9mo		"	* J. P. 4 Apr 1931 James KEHLER		

SOURCES OF INFORMATION
St. Paul's Evang. Luth. * James Kehler md Sara Hodge (itelfenstein)
(pitman)
James is brother of Peter Kehler
Sara died young and James remarried

Kidson or Marsh? Northumberland County, Pa., Court House Record, Deed Book 97, P. 13 in 1887 states George,
Mary, and Sarah are the children of Louisa Kidson. Mary Skelding family tradition recalls Mary's maiden name as
Kidson.
Sarah Hodge Riddle Death Certificate as completed by William, her son, in 1919, states Sarah's father is James
Marsh. Sarah Hodge family tradition recalls Sarah's maiden name as Marsh.

Conclusion: Louisa's first husband, James Marsh, second husband, named Kidson. Court record naming Sarah
Kidson is in error. Should be Sarah Marsh. Perhaps George Kidson is an older step brother to Sarah and Mary Ellen.

189

HUSBAND Curtis H. WILLIER of Eldred twp.

Born	1880	Place
Chr		Place
Mar		Place
Died	1952	Place
Bur		Place Sunnyside (Huntsville) Lavelle

HUSBAND'S FATHER

HUSBAND'S MOTHER

HUSBAND'S OTHER WIVES

WIFE Bertha Mary HODGES

Born	1886	Place Eldred twp. Schuylkill Co.
Chr		Place
Died	1929	Place
Bur		Place Sunnyside

WIFE'S FATHER Joseph Hodges

WIFE'S MOTHER Sarah Marsh

WIFE'S OTHER HUSBANDS

SEX M/F	CHILDREN GIVEN NAME	SURNAME	WHEN BORN DAY	MONTH	YEAR	WHERE BORN TOWN	COUNTY	STATE COUNTRY	DATE OF FIRST MARRIAGE TO WHOM	WHEN DIED DAY	MONTH	YEAR	NECESSARY EXPLANATIONS
1	Mary E.	Age in 1926 census 15				Eldred twp.							
2	Florence M.	14				"							
3	Leona M.	13				"			2 Feb. 1925 Calvin Held				
4	Blanche L.	11				"			McDONALD				
5	Hazel E.	8				"			LEECH				
6	Harry L.	7				"		st.P.	24 June 1941 Pauline M. KELLER				
7	Elsie M.	6				"		st.P.	George E. KRAMER 1909-1972				bur. Sunnyside
8	Curtis H. Jr.	1	1913			"Sonny" "							
9	Robert					"							
10													
11													

SOURCES OF INFORMATION St. Paul's Evang. Lutheran

Researched by Elaine Schwar
3384 Harwood Ln., Reading, Pa. 19608-8811

Kidson or Marsh? Northumberland County, Pa., Court House Record, Deed Book 97, P. 13 in 1887 states George, Mary, and Sarah are the children of Louisa Kidson. Mary Skelding family tradition recalls Mary's maiden name as Kidson.

Sarah Hodge Riddle Death Certificate as completed by William, her son, in 1919, states Sarah's father is James Marsh. Sarah Hodge family tradition recalls Sarah's maiden name as Marsh.

Conclusion: Louisa's first husband, James Marsh, second husband, named Kidson. Court record naming Sarah Kidson is in error. Should be Sarah Marsh. Perhaps George Kidson is an older step brother to Sarah and Mary Ellen.

FAMILY GROUP 00

190

The Authors

Steve Troutman was born in 1952, into a family with many living grandparents, all with roots in the Mahantongo Valley, Pa. He developed an interest in genealogy at an early age due to his parents' interest in family history. Steve studied geology at Franklin and Marshall College, but did not pursue a career in this field. Instead, he continued working for the family business, Troutman Bros. Inc. of Klingerstown, Pa.

Joan (Masser) Troutman's family roots are deep in the soil as she grew up on a potato farm in the Mahantongo Valley. She continued her education at Susquehanna University and graduated in 1974 with a degree in accounting.

The Charles Fetterolf family was rather uninformed about their Hodge connection, as her mother knew very little about her father's parents. Joan was thrilled as new found record were brought to light by researchers in Wales. Steve and Joan enjoyed their trip to Wales researching the Hodge family. It was spiritual in nature. They have been fortunate to travel to Germany several times to see first-hand where the Fetterolfs originated. This is a beautiful area resembling the Mahantongo Valley.

Joan and Steve have written other family histories including <u>Trautman/Troutman Family History, Vol. I and II</u> and <u>The Origin and History of the Jacob Masser Family of Line Mountain, Pa.</u> They have contributed to <u>The Klingerstown Bi-Centenial Album (1807-2007)</u> and <u>The Bi-Centennial Album (1803-2003) A Tribute to Jacob's (Howerter's) Union Church of Upper Mahanoy Twp., Northumberland County, Pa</u>. Other smaller publications they completed include <u>Tulpehocken Trail Traces</u> and <u>The Trevorton, Mahanoy and Susquehanna Railroad and the Susquehanna River Bridge between Herndon and Port Trevorton.</u>

The Troutmans live and work in the heart of the Mahantongo Valley. They enjoy listening to and sharing historical information. Their contact information is below:

Steve & Joan Troutman
1442 Ridge Road
Klingerstown, PA 17941

Phone: (570) 425-3485

Email: troutman425@hotmail.com

www.ingramcontent.com/pod-product-compliance
Lightning Source LLC
Chambersburg PA
CBHW081151270326
41930CB00014B/3109